MOLL FLANDERS:

An Analysis of an Eighteenth Century Criminal Biography

Hymn to the Pillory (Extract)

Daniel Defoe, 1703

"Tell them the men that placed him here
Are scandals to the times,
Are at a loss to find his guilt,
And can't commit his crimes."

MOLL FLANDERS:

AN ANALYSIS OF AN EIGHTEENTH CENTURY CRIMINAL BIOGRAPHY

By

Gregory Durston

MA, DipL, LLM, Barrister,
Associate Professor of English Law,
Niigata University, Japan, Senior Lecturer
in Law Kingston University, England.

Barry Rose Law Publishers Ltd
Chichester, England

ISBN 1 872328 47 4

Jacket cover illustration by kind permission
of The British Museum

Barry Rose Law Publishers Limited
Little London
Chichester
England

Printed in Great Britain by BPC Wheatons Ltd, Exeter

For Philippa

Acknowledgments

I would like to acknowledge the invaluable assistance provided by Louise Doey in proof reading this book.

Thanks are due to Teiko Tamaki of the University of Niigata Law Faculty and the staff at the British Library and Lincoln's Inn for their assistance with the collection of materials. More generally, I would like to thank my students at Kingston University and in Japan over the years for the contribution they have made to the development of my own thought. I would also like to express my gratitude to the University of Niigata Law Faculty, which was my home during the writing of this book; and in particular, to Professors Yamashita, Onozaka, Namazugoshi, Kasai and Kojima. A few short sections have been adapted from several articles that originally appeared in *Justice of the Peace and Local Government Law*, which Journal I would like to thank for permitting their reproduction. I am enormously indebted to the works of a number of major scholars in the field, whose books can be found in the Select Bibliography and in strategically placed footnotes. The spelling and punctuation of contemporary sources is as in the original except where modified to facilitate comprehension. Those parts of the text which relate directly to incidents in Flanders' life are headed in Chancery script, to aid reference to the novel. All mistakes are, needless to say, entirely the author's responsibility.

Gregory Durston
Niigata, Japan
Whitsun, 1996

Contents

Chapter 1

Daniel Defoe and the Novel

*"One of these authors (the fellow that was pilloried, I have
forgot his name) is indeed so grave, sententious, dogmatical
a rogue, that there is no enduring him." Swift on Defoe (1708).*

D aniel Defoe was born in about 1660 in St Giles in London, (the
exact date is uncertain) being the son of a Presbyterian tallow-
chandler and butcher named Foe (the "De" was later added by
his son). Defoe's final years were to be marred by increasing debt and
pursuit by his many creditors, periodically forcing him into hiding until
he died, a rather forlorn figure, in Moorfields, London, in April 1731.
Between these dates he had lived an extraordinary life.

In his childhood and youth he had benefited from an excellent
education at the Dissenters' Academy at Newington Green, run by Charles
Morton. There he received a relatively "modern" type of education, with
all lessons, unusually for the period, given in English. Education was a
particularly strong area for Dissenters, prevented as they were by religious
tests from attending the universities at Oxford and Cambridge. They were
numerous in the capital. The religious census of 1676 revealed that at least
seven per cent of the population of London were Dissenters; if all
Quakers, Presbyterians and Independants were identified accurately,
however, the figure may have been much higher.

Despite being later referred to by Jonathan Swift as an "illiterate stupid
scribbler" Defoe showed an early talent for languages, including his own,

1

a grasp of mathematics and also claimed a good grounding in "natural philosophy, logic, geography, and history". The future Methodist leader, Charles Wesley was to be another famous former pupil who also benefited from the Academy, in the following century. The school, again unusually for the period, as well as possessing mathematical instruments and thermometers also had a fully equipped laboratory.[1] This exposure early on to a broad academic curriculum may explain some of the enormous versatility in Defoe's own life.

Between finishing his education and his death he led a very varied existence, in which he managed to combine training for the Presbyterian ministry (abandoned fairly quickly), brief service in Monmouth's rebel army in 1685 (he was a firm opponent of the Catholic James II), a later career as a government spy (especially involved over the Union of England and Scotland in 1707), being commissioned by the new Secretary of State, his patron, Robert Harley, to travel through England gauging the "temper" of the people (in 1704), numerous (and very often unsuccessful) business ventures that ranged from breeding civet cats to producing ceramic tiles in Essex; being a merchant in the wine, tobacco and hosiery trades, travelling extensively in Europe, and also being, sometimes simultaneously with these activities, a writer of popular "criminal accounts". His first (but not last) bankruptcy, in 1692, appears to have been a powerful impetus to his professional writing career. Additionally, he saw service in the Glass Duty Office, and spent a short spell in Newgate prison, and in the pillory, for publishing an ironic satire, ridiculing the religious intolerance of the new government following the death of William III in 1702.[2] This work, *The Shortest Way with Dissenters* (1702), did not find favour with the Tories, in particular, and much of the Established Anglican Church in general. The House of Commons ordered the book to be burnt and an advertisement was even placed in the official *Gazette* offering a reward for his arrest.

---

1. Watts, M., *The Dissenters, From the Reformation to the French Revolution* (1978), p.303.
2. Allegedly the crowd formed a guard round the pillory and drank his health to show their support.

This experience, combined with his three days in the pillory in July of 1703, his indictment at the Old Bailey on February 24, 1703, his subsequent trial at that court's July Sessions in the same year, and his custody in Newgate, meant that unlike many other writers on criminal justice matters, Defoe was often writing directly from personal experience. This is a crucial point, as much of the value of *Moll Flanders* as an illustration, albeit a highly entertaining one, of the criminal justice system of his time, lies in Defoe's own wide experience and exposure to this facet of life, and the fact that the novel's illustration of the system was not simply an "armchair account" based on hearsay (unlike that of some of his contemporaries, such as John Gay). As a result of this, modern writers have regularly commented on the "powerful sense of authenticity provided by Defoe's novels, especially the criminal novels".[3]

Defoe was to have further brushes with the authorities involving personal custody later in his life. In 1713 he was briefly arrested as a debtor at the behest of a creditor of his from Yarmouth;[4] in the same year he was arrested again and detained for a weekend in Newgate for treason, as a result of publishing *Reasons Against the Succession of the House of Hanover*. In fact, it even appears that on this occasion he was deliberately arrested on a Saturday so that he would be unable to arrange bail before the Monday, forcing him to spend two days in custody. His experiences were evidently somewhat grim and humiliating for a man in his position (he was in his mid-fifties), as he talks in his letters of the time of "having been stripped naked in that jayl". This was particularly unpleasant for him as Defoe considered that he had "a body unfit to bear the hardship of prison", while he also felt that as a "gentleman, the prisons, pillorys, and such like, are worse to me than death".[5]

Simultaneously with other aspects of his work, Defoe was also producing a prolific number of serious books and papers, about 500 in

---

3. Faller, L.B., *Crime and Defoe* (1993), p.37.
4. He was not the only eighteenth century writer to have this experience; John Cleland wrote *Fanny Hill* while in custody for debt in 1749.
5. Letters to the Earl of Nottingham, 1703 and Robert Harley, 1710, at pp.2 and 407, in *The Letters of Daniel Defoe*, Healey, G.H. (ed), (1955).

total. These were on a variety of subjects, ranging from crime, in particular his authoritative analysis, *Street-Robberies Consider'd* (1728), the highwayman and Newgate escapee *Jack Sheppard* (in 1724), histories of the arch-criminals *Jonathan Wild* (in 1725) and to the condition of England, which he considered in great depth in his two volume *A Tour Through Great Britain* (produced between 1724-6). He was also a very active producer of "political" pamphlets, something which periodically created serious problems for him. In many ways Defoe was a profoundly innovative and "advanced" thinker for his times, his *Essay upon Projects* (of 1697) proposing the creation of an income tax, an advanced insane asylum, road improvements and the establishment of a university in London. Inevitably, however, polymath though he was, his knowledge of crime in the London area was especially good, as would be expected from a man with his unusual life experiences, who was also a born and bred native of the City.[6]

Defoe is sometimes considered the father of modern English journalism because of his association with up to 26 periodicals during his life, and his writing and publishing, almost single handed, of the *Review,* from 1704 to 1713 (three times a week for most of this period). This exposure to "journalism" greatly affected his style and perception. Today, however, he is probably best known for a number of important works of fiction, produced relatively late in his career (he was in his late fifties and sixties), of which *Robinson Crusoe* (1719) and *Moll Flanders* (1722) are the most significant, and indeed have some pretensions to being considered as the first "true" modern English novels, showing considerable psychological realism. There were to be three other novels in which criminal activity played a major or significant part. As well as *Moll Flanders*, these included *Roxanna, Colonel Jack* and *Captain Singleton.* In writing these books Defoe drew heavily on the contemporary genre of very loose, but supposedly true, "criminal biographies", a form of literature to which he had been an important contributor when younger, and a tradition that can be seen to have provided the immediate literary

---

6.   Defoe, like Moll Flanders, had of course also had the experience of hiding from creditors, using in his case the pseudonym "Andrew Morton".

"parentage" for his, and other similar, novels. Indeed, he still felt it necessary, in *Moll Flanders*, to make some pretence, in his preface to the novel, for it being a true account of a real person, though he prudently accepted that "... it will be hard for a private history to be taken for genuine".

There is considerable literary debate as to many features of the "autobiography" of Flanders. In particular, is it naive or ironical in its portrayal of her? Was there a single real person on whom the fictional account was based or was it purely fictional? With regard to the latter question, the answer would seem to be "no", though there were undoubtedly a number of genuine individuals on whom his wide experience of the world would have allowed Defoe to draw heavily; some of these can probably be identified by name. For example, an examination of Defoe's earlier life and writings reveals a number of possible "real life" sources for aspects of the character of Moll Flanders.[7] This was a question that was considered by literary commentators from as early as 1723, with different candidates being put forward in a variety of pamphlets (due to its great popularity there were three editions of the novel in 1722 alone, and another edition and an abridgment in 1723). Some of these potential sources appear earlier in the *Review* or in Defoe's many other writings. For example, he had written about the notorious pickpocket Moll King, a "dextrous jade" who specialised in "stealing watches at ladies sides", who may well have been an important source. There have been a number of other female candidates proposed: Moll Harvey, Mary Godson, etc., some of whom Defoe would have personally seen in Newgate either as visitor or inmate. It should also be remembered that there had been a notorious London criminal in the seventeenth century called Moll Cutpurse. To an extent, "Moll" can almost be taken as a generic name for any female criminal of the time. Thirty years later, Henry Fielding, for example, created a character called "Blear Eyed Moll", a raucous female prison inmate in his novel *Amelia* (1752). Defoe himself was the author of a letter dated July 16, 1720, supposedly emanating from one "Moll of

---

7.   On this see also, Howson, G. "Who Was Moll Flanders"? *Times Literary Supplement* (January 18, 1968).

Rag Fair" who was "now in America", and sent to *The Original Weekly Journal* (later *Applebees Journal*) to which he was a major contributor. In this letter the "writer" purported to be by trade "an Elder and well known sister of the file ... in plain English I was in the former part of my life, an eminent pick-pocket", but says that she was unhappily "drawn aside out of my ordinary and lawful calling into the dangerous business of shop-lifting, and being not half so clever and nimble at that as I was at my own trade, I was nab'd by a plaguy Hawks-Ey'd Journeyman Mercer". She was subsequently transported to America, like Moll Flanders in the novel.

Earlier, there had also been the exceptionally popular work by Captain Alexander Smith *The history of the lives of the most noted highway-men, foot-pads, house-breakers, shoplifts, and cheats of both sexes ... for above 50 years last past* (published in London in 1714). By 1719 it had run to five editions. A number of female criminals who may well have influenced Defoe's writing were portrayed in its pages. Foremost amongst them might have been that of Moll Hawkins a "shop-lift" for whom "adultery and fornication were her common recreations, as well as shop-lifting". However, she also had the habit of "putting herself into a good handsome dress" to carry out her work (clear echoes of Moll Flanders there); she was executed in 1703. Additionally, in this work, there was the portrayal of Anne Holland, a "pick-pocket" who, similarly to one of Flanders' marriages, was "marry'd to one James Wilson, an eminent highway-man, very expert in his occupation". Another felon discussed in this work, was Mary Carleton, who was a "cheat, thief, and jilt" and who was regularly "indicted for having two husbands, but so carry'd the matter that she was acquitted". Together, facets of these real women almost provide a complete composite picture of Flanders. Most likely, then, Moll Flanders was a fictional and composite character drawing heavily on a small group of women prisoners personally familiar to Defoe, and other real female felons portrayed in contemporary literature.

Some incidents in *Moll Flanders* clearly came direct from Defoe's own observations of London; thus the pandemonium surrounding the fire at a gentlewoman's house can probably find its source in a fire that he personally witnessed and wrote about in the *Review* in January 1713, an

6

incident in which he observed furniture and furnishings (equal in quality, he felt, to that which formerly would have belonged to the nobility) "thrown into a street flowing a foot deep with water and mud, trodden under-foot by the crowd".

On the question of Defoe's social realism, it has very rightly been remarked that his novels are "packed thick with evidence of [contemporary] social conditions". Many of the individual instances in Flanders' criminal life are well evidenced by numerous other contemporary accounts of criminal trials from the time, some of them being almost classic criminal scenarios (such as her shoplifting ventures). However, it has also been observed that some of Defoe's social analysis was simplistic, and it has consequently even been said that he "can hardly be ranked as a thinker, he is rather a peculiarly vivid photographer, to whom nothing is too humble or too sordid for his camera".[8] While in many respects a very broad minded thinker, as evidenced by his attack on a narrow form of nationalism (in particular the resentment at the foreign birth of William III) in *The True-born Englishman* (written in 1701), Defoe does appear, from his serious writings, to have had a relatively "straightforward", robust and perhaps sometimes even naive attitude to some of the structural social problems of the England of his time, and London in particular, ascribing, as he did, much poverty to drink and idleness and only allowing for unforeseen accidents as a justified extrinsic source of individual misfortune. To an extent, in Defoe's attitude can be seen a fore-runner of the later fairly rigid Victorian distinction between the poor, one that identified two separate classes, the "deserving" and the "undeserving". The former included anyone thrown into financial straits by events beyond their control, such as illness or old age, etc. The undeserving poor were made up of people who deliberately refused to work, and who appeared to live from begging or property crime. As a religious and slightly puritanical man, Defoe would have had limited time for many modern explanations for hardship or crime. However, rightly or wrongly, this in no way detracts from the quality of his observance of

8.   Hearnshaw, F.J.C. (ed) *The Social and Political Ideas of Some English Thinkers of the Augustan Age, A.D. 1650-1750* (1928), p.174.

his own society.

Contemporary Political Events

The years around the period that Defoe was writing *Moll Flanders* were momentous ones for the nation. The previous year, 1720, the South Sea "bubble" had "burst", the ensuing financial scandal almost implicating the King, the somewhat unpopular German monarch George I (reigning from 1714 to 1727), a man who could barely speak English and who kept a pair of widely loathed mistresses. Two years earlier, in 1719, there had been an attempted, if rather desultory, Jacobite invasion (much less threatening than that of 1715). The year afterwards, 1722, there was another Jacobite conspiracy and Robert Walpole became Prime Minister, to be a dominating political presence in Britain until his retirement, with an earldom, in 1742.

Format of the Novel

The novel, written in 1721 and published early the following year, purports to be a historical autobiography of Flanders, though Defoe himself admits, in the preface, to refining it "... the copy which came first to hand, having been written in language more like one still in Newgate, than one grown penitent". It was supposedly written towards the end of her life, as an old woman, in 1683. This would place much of her criminal career in the 1660s and early 1670s. However, a great deal of the book is clearly anachronistic, being more an accurate record of features of urban life and crime in the early eighteenth century, the period when it was written, rather than the slightly earlier period in which it was supposedly set; as has been observed by literary commentators, "the setting and events conform more closely to the 1722 date of publication", though, a little confusingly, this is not always the case.[9]

Essentially, the book recounts the life experiences of Moll Flanders through many vicissitudes, from her birth in Newgate prison to her inmate mother, till her contented retirement as a by then honest woman in England in her seventies. In particular, Defoe's account of Flanders' 12-year criminal career, embarked on when she was well into middle age, provides an acute and perceptive introduction to the period, its criminal procedure, punishments, and law and order problems, and is also highly illustrative of those issues. Most importantly, it is a largely accurate portrayal of London's criminal scene, though there is, necessarily, no suggestion in the work that Flanders is herself a "typical" London criminal. She has absolutely no intention, as her career develops, of joining the "poor unhappy thieves" who commit crime out of a basic instinct to survive. *Moll Flanders* is, of course, within the "picaresque" tradition (popular in the eighteenth century, and attracting other English writers such as Tobias Smollett), and it is as much aimed at entertainment as instruction; however while the *totality* of Flanders' life may be rather implausible, the parts in themselves are nearly always highly convincing.

It was not to be Defoe's only such fictional portrayal of crime through a pretended autobiography. Two years later, in 1723, he published *The Life of Colonel Jack*, the first part of which was the portrayal of a young male thief (rather than a middle-aged female one), supposedly being that of a man who was born a Gentleman put "prentice to a pick-pocket was six and 20 years a thief, and then kidnapped to Virginia", before becoming a soldier.

The account of Flanders' life is at its weakest in those few areas that deal with lacunae in Defoe's own life experiences. For example, his understanding of the opportunities for those transported to America, a place that he had never been to, is certainly a little idealistic. Generally though, as the thoroughly educated son of a Dissenter he was well situated to observe the society and establishment of which he was an integral but, to a small degree, not quite a full, member. Consequently his portrayals

---

9.   Howson, G., "Who was Moll Flanders"? *Times Literary Supplement*, no.3438, (January 18, 1968).

have a "ring of truth"; his heroes are never flawless and his villains never evil caricatures, while he also has a great eye for minor detail. It is this detail which may explain why, in the nineteenth century Sir Leslie Stephen, a literary critic (and brother of the famous Victorian Judge) was to say that the novel "could not claim any higher interest than that which belongs to the ordinary Police Report, given with infinite fullness and vivacity of detail". While this is grossly unfair to the work's literary merit, the student of early eighteenth century London crime and criminal justice could ask for no greater recommendation.

Chapter 2

Law and Order in
Early Eighteenth Century London

"Nature has left this tincture in the blood, that all men would be tyrants if they could." Defoe, The History of the Kentish Petition (1712).

Crime in London and England at this Time

Flanders spent most of her criminal career in London, though occasionally she moved out into the provinces (especially East Anglia). It is thus worth considering some of the general features of crime in England, and in London in particular, in the late seventeenth and early eighteenth centuries.

In this period, law enforcement in the nation generally, and within the London area itself in particular, varied enormously in its intensity; some locations in the seventeenth and eighteenth centuries were virtually "lawless" zones, others comparatively efficiently policed. Additionally, the judicial practice of local courts sometimes also varied greatly from region to region. England in the early eighteenth century was a very decentralized country in which there was no serious suggestion that the government writ should run uniformly; this was much less so, even, than in the highly centralized France of Louis XIV. There were numerous local power centres in the country and the towns that vigorously resisted central control and which had to be dealt with circumspectly. This contributed to a process whereby the administration of criminal justice in the nation

11

at the time can be compared to a series of sieves; from start to finish there were many factors that might preclude a criminal being caught, convicted and punished.

However, it does appear that at this point London was beginning to experience the onset of an apparent (or at least perceived) crisis in law and public order, and consequently posed policing problems far ahead of those of the rest of the nation. It has even been asserted, albeit with very considerable exaggeration, that "in eighteenth century England crime was overwhelmingly a London phenomenon".[1] There are some attractive potential explanations for this. For example, the explosion in gin drinking was already well under way by the early 1720s, initially even being helped by specially favourable government tariffs, but ultimately encouraging a downward cycle in the physical and moral health of the populace that could easily lead to crime. Its ready availability and deleterious effects were to be graphically illustrated in later prints by Hogarth, and caught by the popular contemporary advertisement for a tavern, "drunk for a penny, dead drunk for tuppence, straw free".

Gin Consumption

The explosion in spirit drinking which started significantly before 1720, and peaked in the 1740s (before reducing gradually from about 1750), prompted widespread public concern in the year in which *Moll Flanders* was written, though Thomas D'Avenant had seen the potential dangers as early as 1700, when he observed that "this a growing vice among the common people, and may in time prevail as much as opium with the Turks". Indeed, right at the inception of the consumption of the new spirit, Sir Thomas Overbury had noted its damaging potential, when, in 1615, he remarked of the poor Dutchmen already clustered round St Katharine's near the Tower "now this new trade of brewing strong waters makes a

---

1.   McLynn, F., *Crime and Punishment in Eighteenth Century England* (1991), p.1. The greater number and accessibility of contemporary sources in London also contributes to this perception amongst some modern historians of crime.

number of mad men". In 1721, even while Defoe was writing, the Westminster Justices were conducting an inquiry into the issue, and opined that the great increase in the number of alehouses, brandy and "geneva" shops was the "principal cause of the increase of our poor and of all the vice and debauchery, as well as of the felonies ... about this town".[2] Cheap alcohol, especially gin (it was usually drunk with fruit cordial "mixers" by the "quartern", and largely unregulated in its sale) can at times have been said to have had as deleterious an effect as crack cocaine and heroin in the modern inner city, perhaps less potent in effect but far more widespread in its consumption. In rural areas, moreover, there was a firm basis of economic support for the distilling industry encouraging its high level of production. Much distilling was carried on by small almost unregulated enterprises which often retailed direct to the London populace and were, in Defoe's opinion a "a collection of sinners against the people, for they break almost all the known laws of government in the Nation".[3] Drunkenness is a periodical motif in *Moll Flanders* and explains the total incapacity of one of her gentleman victims (she herself did not overindulge in this vice).

The statistics were highly alarming. By the 1740s the average weekly consumption was to be two pints for every man woman and child.[4] Even in the 1720s the gin houses were numbered in their thousands. The magistrate, Henry Fielding, in the mid-eighteenth century, was to claim that "this poison called gin" had become "the principal sustenance (if it may be so called) of more than a hundred thousand People in this metropolis". As such, it acquired a number of "cant" or colloquial names, "Blue Flash" and "Lightning" amongst them. Not only was gin cheap, but other spirits were also easily affordable (smuggled French brandy was fairly inexpensive, while "British Brandy" was only 4s. a gallon).[5] In the 1730s 14 gallons of spirits (of all types) were consumed per adult male a year (though it should not be forgotten that women, and sometimes even

---

2.   George, D., *London Life in the Eighteenth Century*, 2nd ed (1930), p.31.
3.   Defoe, D., *Complete English Tradesman* (1727), ii. Part II, p.80.
4.   Porter, R., *London* (1994) p.181.
5.   Rude, G., *Hanoverian London* (1972), p.72.

children, also drank a lot of this).

Attempts by the authorities to contain the situation, such as the hugely unpopular Gin Act of 1736, which introduced strict licensing requirements for selling the spirit, were largely ineffectual. Nevertheless, the potentially criminogenic properties of this torrent of alcohol was something that other near contemporaries of Defoe were also well aware of. In his later *Inquiry* (of 1751) Henry Fielding observed that "so many temporal mischiefs arise from it, amongst which are frequently robbery and murder itself".[6]

Problems with Discharged Soldiers and Sailors

However, alcohol abuse (yet to reach its worst level) was by no means the only pressing social problem in the Metropolis in the early 1700s. There were also increasing problems from the considerable numbers of discharged soldiers and sailors present in the streets.[7] As early as 1693 a pamphlet, "offered for the consideration of parliament", expressly raised the problems faced by such men and the "deplorable condition of the Reduced and discharged men" from the army; these were veterans who had previously "served his majesty in the reducing of Ireland and in the wars in the low countries". The growth of this problem was linked to the numerous ongoing wars combined with the military revolution of the period (characterized as it was by ever larger armies and navies).[8] Indeed, there were almost 200,000 men under arms, in various forms, in Queen Anne's time alone (1702-1714). The ending of Marlborough's wars in 1713, and the accompanying demobilization, a few years before Defoe was writing *Moll Flanders*, caused especially acute problems with large amounts of tradeless young men, familiar with weapons, and accustomed to danger, returning to England, and especially to London. Sometimes these men had been recruited direct from prison in the first place. This

---

6. *Inquiry into the Causes of the Late Increase of Robbers* (1751), Barnes and Noble (edn) (1967), p.19.
7. Beattie, A.J.M., *Crime and the Courts in England 1660-1800* (1986), p.228.
8. *Cf.* Parker, G., *The Military Revolution* (1988), p.45.

was alluded to by Defoe himself when he was threatened with imprisonment for his publication of *The Shortest Way with Dissenters*. He offered to serve in Queen Anne's army in the Netherlands for a year in lieu of prison, noting in a letter to the Earl of Nottingham that "felons and thieves whose punishment is death are frequently spar'd upon entering into Her Majesties service".[9] Defoe identified the military of the early eighteenth century as a fertile source of recruitment to the ranks of criminals. In *Street Robberies Consider'd* he stated that "I hope that the honest part of the soldiery will forgive me, if I think we have many incorporated in their companies as fit for the triple tree". This was, he felt, partly because they were often under-employed "their time hangs upon their hands", while some were also "idle and lazy". He suggested that particular "inquiry ought to be made concerning those [soldiers] that go better dress'd than their Stations will admit".[10]

Even allowing for some exaggeration on his part, it is certainly the case that Press Acts for the compulsory recruitment of debtors, vagrants and other "marginalized" members of English society, to the military were in force in the years 1704-12 (and also at other critical times later in the eighteenth century).[11] There was a well known and marked correlation (by both contemporary writers and modern social historians) between the onset of peace and rising levels of crime.[12] Not only were young men released onto the streets rather than taken away from them, but war industries, such as armaments and uniform manufactures, were likely to cut back heavily on employment. It was also widely believed that discharged soldiers found readjustment to normal labour and regular hours of work very difficult, especially as, unlike sailors they usually had no obvious "trade" to ply.

9.   Letter of January 9, 1703, in *The Letters of Daniel Defoe*, Healey, G.H. (ed) (1955).

10.   Page 49.

11.   Anderson, MS, *War and Society in Europe of the Old Regime, 1618-1789.*

12.   Hay, D., *War Dearth and Theft in the Eighteenth Century, Past and Present*, no.95 (1983), p.127.

Other Social Problems in the Metropolis

However, gin and discharged servicemen were merely contributory factors to a more serious developing urban problem. There were other fundamental structural causes for an incipient crisis in policing in the capital. These can be ascribed in large part to the unusual size of the "Metropolis", that is the conurbation that comprised the two adjoining cities of London and Westminster and some adjacent parts, and which by 1712 were completely joined together. By this time they had a total population of about 500,000 (some accounts place it significantly higher),[13] and 11 per cent of the total population of England.[14] In defining this greater "London" in his *Journal of the Plague Year* (1720), Defoe stated that this was to "mean the whole mass of buildings, city, liberties, suburbs, Westminster, Southwark, and altogether".

Long before 1700, London had started to explode out of its historic boundaries. Indeed, around the turn of the eighteenth century, Celia Fiennes had been struck by how there was no longer open space between the two neighbouring cities "it makes up but one vast building with all its suburbs". In 1560, 73 per cent of London's population had lived in the city (the area surrounded by its ancient walls); by 1680, however, the proportion had fallen to 24 per cent and was set to fall steadily further as its burgeoning suburbs, such as Southwark, expanded. London in 1550 was still clearly discernible as a medieval city, largely concentrated inside its historic walls; this was to have changed totally 200 years later.[15] It was easily the largest city in Europe, rivalled only (and remotely) by Amsterdam. It was (Edo in Japan possibly excepted) the greatest conurbation in the world. It dwarfed its nearest English provincial rivals, Norwich and Bristol, which had only 30,000 inhabitants apiece at the start of the 1700s. Its continuing expansion seemed inexorable to

---

13.   Howson, G., *Thieftaker General* (1970), p.22 and Summerson, J., *Georgian London* (1978). At p.25 he places the population of the London area in 1700 at about 674,500.

14.   Wrigley, E.A., *A simple model of London's Importance in Changing English Society and Economy 1650-1750, Past and Present,* no.37, (1967), p.44.

15.   Sharpe, J.A., *Early Modern England, A Social History* (1987), p.86.

contemporaries; observing that the villages of Chelsea and Marylebone were being drawn into London's ambit, Defoe was to ask, in a sense of bemusement, in 1724 "whither will this monstrous city then extend"?

As the death rate in London for this period exceeded the birth rate to a considerable degree, the increase was necessarily the result of a large scale immigration of people from all parts of the British Isles. London, unlike other cities in Britain, exerted a nationwide "pull". Rather than recruiting merely from its immediate hinterland, it received people from as far afield as Ireland and Scotland and even from overseas. By the early eighteenth century it had colonies of foreigners from several other European countries, such as Holland (the Dutchmen living mainly near the Tower), as well as a small community of African descent living near the riverside docks. This supplementing of the native population was crucial. Between 1750 and 1769, 63 per cent of children in London died before the age of five (of those born in workhouses or received there before they were one, the figure was over 90 per cent, something that Flanders herself alludes to in the novel when trying to decide on the future of one of her many offspring). The situation was to improve somewhat from the 1750s as mortality rates fell, inevitably though, in the early eighteenth century, many of the city's inhabitants were immigrants to London, often the young, poor and energetic from the provinces.

This influx of young uprooted people produced an attendant reduction in those informal and traditional methods of social control which had worked comparatively well in rural areas where there were few strangers, and where recourse to the regular criminal process was often very much a "last resort" for minor offenders. This was inevitable as in London a far higher proportion of day-to-day contacts were on a "casual" basis between comparative, or total, strangers, in a city that was already significantly larger than present day Edinburgh. While the harsh exigencies of early modern life inevitably meant that for much of the "lower orders" of society, "Merry England" was only merry on a number of widely separated occasions (rural communities could be rife with internal tensions), the feast days and communal customs of "traditional" England, whether the apprentices' raucous celebration of Shrove Tuesday, or the widespread celebration of Mayday, probably really did give the ordinary people "a sense of the rhythm of the world in which they lived and perhaps helped foster a sense of belonging".[16] This was to be progressively lost in the Capital.

The political philosopher, Adam Smith, later in the century, was to specifically identify the city as a potentially corrupting force because of this lack of social solidarity, saying that in the intimate context of a village a man of "low moral character" could be controlled, but "as soon as he comes into a great city he is sunk in obscurity and darkness, and he is very likely to ... abandon himself to every sort of low profligacy and vice". He was not original in suggesting that cities could be corrupting, a pamphlet writer from 1716 even opining that as a result of this process "... there is no populous city whatsoever, but abounds with knaves and cheats".[17]

Additionally, this huge city still preserved its rather ramshackle, largely medieval, and highly varied, system of local government.[18] The City of London itself was *sui generis* in the whole country, with its ruling Lord Mayor, Sheriffs and Aldermen acutely jealous of their ancient privileges. This was unlike the situation in neighbouring Westminster, which had never become a municipality in the full sense, being unable to elect, at this time in its history, a proper Lord Mayor and Court of Aldermen. It was nominally governed by a court of 12 Burgesses. Other parts of the Metropolis were still governed by the Middlesex JPs, in, at least theoretically, the same way as other parishes in the country (Middlesex being the county immediately surrounding the two cities North of the river; large parts of it were urbanized by 1720). These JPs also had an important function in the government of Westminster generally (but not the City), while in the built up areas south of the river, the Surrey JPs held sway (except, after 1550, in the City dominated and controlled borough). This historic diffusion of power was backed up by an increasingly archaic system of policing, based on local nightwatchmen and part-time, usually unpaid, parish constables, recruited, sometimes

16.   Sharpe, J.A., *Early Modern England, A Social History 1550-1760* (1987), p.282.
17.   "The Case of Richard Gascoigne", printed and sold by J.Roberts of Warwick-Lane (1716), p.5.
18.   Plumb, J.H., *England in the Eighteenth Century* (1950), p.14.

against their will, to fulfil the office for a year or two by their Anglican parish vestries.

Adding to these problems were the socio-economic changes brought about by the ongoing commercial and agrarian revolutions of the period. These were second in importance only to the industrial revolution of the late eighteenth century. In 1700 England was economically the most advanced nation in the world, with a cash and market economy aimed at producing an agricultural and manufacturing surplus.[19] To call it "pre-industrial" (as opposed to pre-factory) can be misleading. England had moved from a position of relative backwardness in the mid-sixteenth century to become a European leader in many industries. There were already a few signs as to what would happen later in the eighteenth century. The engineer Thomas Savery had effectively pioneered the steam engine with his "miner's friend" of 1698, used to pump out water from coal mines, although it was still a very crude device. This change had been greatly aided by the growing "consumer" society which was creating a nation-wide market, and was centred very much on London.[20] In 1705, 157,000 tons of goods arrived in London from foreign ports alone (this excluding a substantial coastal trade from within the realm). Defoe himself was to say (in 1724) that the whole of Britain depended on London "for the consumption of its produce".[21] Additionally, as well as importing commodities, London became the national centre for the production of a range of high value, and even luxury goods, such as silk weaving (particularly in Spitalfields where it had been pioneered by Huguenot immigrants from France), brewing and gin distilling, cabinet making and the manufacture of glass, soap, clocks and watches.[22] This new "consumer" society was also reflected in an unprecedented degree of mobility in the nation, and substantial new amounts of portable wealth, Henry Fielding's later "torrent of luxury".

This increase of wealth was also, in itself, to be a popular explanation

---

19. Evans, E., *The Forging of the Modern State* (1983), p.11.
20. Sharpe, J.A., *Early Modern England, A Social History* (1987), p.142.
21. Radzinowicz, L., *A History of English Criminal Law*, vol.2, p.350.
22. Wrigley, E.A., *ibid.*, p.62.

amongst contemporary writers for increased crime in London; more than 80 years after Defoe was writing, Patrick Colquhoun felt that "wherever riches are placed in one scale, the apparent good is counterbalanced by an increased quantum and profligacy of crimes in the other".[23] In part this was because it inevitably provided attractive targets for crime, especially in a city like London, which was the location of the Royal Court and the law courts, and thus the focus for the richer elements in the entire country, many of whom kept town houses for part of the year. There was a greater and much more widespread abundance of material goods to steal. It has been observed that in 1530 the majority of Englishmen not only lived in rural communities but also wore sackcloth, skin, canvas and leather clothing and ate black bread from wooden trenchers without the use of forks or pocket handkerchiefs, while by 1780 brick houses, cotton clothes, white bread, plates and cutlery were becoming accessible to even the lower classes of society. Even in Defoe's day what had been considered normal a century earlier was changing as he expressly remarked when examining the contents thrown from a "middle order" house that had caught fire.[24]

London was also socially well "ahead" of the rest of the country in fashions, behaviour and social attitudes; in many ways it was the clearest illustration of the newly "individualistic" culture of Defoe's age. Flanders herself noted the increased cynicism of all classes in London, observing that usually "Marriages were here the consequences of politick schemes for forming Interests".

As Fanny Hill was to note in John Cleland's early pornographic novel by that name (written in 1749), arrival in London from the provinces (even, as in her case, nearby Kent) was an extraordinary and disorientating experience "as we passed through the greatest streets that led to our inn, the noise of the coaches, the hurry, the crowds of foot passengers, in short, the new scenery of the shops and houses, at once pleased and amazed me". Earlier, in 1689, the Reverend Robert Kirk from Perthshire, visiting

---

23.   Colquhoun, *ibid.*, p.34.
24.   See on this Hill, C., *Reformation to Industrial Revolution*, Penguin Economic History of Britain (1992), p.20.

London to seek a publisher for his Gaelic Bible, noted in his diary that "The city is a vast wilderness. Few in it know a fourth part of its streets".[25] The streets were noisy, crowded and very dirty, something well caught by Swift's description of the aftermath of a city rain shower:

> "Sweepings from butchers stalls, dung, guts, and blood,
> Drowned puppies, stinking sprats, all drenched in mud,
> Dead cats and turnip-tops come tumbling down the flood."[26]

In the rapidly expanding and changing Metropolis, the traditional patterns of social organization and policing, including, for example a customary tolerance for "collective bargaining by riot", were becoming inappropriate by the early decades of the eighteenth century. There was a growing sense amongst "respectable" people in London of a "loss of control". Later in the century Henry Fielding was to say of the Metropolis, "a thief may harbour with as great security as wild beasts do in the deserts of Africa or Arabia, in the cities of London and Westminster, with the late vast addition of their suburbs". Of course, it is important not to fall into the mistake of "discovering" artificial watersheds in London's policing history; there were already serious social and criminal problems in the early seventeenth century city, and even before.

It must also be remembered, when considering the apparently higher rate of criminal activity in the Metropolis (compared to the countryside) throughout the early modern period (1500-1750), that in rural areas it was a lot more difficult and expensive to use the formal court structures than in London; courts sat less frequently and were usually much more distant and widely spaced apart, making attendance to give evidence, for example, significantly more onerous and costly than in London, and in turn probably increasing reluctance on the part of private prosecutors and witnesses to become involved in such action rather than having recourse to the informal resolution of crimes. This, as much as any other social factors, may, in part, explain the apparently higher rates of crime in

---

25.   In Carswell, J., *The South Sea Bubble* (1960), p.1.
26.   Swift, J., from "A Description of a City Shower" (1710).

21

London.

Even so, making full allowance for this criminal legacy from earlier times, and a differential rate of reporting compared to the countryside, it does appear that the policing problems of London assumed a much more serious stamp at the turn of the seventeenth century.

The Criminal Geography of London

In the early eighteenth century London was still not yet very heavily differentiated on a social basis, the varying classes generally living in relative proximity, and small employers and workers living close in to the most fashionable areas. Nevertheless there were a few areas which had already acquired a reputation for being largely poor, and sometimes also dangerous by 1700. These included places such as St Katharine's by the Tower, where so many poor people had congregated that, in 1690, at Quarter Sessions, they even petitioned to be released from having to fund double watches "... the inhabitants of the said hamlets being generally very poor, and unable to sustain the charge".[27] Others areas, such as Bethnal Green, Whitechapel, and St Giles in the Fields and Covent Garden were slowly beginning their descent to such a status. London's social medley was beginning, very slowly, to become less mixed. Later in the century the magistrate, Saunders Welsh was to tell Dr Johnson that a score of people died every week from malnutrition in these poorer areas.[28]

This process of gradual social differentiation can be seen in several other parts of the Metropolis. In 1730 the shopkeepers and traders of Westminster complained, to the Westminster Sessions, that several people "of the most notorious characters and infamously wicked lives and conversations" had taken up residence in their parish. This was felt to be especially the case in the immediate neighbourhood of Drury Lane which was "infested with these vile people", the presence of whom apparently resulted in "frequent outcries in the night, fighting, robberies and all sorts

---

27.   Hardy, W.J., *Calendar of the Sessions Books 1689 to 1709* (1905), p.17.
28.   Rude, G., *Hanoverian London*, p.86.

of debaucheries".[29] In some parts of London, Henry Fielding was to note in the 1740s "a rogue no sooner gives the alarm, within certain purlieus, than 20 or 30 armed villains are found ready to come to his assistance". Although the eastern parishes, in particular, were becoming problematic, some of the worst areas, such as parts of Holborn, Alsatia and St Giles, were not to the East of the City, while Southwark to the south of the river still maintained its position as easily the most unruly part of the Metropolis in 1700, criminals escaping across London Bridge to its relative safety.

A provision that was to facilitate the increasing differentiation of London throughout the eighteenth century was the extensive use of local Acts of Parliament to allow for the levying of special rates to provide enhanced services, especially those relating to security. Thus local statutes allowed Marylebone, St Andrews Holborn, and Peckham to raise a superior local force, cost. This increased the growing division between "good" and "bad" areas - poor locations not being able to raise the funds necessary to carry out such programmes.

Population was expanding at a particularly rapid rate in those parts of the Metropolis where the City's controlling writ was weakest, there having been constant proclamations from the early 1600s forbidding London's expansion (none of them successful). This accounts, in part, for the crowded population, at an early date, of poor people in St Katharine's by the Tower, and of places in the Liberty of Stepney and Hackney.

However, even when all of this is considered, in 1700 very few parts of London were more than a stone's throw from a "criminal" street or even a full and historic thieves' "sanctuary".[30] Society was much less segregated than is the case today, let alone the Victorian period.

Contemporary Concern Over Law and Order in London

Although the law and order problems in London were not yet so severe

---

29.   Quoted George, D., *ibid.*, p.83.
30.   On the presence of thieves' "sanctuaries" see below p.99.

that the major inquiries into policing to be carried out in the mid-century were not still some way off (for example the magistrate Henry Fielding's *Inquiry into the Causes of the Late Increase of Robbers*, written in 1751, along with that of the House of Commons' Committee of 1750, set up specifically to examine the issue),[31] they were already felt to be fairly bad in Defoe's time. A pamphlet from 1677, dealing with a famous theft from the Lord High Chancellor himself, even observed that "many and intolerable are the injuries and abuses that are committed almost daily within the city and suburbs of London". There were three "Presentments" of the Grand Jury of Middlesex in 1728, 1741, and 1744 considering the mounting problems of beggary and gin drinking in London and its environs (most of the Metropolis outside the City, including the Borough of Southwark and City of Westminster was within its consideration). In 1718 the City Marshal, Charles Hitchin, in the then relatively better policed city jurisdiction, was able to note (perhaps a little ironically for a man who had been a friend and fellow "thief-taker" of Jonathan Wild and who was at one point considered every bit as bad as Wild) that people were "afraid when it is dark to come to their houses and shops for fear that their hats and wigs should be snitched from their heads or their swords taken from their sides, or that they might be blinded, knocked down, cut or stabbed."[32] Later in the eighteenth century, in his Throne Speech to Parliament in 1751, even the King felt moved to urge that body to take effective action against "those audacious crimes of robbery and violence, which are now become so frequent, especially about this great capital".[33] These mid-century reports had some important policy consequences. However, when Defoe was writing in 1721 attempts to combat Metropolitan problems were still in their infancy.

---

31.   Interestingly, a century later, Patrick Colquhoun in his "Treatise on Indigence", written in 1806, felt that "the indigent of the present period ... are not only on the whole less moral; but also ... more dissolute" than a century earlier. At p.33.
32.   Tobias, T., *Crime and Industrial Society in the Nineteenth Century* (1967), p.26.
33.   Cleary, T., *Henry Fielding: Political Writer* (1983), p.283.

Other Explanations for Increased Sensitivity to Crime in this Period

The population increase in London and the expansion of commerce are probably not sufficient in themselves to fully explain the phenomenon of a greater general concern about crime. To some extent there also appears to have been a changing attitude towards property and crime itself underway at this time, perhaps linked to the commercial revolution of the period, and which may have brought with it a heightened awareness of, and sensitivity to, such crime (especially instrumental crime against property). This is a very difficult subject to assess. If such a process was afoot, it was still in its early stages when Defoe was writing. The manifestations of a general change in attitudes to possessions can be seen to be present in the work of philosophers such as John Locke writing from the latter half of the seventeenth century onwards. This was well caught by Locke's famous comment that "government has no other end but the preservation of property". This change in attitude also appears to have contributed to a significant transformation in the legal concept of "property" itself. For example, William Blackstone in his famous *Commentaries* from the 1760s was to describe property as being the "... sole and despotic dominion...in total exclusion of the right of any other individual in the Universe".[34] Some common lawyers in the latter part of the previous century (the 1600s) had also shown a greater belief in an unmitigated extent of "property" rights, demonstrated, for example, by a willingness to give "ownership" of wild animals to those who "owned" the land on which they roamed, and to allow the enclosure of land.[35] This attitude sometimes contrasted markedly with that of sixteenth century commentators who more readily accepted the notion of restricted rights

---

34.   Blackstone, as the first Vinerian Professor of English law in his *Commentaries on the Laws of England*, which was published in four volumes between 1765 and 1769 and was based on his earlier lectures at Oxford in 1758, remedied the lack in England (compared to other European countries) of a comprehensive and relatively clear statement of its modern law and legal system. His views were enormously influential and thus are deserving of consideration on many issues.
35.   *Cf.* "The concept of Property in the Early Common Law", David Siepp, p.83, *Law and History Review*, vol.12, no.1, (1994).

of ownership.

It thus appears that extrinsic theoretical limitations on the extent of property rights, limitations which had existed for many years, were becoming attenuated in this period (the turn of the seventeenth century) in favour of a concept of "absolute" property rights, in which "ownership" was subject to no limitations. This can, perhaps, be seen to be most obviously manifest in the new legislation dealing with (usually forbidding) gleaning, poaching, the taking of perquisites by artisans and employees (such as stevedores) and enclosure of common ground. By way of an early illustration (admittedly extreme), of this new attitude, can be considered an imaginary dialogue from a pamphlet from 1677 considering these issues; the criticisms of enclosure by the poor are dealt with quite dismissively "for the cry that the poor will be starv'd, it is not worth a rush, for few of them make the benefit for lack of stock", even though the commentator accepts that there is a question mark as to the legality of many enclosures he feels that it was enough "that I have prov'd it profitable".[36] This was in sharp contrast to the attitudes of the older common lawyers of the mid-1600s, men such as the former Lord Chief Justice of Kings Bench, Mathew Hale (1609-1676; Chief Justice from 1671 to 1676, at that time the highest judicial office), who retained the opinion that God "hath left the poor as his pupils, and the rich as his stewards to provide for them".[37]

This change in attitudes *may* (it is quite unprovable) have contributed, in turn, amongst many parts of English society, to an increasing sensitivity to theft, the ultimate violation of these "absolute" property rights, and thus also a belief in the increasing level and threat of crime. It does also appear that English and London society had been becoming progressively more nervous of vagrants from the Tudor period (with its fear of "sturdy beggars") onwards. The post-medieval period appears to have coincided

---

36.   "England's Great Happiness", anonymous pamphlet ("by a real and hearty lover of his King and Countrey") published in 1677. Printed by "J.M." for Edward Crof.

37.   From the Preface to ""A Discourse touching Provision for the Poor". Written by Sir Mathew Hale, late Lord Chief Justice of the Kings-Bench, printed for William Shrowsberry (1683). Published posthumously.

with a growing degree of intolerance towards "petty" crime in general, manifest, for example, in the establishment of the London Bridewell in 1552, which was to become the precursor of a system of "houses of correction", where such people could serve short sentences of imprisonment or be whipped (indeed these were the first institutions to widely adopt custody as a punishment rather than merely a holding measure pending further action, as was normally the case in the more mainstream prisons for felons). These houses of correction were a well established type of institution in the early eighteenth century. There was to be a surge in the creation of such prisons around 1700. The decrease in tolerance for much minor crime may also, therefore, have been linked to the general "awareness" and fear of crime amongst the literate.

Mobility of the English Population and Attendant Problems

There were also much larger numbers of people (and thus labour), on the move in 1700, in numbers that would have been unthinkable a hundred years earlier, though the Tudor problem with vagrants can be said to have heralded the difficulty. This was in a society that had, for centuries, historically been based on more stable relationships and had yet to develop different types of social arrangement to deal with the increasingly fluid situation. There were constant proposals throughout the late seventeenth and the eighteenth centuries for dealing with this problem. Writing in 1753, the sometimes draconian magistrate, Henry Fielding, felt that a deficiency in the laws dealing with vagrancy from the Tudor time onwards was that though they punished certain acts "... yet vagrancy itself, or wandering about from place to place, is not itself alone punishable".[38] He wished "that it shall be lawful to seize all suspicious persons &c." This was despite the fact that there had been a new and more "robust" Vagrancy Act passed into law in 1740.

---

38.   Fielding, H., *A Proposal for Making an Effectual Provision for the Poor* (1753).

Perception of Crime Due to Increased Publicity

It is also very possible that the levels of crime were *perceived* as being worse, or at least much more novel, than was actually the case because of their much wider publicity, something that was largely due to the recent rapid growth of popular literature. Between 1600 and 1700 there had developed a new "culture" of printed material available cheaply to the public (itself increasingly literate), broadsides, chap-books, pamphlets, newspapers and "ballads", the latter being largely dominated by specialist London booksellers such as the Cole and Wright families. Provincial printing grew steadily after the 1690s, but London was the traditional centre for chap-books and pamphlets. Some of this work was religious or morally improving in character, but a considerable amount dealt, in often gruesome detail, with sensationalist crime or disaster. It has, as a consequence, accurately been observed that "Defoe lived in a period notably troubled and fascinated by crime".[39]

Periodic newspapers were well established quite early in the seventeenth century, though London's first newspaper in a regular sense, The *Daily Courant*, only appeared in 1702.[40] By the end of the eighteenth century there were to be twenty London papers. The enormous growth in the numbers and circulation of newspapers at this time, and their wider availability at coffee houses and other common places, the increasing emphasis on public socializing and discussion in such coffee shops, and the attendant growing numbers of clubs and "tea gardens" attracting the leisured classes in the Metropolis at various levels (whether successful merchants or aristocrats) provided greater forums and opportunities for the discussion of contemporary issues, including crime, and can only have increased public alarm.[41] This, with the printing of huge quantities of

39.   Faller, L.B., *Crime and Defoe* (1993), p.xi.
40.   Burke. P., *Popular Culture in Seventeenth Century London* (1976), p.154.
41.   There were over 3,000 coffee houses in London in 1708, as well as serious journals, such as *The Spectator* from the 1720s and *The Gentleman's Magazine* which also considered the question of crime, again raising consciousness of it. See *The Later Stuarts 1660 -1714*, Clark, G.N. (1956).

popular and sometimes lurid criminal "accounts" (of some of which Defoe himself was probably the author), may have contributed to an increased fear of crime generally. The sometimes dubious reliability of these accounts, and the extent of this trade in crime stories, is illustrated by the famous highwayman, Jack Sheppard, who was the subject of dozens of such works. Significantly, after one of his celebrated escapes he delivered a letter to the well known specialist printer, Mr Applebee, in Blackfriars, ridiculing his publishing of "dying speeches" as well as the efforts of the Ordinary of Newgate in writing them (the Ordinary was the author of a famous periodic *Account*). As with today's popular newspapers, the accounts of crime concentrated overwhelmingly on the most notorious felonies, the most appalling and bloody murders, or the "heroic" and glamorous, such as tales of the daring Sheppard, rather than the more routine crimes of theft which most of those hanged at Tyburn had committed. This might well have served to heighten anxiety in the same way that, it is sometimes argued in the twentieth century, "popular" television reconstructions of "true crimes" do. However it occurred, while many historians would not agree with Martin Kayman's assertion that the eighteenth century was not witnessing more crime, but rather merely the better apprehension and recording of crime, most would agree with him that there was a much greater contemporary concern with crime than amongst earlier generations.[42]

Finally, there were also much higher expectations of government action by 1700. In England from the late seventeenth century there was the growing appearance (and reality) of state sovereignty. This was manifest, for example, in the founding of the Bank of England (1694) which was to compete successfully with the small private banks that had grown out of the city's goldsmiths, and which would quickly control the nation's money supply by setting the bank rate for commercial banks. It could also be seen in the rapidly growing numbers of men in government employment, both in the military and the emerging civil bureaucracy.[43] It is thus probably the case that there were greater expectations of, and

---

42.   Kayman, M., *From Bow Street to Baker Street* (1991).
43.   Shennan, J.H., *Liberty and Order in Early Modern Europe* (1986), p.5.

pressure on, government to be seen to be "doing something" about the problems of law and order than would have been the case a hundred or so years earlier. There was a growing awareness of law as a regulator of social conduct in English society. Along with a progressively greater desire for a more thorough and regularized *system* of police there appears to have been an increasing dissatisfaction with the existing state of law enforcement. This was a dissatisfaction that was based as much on new and higher expectations of what could reasonably be expected from policing agencies, as much as any inherent deterioration or inadequacy in the old system used to combat crime (many of the manifestations of which were certainly not new in the 1700s).[44]

Policing Reform in Defoe's Era

Some piecemeal steps were already being taken in Defoe's day to counter the apparently increasing public order problems and the fear of growing crime. For example, there was the large scale introduction of state rewards from 1693 for those who captured and convicted felons, whether members of the public or professional "bounty hunters" (these could be up to £40 for a captured highwayman),[45] while in some specific cases special extra rewards of great amounts would be offered. One example, from 1725, even providing that "His Majesty has been graciously pleased to promise a reward of £200. For discovering and convicting the Author or authors of a villainous Attempt to poison Mr St Andre, an eminent surgeon and also a pardon to any person concerned therein (except the chief actor or contriver) who shall make such discovery".[46] The Riot Act of 1715 was introduced to deal with growing street disturbances and the Transportation Act of 1718 to increase available secondary punishments (those other than

---

44. See on this Styles, J., "The Emergence of the Police - Explaining Police Reform in Eighteenth and Nineteenth Century England", *Brit.J. Criminol.,* Vol.27, No.1 (1987).
45. Howson, *ibid.,* p.3.
46. *The Original Half-Penny London Journal,* Saturday, February 27, 1725.

death); there were improved street lighting initiatives, including rather laxly enforced legislation requiring every household in the city to hang a candle in a lamp outside their front doors (the Lighting Acts of 1716 and 1736).[47] There was also legislation in the 1690s against handlers of stolen goods, making the receiver an accessory after the fact who could face transportation.[48] There were further Acts reinforcing this in 1702 and 1706. Additionally, there was the drastic and notorious Waltham Black Act of 1722, an emergency measure that lasted till 1823 and caught a potentially huge range of crimes committed at night or in disguise.[49] Throughout this period more and more offences were withdrawn from benefit of clergy or new offences introduced which did not allow for "clergy", such as the Shop Lifting Act of 1699 which made it a capital offence to steal more than 5s. from a shop, or that of 1713 which made theft of 40s from a house also a death penalty offence.[50] At the level of private initiative there was activity on the part of the Society (or area-based societies) for the Reformation of Manners from 1691 onwards; it brought 99,380 actions in London alone in 1735.[51] The original inspiration for the movement to reform manners had come, in 1689, from the court of the newly crowned William III, prompted as it was by a fear on the part of the King and some of his courtiers that there was, as William himself phrased it, a notorious "overflowing of vice" in the nation. This in turn appears to have prompted the Westminster justices to begin rounding up large numbers of prostitutes and "disorderly persons" for commitment to the Westminster house of correction, and subsequently also spawned numerous private societies to combat vice.[52] These societies, starting, perhaps significantly, in the Tower Hamlets area, soon attracted considerable official support and also developed links with the city authorities. The *Daily Courant,* for January 4, 1704, was to note that

---

47. Besant, W., *London in the Eighteenth Century* (1903), p.484.
48. 3 Will and Mary, ch.9, s.4.
49. Kayman, M., *From Bow Street to Baker Street* (1992), p.36.
50. On benefit of clergy see below, p.82.
51. Plumb, J.H., *England in the Eighteenth Century, 1714-1815* (1950), p.31.
52. Shoemaker, R.B., *Prosecution and Punishment* (1991), p.238.

"Yesterday the Right Honourable the Lord Mayor, with several of the Aldermen, the Sheriffs and other persons of Quality, &c. were present at the Sermon preach'd to the Societies for Reformation of Manners at Bow-Church, by the Reverend Dr Willis, Dean of Lincoln, &c." There were also similar Societies for the Suppression of Mendicity, Associations for the Defence of Liberty and Property, and a growing number of prosecution associations, starting in the 1690s (though increasing especially fast from the 1740s), to share the heavy private costs of taking criminals to court.[53] Moreover, there was the emergence of professional "thief takers", effectively bounty hunters, profiting from the rewards on the heads of captured and convicted felons. Many of them were incorrigible criminals themselves, such as Jonathan Wild, who in this period was at the summit of his powers, despite an Act of 1717, to combat his *modus operandi*.[54] This Act was aimed at the "... divers persons, who have secret acquaintance with felons, and who make it their business to help persons to their stolen goods, and by that means gain money from them". Essentially he returned goods to their losers for a substantial price, having received them direct from the thief who stole them. If they "stepped out of line" he would claim the reward on their heads. Even so, thief takers were a very important part of the contemporary justice system.

Thief Takers

In the mid-eighteenth century the collation of witnesses whose names appear on the back of indictments for the Metropolis and adjacent counties, and an examination of the names of those to whom rewards were regularly paid, produces a list of 12 important thief takers in the London area at this time and another dozen regular, but less committed, ones. These men generally appear to have broadly similar backgrounds; usually

---

53.   *Cf*. Adrian Shubert, *Private Initiative in Law Enforcement: Associations for the Prosecution of Felons, 1744-1856, in Policing and Punishment in Nineteenth Century Britain* (1981) (ed) Bailey, V., at p.25.

54.   Thompson, E.P., *Whigs and Hunters* (1975), p.163.

they were skilled artisans such as McDaniel, the sword cutler, or Harris who was a hatter. Interestingly, many appear to have lived in criminal areas despite the perceived unpopularity of such men in these places. Some were of Irish origin (more than the proportion of the London population that was Irish). Nearly all of them had some previous criminal record of their own, however, not all were as bad as the most infamous of their number.[55] The magistrate John Fielding in the 1750s was keen to distinguish between those "thief takers", like the notorious perjurer McDaniel who entrapped men into crime to claim the rewards, and "real and useful thief takers" who "deserve to be considered with regard and esteem". He noted that when his brother Henry had become a justice "the town was infested by a daring gang of robbers, who attacked several persons of fashion". He felt that they were crucial to the administration of justice, noting that London, and its immediate environs to a range of about 20 miles had more highway robberies than the rest of the country, of whom "not one in a hundred of these robbers are taken in the fact".[56] He also observed that there was an apparent growing reluctance on the part of some members of the public to become involved in risky operations against thieves, citing the case of an officer who had been attacked on Hounslow Heath and who had then pursued his attacker through a local town crying out for assistance "yet no one join'd the pursuit".[57] Good thief takers were probably an important part of the arsenal in the fight against crime, though after the mid-century entrapment scandals in which members of London's population of marginal drifters were involved in "put-up" criminal acts with a view to claiming the rewards for their capture sent a judicial "shockwave" through the criminal justice system, the levels of reward were reduced. The most famous of

---

55.   Paley, R., "Thieftakers in London in the Age of the McDaniel Gang, c. 1745-1754, p.303 in Hay D. and Snyder R. (eds) *Policing and Prosecution in Britain 1750-1850* (1989).

56.   Fielding, John, *A Plan for the Prevention of Robberies Within 20 Miles of London*, p.7, MDCCLV, London.

57.   Fielding, John, *A Plan for the Prevention of Robberies Within 20 Miles of London*, p.8, MDCCLV, London.

these cases involved a group of thief-takers led by Stephen McDaniel (who had already prosecuted several men to their deaths) who lured two youths, Peter Kelly and John Ellis, into committing a robbery (against one of his colleagues, known as a "decoy duck") in Deptford (which parish offered an extra £20 reward for the apprehension of such offenders).[58] When the details of the case were exposed the two youths were discharged and McDaniel and his companions pilloried, one of them, Eagan, being stoned to death by the infuriated "mob". Henry Fielding, employing thief-takers in 1753, felt obliged to stress that he had chosen men who were all "of known and approved fidelity and integrity".[59] It appears that they would work by cultivating contacts and informers, and developing an almost encyclopedic personal knowledge of criminals, their appearances and their regular haunts. Sometimes they would follow the developing criminal career of a promising candidate till there was a satisfactory reward on his head, when he would be "taken". Thief-takers are referred to at several points in *Moll Flanders*.

Private Suggestions to Improve Policing

Private recommendations on how to combat the apparent crime problem also abounded. Amongst them were suggestions as to how to make execution even more terrifying, for example the anonymously published tract *Hanging Not Punishment Enough,* which came out in London in 1701, and suggested the introduction of aggravated forms of the death penalty, such as breaking on the wheel, starving and whipping to death, to increase its deterrent effect.[60] There was at least some widespread support for this even amongst educated people. That there was a general feeling amongst many of the literate sections of society, that extreme severity should be the consequence of extreme crime is clear from the approval occasionally given to the more widespread use of aggravated

---

58.   Radzinowicz, L., *A History of English Criminal Law*, vol.2, p.326 (1956).
59.   Fielding, H., *The Voyage to Lisbon* (1754), Everyman (edn) (1952), p.192.
60.   Radzinowicz, L., *ibid.*, vol. 1, p.232.

forms of the death penalty in other countries. Thus a newspaper could note of a young Frenchman who murdered a widow and her children and then stole their money, having previously been their lodger "they write from Nantes in France that a young Student there has lately been broken Alive on the wheel, where he lay in Torment four hours, and had it been fourteen he had well deserved it".[61] Defoe himself appears to have had some sympathies with this approach. In *Street Robberies Consider'd* (1728) the fictional narrator takes a decidedly "robust" attitude to punishment (given that he was allegedly a reformed criminal himself) "I know I shall be tax'd with barbarity, when I say, in my opinion, our punishments are too mild". While observing that it was reasonable for women accused of coining to be strangled prior to burning he felt that "in the case of murder, both male and female should be burnt alive". With regard to murder, as this passage suggests, there were especially widespread and regular suggestions that "hanging does not seem to be an infliction adequate to so horrid a crime".[62]

To some limited extent the government was to follow this line of thinking in 1752 when the Murder Act of that year made greater provision than existing practice for allowing executed felons' bodies to go for dissection by trainee surgeons, or to be gibbeted for public display (usually having first been "tarred" to preserve them from rapid decay), on the order of the condemned person's trial Judge. The effectiveness of the latter of these deterrent methods may be open to considerable doubt; as a newspaper laconically noted in 1723 "early on Monday morning last the *Bristol Mail* was robbed by one highwayman, near Longford, where Hawkins and Simpson hang in chains for the same crime".[63] It was though, clearly the case, that dissection by surgeons, as opposed to Christian burial, was greatly feared and disapproved of by the general populace. On several occasions the crowd at executions prevented bodies going to

---

61. *The London Journal*, May 25, 1723.
62. Proposals to the Legislature for Preventing the Frequent Executions of Convicts. In a letter to the Right Honourable Henry Pelham, "By a student of Politics", 1754.
63. *The London Journal*, February 9, 1723.

the surgeons or recovered those that had already been taken, as can be seen from many contemporary reports; "the surgeons of this city having had a warrant from the Sheriff for a body of one of the malefactors executed on Monday last, and they having received it accordingly, the mob took it from them and carried it off, but the surgeons recovered it next morning".[64]

In this connection, it is also worth observing that the serious shortage of available bodies for London's growing population of medical students, could itself prove a fruitful source and motivation for crime, in particular "body snatching". Another newspaper account of the time (from 1723) mentions that "it having been a trade for some time past to plunder church-yards of the dead bodies, and several having been taken out of the Burying-Ground of St Giles; the grave-digger, one Samuel Buxton, hath been committed to Newgate for the same. He is charged with stealing a shroud and coffin, and selling the corpse of a female child to a person unknown".

The London "Mob", Urban Disturbances and Public Order

At various points in *Moll Flanders* it is possible to detect the presence, and the authorities' fear and need to consider the feelings of, the volatile nature of the common Londoner *en masse*, or, as many contemporaries termed them, the "mob". There were endemic riots and popular disturbances in the Metropolis throughout the seventeenth and eighteenth centuries.

There had been riots in Charing Cross and Fleet Street in 1628 and 1629, largely made up of a mixture of apprentices, sailors and soldiers; in 1675, there were serious riots by the capital's weavers. Disturbances were to get worse in scale as the eighteenth century advanced, culminating in the anti-Catholic Gordon Riots, easily the worst of the century, in 1780. There were major riots in London in 1710 (over religion, in the form of

---

64.   *The London Journal*, January 5, 1722.

the Sacheverel and High Church riots), 1715 (over the Hanoverian Accession), 1716, and 1719, as well as large anti-Irish riots in 1736, the "Penlez" Riots in 1749, the Wilkite Riots in 1768, and anti-recruiting riots in 1794, amongst numerous others. Popular disturbances in London could have an enormously diverse range of precipitators: political, religious, trade matters, etc., though on examination, an economic grievance can, fairly frequently, be observed as an underlying cause in many (though certainly not all) outbreaks. A classic illustration of underlying economic grievance behind popular unrest were the riots that occurred in East London in 1736. According to one of Sir Robert Walpole's informers at the time "it is evident that there are great discontents and murmurings through all this mobbish part of the town".[65] The reason for this was the presence of Irish workmen who had been undercutting English labourers in building work (where they were willing to work for half to two-thirds of the latters' rate of pay). This prompted violent confrontations from whence the riots spread to Whitechapel, Spitalfields, and the Irish "colony" in Rosemary Lane.

There were also several riots over attempts to control the sale of cheap gin, industrial disputes amongst weavers, and political activities. Almost anything could be the precipitator of a disturbance. Any extra social stress, whether caused by bad economic conditions or plague, could make the London "mob" even more volatile than was normally the case. This was well appreciated by the city authorities, and some richer private citizens, who often took care, in this period, to make some attempt to ameliorate especially hard times. In his *Journal of the Plague Year,* loosely based on the events of 1665, but written in 1720, Defoe noted that had not sums of money contributed as charity by well-disposed people "been prodigiously great, it had not been in the power of the Lord Mayor and Sheriffs to have kept the public peace. Nor were they without apprehensions, as it was, that desperation should push the people upon tumults, and cause them to rifle the houses of rich men and plunder the markets of provisions". Fortunately, however, the "prudence" of the Lord

---

65.   Rude, G., *Hanoverian London* (1971), p.188.

Mayor and the Court of Aldermen [also *ex offico* magistrates] within the city, and of the Justices of Peace in the out-parts, was such, and they were supported with money "from all parts so well, that the poor people were kept quiet, and their wants everywhere relieved, as far as was possible to be done".

Large scale riots from the era are well documented, but there were also numerous, less well recorded, small scale disturbances, which tend to be overlooked. To an extent these were simply a part of everyday life, and sentences for low level disturbances which did not "get out of hand", and did not have a large political motivation, could even be quite lenient. Thus a newspaper of the time noted that Edward Dunn, who was, in February 1721, "together with Edward Galloway and Charles MacCave since dead, convicted at the Old Bailey, for the riot in Drury-Lane and fined £50, ordered one years imprisonment, and to give sureties for his good behaviour, was on Monday last discharged out of Newgate".[66]

The "mobs" involved in riots in London were, it appears, primarily made up of local, employed men who had joined spontaneously, "on the spur of the moment", but who were led by more committed "captains", men with charismatic personalities, enjoying a real, if temporary and localized, authority. The action of the crowds, the targets chosen for destruction etc., were often more selective than might be imagined from some fairly lurid contemporary accounts.[67] In 1715 there were a number of these manifestations of crowd unrest. Hanoverian supporters sometimes being attacked in the streets, mobs shouting "No Hanoverian, No Presbyterian Government" etc. These anti-Whig and anti-Hanoverian sentiments even permeated some of the lower ranks of the law enforcement agencies themselves. The efforts of Whig Aldermen in the City of London to deal with the trouble were often rendered nugatory by the recalcitrance of some parish constables who sympathized with, or were afraid of, the Tory crowd, along with disaffection in the part-time militia

---

66.   *The London Journal*, April 6, 1723.
67.   Rude, G., *The Crowd in History*, p.60.

and trained bands of the City.[68] A letter from one of the captured Jacobite Highlanders of the Northern Rebellion of that year, sent for trial in London, reveals how potent the crowd could be, "the mob stopped our coach and notwithstanding that our coach hade six sojers, they bade almost drawen us out".[69]

These disturbances, sometimes with distinct political undertones, provided the immediate backdrop to the introduction of the Riot Act of 1715, the Whigs being persuaded that common law and the existing statutes on riots were unsatisfactory. Prior to 1715, these had distinguished between riots against the state, for which the penalty was the same as for treason, and those of a private nature (which were merely misdemeanours, unless other crimes were committed in the course of them, and as such treated relatively leniently). This gave the Grand Jury considerable discretion in its interpretation of popular disturbances when deciding whether to indict and on what charges, and where they were deemed to be merely of a private nature also meant the civil and military authorities could themselves be liable for prosecution for unnecessary injuries inflicted in dispersing such rioters. This could be a powerful dissuader against forceful action by the authorities. Under the new statute rioters numbering a dozen or more were guilty of a capital felony if they failed to disperse within an hour of the appropriate proclamation. This greatly increased the opportunities for the speedy judicial suppression of public disorder.[70]

Nevertheless, despite the new Act, there was another major outburst of rioting in 1719, only two years before *Moll Flanders* was written. This had been aimed at the weavers of cheap printed calicoes, amongst others, people who were felt to be driving weavers out of work. Their endemic economic difficulties also explains why weavers from London figured heavily at various times amongst the indentured labourers going to

68.   Rogers, N., *Popular Protest in Early Hanoverian London, Past and Present*, no.79 (1978), p.73.
69.   Quoted, *ibid.*, p.81.
70.   Rogers, N., *ibid.*, p.75.

America.[71] The potential for a riot to do damage and to gain
reinforcements quickly was much greater in a huge city than in the
countryside. In narrow streets it was enormously harder to control such
outbreaks when once under-way.

If there was large-scale disorder the bulwark for the authorities was
the military, either regular soldiers (some of which were themselves of
doubtful reliability) or one of the Metropolis's numerous part-time military
bodies. In the seventeenth and eighteenth century the need for a reliable
potential military response to trouble led to the widespread formation of
localized Military Foot Associations. The Westminster Military Company,
for example, partly based on the predecessor to the Honourable Artillery
Company (which was based in the City), was founded in 1615 and was
still in existence in 1708 (though exactly when it was replaced by other
part-time military bodies is not clear). Its only recorded active use,
throughout its entire history, was in occasional Metropolitan riots. The
military were consequently a regular but not constant feature at
disturbances large and small in the capital. That they were not
permanently on the streets was a measure of the normal success of the
authorities in dealing with such problems.

In many ways the urban, indeed London, "mob" was to be the main
criminal caricature of the century, widely portrayed by cartoonists and
illustrators. Perhaps this in part explains why some literary accounts of
the social composition of rioters, portraying them as hardened criminals,
do not seem to tally with what is known of those who were often executed
for the crime. Certainly, however, it explains the cautious and at times
deferential attitude taken to the crowd by some of the characters in *Moll
Flanders,* such as the arrested mercer who mistakenly holds her for

---

71.   It should, perhaps, be observed that the indentured servants who, unlike the
transported convicts, went to America and to a degree of servitude voluntarily,
were not that dissimilar in their legal status to the London apprentices who
remained at home, and whose relationship with their masters for the seven years
of their articles was, at least in theory, subject to draconian legal restrictions and
controls, enforced by the courts (though the reality in many cases was probably
often rather less rigorous).

shoplifting and is himself subsequently detained for false imprisonment and followed by a crowd, pelting him with dirt, to the local justice.

Eighteenth Century Political Resistance to Policing Reform

Despite the policing problems in London there was enormous resistance by the "political nation" (essentially the gentry and aristocracy) to any expansion of state power at the expense of the political settlement of 1688, which had given them an unprecedented degree of influence and freedom from centralized control. Reforms were only politically acceptable on a gradual basis, when fear of the "threat from below" appeared to outweigh fear of that "from above". There was a widespread awareness of the greater provision for policing in France, where Paris had a *lieutenant general de police* and where there was also a military police to patrol the main roads of the nation, as well as the extensive urban police forces and Marechaussee, but this was seen as inimical to the freedom of "freeborn" Englishmen. The notion that a large uniformed body should patrol the streets of London was particularly unthinkable, having connotations with the absolutist foreign governments so despised by the English. There were, of course, important but usually unconsidered historical explanations for the more developed nature of French policing agencies. In particular, the need for central government there to effect control in what had been, till the 1600s, a very decentralized and localized country, in a way that was not the case in England (where local people of eminence had for centuries represented the state, in the guise of JPs). However, it is also important to note that in some respects England was already very singular compared to other European countries; in particular there were a number of important differences between the English "political nation", largely the untitled gentry, and the upper classes on the continent, for example, the French nobility (actually about one per cent of the French population, unlike the tiny English aristocracy). Gentility in England was largely a matter of culture and money. The upper echelons of English society may not have been easily penetrated but they were never a closed circle to new people who could afford to live in the appropriate style.

Most importantly the gentry were, legally speaking, theoretically indistinguishable from the rest of English society, not exempt from any form of taxation or any of the laws of the country, and subject to trial (unlike the numerically very small aristocracy) in front of the same juries as everybody else.[72] While the practical reality was obviously different to a degree; this equality of legal status was still important, especially at a time when in many European countries (apart from The Netherlands) there was no pretence at applying the same laws to the different social groups.

Although, to an extent, the notion that all members of English society were equally subject to the same law, regardless of location or social status, may have been a myth it was a popular belief that does appear to have gained a degree of support from plebeians as well as patricians. That England was also unusual in the amount of licence permitted to the ordinary man can be seen in the reactions throughout the eighteenth century of visiting foreigners, who clearly felt that they were witnessing a strange phenomenon (in European terms). The English criminal justice system may have displayed a thinly veiled class control, but, unlike nearly anywhere else in Europe, it *was* veiled.

Equality of treatment before the law was also, in part, a reality, and not purely a myth; it was something that was accepted, largely, by the highest orders of society. It should, perhaps, be noted that as a Lord, Earl Ferrers, when accused of a homicide, was tried not in the normal courts (such as the Old Bailey), but before his peers, in a trial in the House of Lords in April of 1760 (one which, because of this feature, lasted the highly unusual length of three days). Despite the Earl's very strange behaviour and a proven family history of lunacy, supported by the first documented use of psychiatric testimony, he was condemned to death (and subsequently executed, allegedly with a silken rope) for the murder of his lowly factor, one Johnson. Even Ferrers, like any other defendant in a non-treason trial for felony, was not allowed to be represented by counsel except when a point of law arose.[73] His fellow peers clearly did not

---

72.   Shennan, J.H., *Liberty and Order in Early Modern Europe* (1986).
73.   Walker, N., *Crime and Insanity in England* (1968), vol.1, p.59.

exercise "class solidarity" in considering the evidence against him. The "rule of law" was widely seen as the birthright of all Englishmen and one of the things that distinguished them from the inhabitants of other European countries.[74]

This phenomenon, and its popular acceptance, possibly goes some way to explaining the ability of the dominant social group (the upper gentry) to rule without a huge repressive apparatus, despite the fact that the number of people even theoretically qualified to become Justices of the Peace in rural areas probably numbered significantly less than three per cent of the adult male population. The authorities could not exercise power in a totally untrammelled manner if they were not to lose the legitimacy that this widespread perception of English justice conferred on them, and which in turn allowed England to be policed by a markedly smaller, less powerful, and less expensive criminal justice and policing system than most other European countries, and France in particular (the contrast with France was particularly widely noted and remarked on by contemporaries).

The effectiveness of this control, especially in rural areas (in fact, outside London generally), meant that root and branch reform would be delayed till the end of the century and even beyond (the Metropolitan Police only being established in 1829); reform was postponed by a century of gradual, though certainly not insignificant, changes.[75] Ultimately, however, the existing penal system did not serve adequately a new urban society in which large amounts of portable (and thus stealable) property provided constant temptations and targets for significant parts of the population. In particular, a new or reformed system of criminal administration and policing was needed by the growing "middle ranking" commercial class of the capital, those men earning between £50 and £150 a year, men that Defoe referred to as "tradesmen", as opposed to "mere labouring people" or "the gentry" (he included ordinary farmers amongst the tradesmen, and lawyers of barrister rank and above amongst the

---

74.   Brewer, J. and Styles, J. (eds), *An Ungovernable People* (1980), p.13.
75.   It is a mistake to view 1829 as a total revolution; policing in London was already very different in 1810 compared to the situation in 1710.

gentry). Any new system would necessarily be one that would encourage the prosecution of felons, take away the financial burden of the middle-ranking private prosecutor, and would be more of a deterrent to other criminals from re-offending. One of the principal problems facing the political nation was that what was necessary for London in 1700 might well be unnecessary for Norfolk but would inevitably provide a precedent for that county. To an extent, some tolerance of higher rates of crime in London was the price to be paid for preserving a traditional system of organization in the rural counties, where it still worked reasonably well.

Chapter 3

Moll Flanders' Early Life

"Laws grind the poor, and rich men rule the law."
Oliver Goldsmith, The Traveller (1764).

This analysis is primarily concerned with Moll Flanders' 12-year criminal career. Ignoring her early involvement as a prostitute, Flanders' participation in crime only begins after she has turned 48, quite old for the period, and late in any time to start on a life of crime (Defoe dealt with a much more conventionally aged start to a criminal life in *Colonel Jack*, two years later). Flanders' motivation was originally economic hardship, and indeed she provides an interesting portrayal of the move from desperate opportunist thief to calculating and sophisticated professional criminal. It has been asserted, fairly convincingly, that the former was the more characteristic criminal in the early eighteenth century, that for many people crime was a "normal" response to their situations and that those who went to Tyburn were largely the unlucky ones who were caught. Though this is probably exaggerated, it does seem to be partly supported by what is known of the lives of many of those who were executed; a substantial part of the men had at least started formal apprenticeships, with a view to learning a trade, and were thus "ordinary" Londoners in this respect. Flanders' experiences, however, do raise the problematic issue of the extent of professional, as opposed to casual, crime. London was, it appears, a place apart in having a significant amount of such crime from relatively early on in its history, even if most crime was still casual and impulsive.

Prostitution

Moll Flanders' initial involvement in "illicit" activity, up till late middle age (for the period, given life expectancy at that time), had been largely limited to prostitution. By 1700 there had been, for well over a century, the professional organization of prostitution in London. For an illustration of this can be considered the case of Margaret Ferneseed, who was burnt for murdering her husband in 1608.[1] She admitted, before execution, to a lifetime of ensnaring women and young girls into prostitution, then blackmailing them, and receiving "10 shillings a week out of their gettings".[2] There were also long established organized brothels in London, especially on the south bank of the Thames, along with attendant "red light" areas, largely catering for the lower class of prostitute, particularly in Southwark, across the river from the City. Although there was a degree of tacit tolerance for discreet or territorially confined prostitution, prostitutes were always vulnerable to punishment and clampdowns on vice by the authorities; this usually involved a degree of public disgrace or humiliation for the women, such as the stocks or pillory,[3] being paraded through the streets on a cart, branding, or even being sent for a short period to the house of correction. Prostitutes were often scapegoats for outbreaks of venereal disease, a constant eighteenth century preoccupation, and which sometimes also prompted official action. Most of the vice trade, however, was probably carried out on a very casual basis. Women who wished to work on their own account, as seems to have been the case with Flanders, were usually able to do so, many drifting in

---

1. Women were burnt, not hanged drawn and quartered for treason, whether coining, see below, p.137, or "petty treason", the murder of their husbands; the last such execution for husband murder being in 1789.
2. Sharpe, J.A., *Crime in Early Modern England 1550-1750* (1984), p.115.
3. Stocks constrained the individual at the ankles, the pillory, the less comfortable of the two, at the wrists and neck.

and out of the "profession" as their circumstances dictated. Although Flanders describes herself as a "whore", and though her mother was a prostitute before being transported, making her daughter the "offspring of debauchery and vice" (as Defoe states in his preface), Flanders appears to have catered for the higher end of the "trade". She was, for much of her career, almost a serial mistress, rather than hardcore prostitute. For example, between her first meeting with, and her marriage to, the bank clerk (one of her earlier spouses), a period of many months, she had, only "lain with 13 men". She was clearly superior to the hundreds of young maidservants who according to Defoe (writing a few years later in 1725), when finding themselves without work, were forced to "prostitute their bodies or starve" (though in his opinion they made "neither good whores nor good servants"). In London they were also the target (largely unsuccessful) of the Society for the Suppression of Vice, which in the early 1700s was busy trying to drive them off the streets.[4] Flanders' own name may contain a joke with regard to this subject, as foreign women from that part of the Low Countries were notorious in London for their involvement in professional prostitution, especially in Southwark.

Flanders' Early Life

The full title of Defoe's novel also briefly sums up Flanders' life, being "The Fortunes and Misfortunes of the famous Moll Flanders, &c, who was born in Newgate, and during a life of continued variety, for threescore years, besides her childhood, was 12 years a Whore, five times a wife (whereof once to her own brother), 12 years a thief, eight years a transported Felon in Virginia, at last grew rich, lived honest and died a penitent".

Briefly, her start in life was unhappy. She was born to a prisoner in Newgate, who successfully "pleaded her belly",[5] and was subsequently

---

4. Stone, L., *The Family, Sex and Marriage in England 1500-1800* (1979 edn), p.392.
5. See below, p.166.

transported to America for petty theft, leaving her baby to fall into the hands of a "crew of those people they call gypsies, or Egyptians" who abandoned her (or from whom she managed to hide), when she was three. This occurred in Colchester (a town that Defoe was personally very familiar with). It was not an auspicious start to life given that gypsies had a decidedly marginal position in English society, and were commonly associated, in the popular mind, with crime. Blackstone himself was later to comment that they were "outlandish persons calling themselves Egyptians or gypsies," who were given to "chiromancy, begging and pilfering". He observed that they had formerly been subject to severe penalties though these had not been applied since the Restoration, due, he felt, to an increased spirit of humanitarianism.[6] Despite this beginning, Flanders subsequently managed to avoid becoming involved in serious crime for the bulk of her adult life and grew up to become a domestic servant.

Though the circumstances of her birth made her an outcast from the "middle orders" of society her education appears to have been a little above her station, something that was to be important to her later criminal operations. She was later seduced by her employer's elder son, and married the younger one, who then died five years later. She next married a spendthrift draper who swiftly became bankrupt, being a tradesman who was "rake, gentleman, shop keeper, and beggar all together". He was reluctant to take refuge from legal process for debt in the "Mint", absconded to France and disappeared from her life.[7] Subsequently, Flanders managed to secure a marriage to a sea captain, with whom she went to Virginia, only to discover that he was her half-brother, by her natural (and still living), transported mother. She agreed to return to England so that he could pretend that she had died and marry again. After further romantic adventures she married a Lancashire man whom she believed to be rich, only to find that like herself he was a fortune hunter,

---

6.   Blackstone W., *Commentaries on the Laws of England* (1768), vol.iv., p.165.
7.   On the "Mint", a debtor's sanctuary, see below, p.99.

and they also agreed to separate,[8] he to return to highway robbery and she to go to London, where she had a baby by him.

Although strictly speaking bigamy had been a felony since 1604 and as such could be punished in the secular courts with a sentence of death, this was quite rare in practice, as it was almost impossible to enforce or prove with the poor records of the period. Prior to this date it had only been punished in the religious courts (such as the Archdeacon's court), which were already beginning their gradual decline in 1604.[9] The impracticality of enforcement of this law in the seventeenth and early eighteenth centuries explains Flanders' numerous marriages while some of her husbands were still alive. Until Lord Hardwicke's Marriage Act of 1753 introduced stricter recording and witnessing practices, marriage to more than one person was especially easy.[10]

An examination of the Old Bailey Sessions Papers from the late 1600s and early 1700s, reveals that the court was often quite realistic and lenient about situations where couples had become separated or there was real mitigation.[11] They also show that by far the most frequent reason for prosecution was the action of an aggrieved former spouse bringing the matter to court, as was the case with Margaret Haines in 1681, whose husband had apparently deserted her for 18 years and having "spent all she had, indicted her to take away her life, thereby to make way for another". Hearing this, the "Court took pity on her, and directed the jury to acquit her".[12]

The baby of Flanders' marriage to her Lancashire husband was placed

---

8. This may appear cynical on Flanders' part but was only a blatant example of something that was not at all uncommon in her social milieu at this time, *cf.* Stone L., *The Family Sex and Marriage*, p.197.
9. Laurence L., *Women in England 1500-1760 A Social History* (1995), p.49.
10. *Cf.* Stone, L., *The Family Sex and Marriage* (1979) (edn), p.32.
11. For an important discussion of the value of these pamphlets as records see Langbein, J., "The Criminal Trial Before the Lawyers' *University of Chicago Law Review*", vol.xlv (winter 1978). I have made extensive use of these documents and have followed Professor Langbein's method of citation ("OBSP" followed by the date of the Sessions).
12. OBSP, October 17-19, 1681, p.3. For a note on these papers see the bibliography.

out to a nurse (Flanders' later "Governess" and an influential figure in her subsequent criminal career). She next married a bank clerk and had five years of happiness and two children by him before his death again left her destitute and ultimately turned her to a life of crime. Throughout her early life Flanders was adept at finding people to take the responsibility for her children off her hands, effectively leaving her as a single woman when her criminal career began (though it must also be said that Defoe, in the novel, left a number of "loose ends" unresolved).

Chapter 4

The Start of Flanders' Criminal Career

"Wealth, howsoever got, in England makes Lords of mechanics,
gentlemen of rakes; antiquity and birth are needless here; `thi
impudence and money makes a peer'." Defoe, from:
"The True Born Englishman" (1724).

Although Flanders had a fairly long life as a prostitute and mistress (sometimes at the very highest level), her real involvement in criminal activity only began at the age of 48, as a result of the death of her fourth husband. She was left destitute and under enormous temptation, having lived frugally on her previously saved assets for over a year. Pressing poverty and the consequent dreadful temptation resulted in "all the strength to resist" being taken away.[1] She could see nothing ahead of her but the utmost distress, and fancied that "... every sixpence [she] paid for a loaf of bread was the last [she] had in the world, and that tomorrow [she] was to fast and be starved to death". As a result, when the opportunity suddenly presented itself to steal a bundle that she saw in an apothecary's shop in Leadenhall Street, she acted on impulse and took it while the apprentice and the maidservant in the shop had their backs to her (though she felt in retrospect that she *may* have gone abroad that day

---

1. Quotations from the First Edition, printed and published by W. Chetwood and T. Edling, 1721, reproduced by W.W. Norton and Company (1973), editor, Edward H. Kelley. All subsequent quotations from the first edition.

with the vague intention of stealing something).

That hardship could have propelled Flanders into committing an offence is not surprising. Although a much (and inconclusively) debated issue there does appear to be a degree of correlation at this time with changes in food prices (caused, for example, by bad harvests), and fluctuations in the rate of indictments for property crimes, though assault and drunkenness may exhibit the inverse relationship (perhaps as the result of a lack of disposable income to spend on alcohol).[2] Many casual thieves were probably prompted by sudden hardship combining itself with an unexpected opportunity. At times Flanders herself explicitly alluded to the structural pressures that could compel someone into crime, saying "give me not poverty lest I steal". While in the late twentieth century criminological paradigms linking unemployment (and thus poverty) with rates of crime have been less empirically supported than is sometimes believed, this does not mean that such was not the case in the seventeenth and eighteenth centuries.[3] Indeed it has been argued that in this respect the mid-nineteenth century appears to have been a "watershed" with years of hardship and crime correlating fairly closely up to this period, but much less so in the remaining part of the nineteenth and in the twentieth centuries. A possible explanation for this phenomenon is that in the earlier period, hardship was hardly ever alleviated by even the limited amounts of charity, and the greater general prosperity, of the late Victorian period. Hard times were really hard. Flanders' fears of starvation were entirely reasonable, not fanciful. People did regularly die of malnutrition in the poorer parts of London. Significantly, later in the eighteenth century the magistrate, Saunders Welsh, was to tell Dr Johnson that a score of people died every week from malnutrition in these poor areas.[4] This fear probably induced real and total desperation, a feeling that may well have been shared by many others in a similar situation at the time.

Flanders immediately felt great remorse for the initial theft from the

2. Hay, D., *Crime and Justice in Eighteenth and Nineteenth Century England*, p. 65.
3. See for example, J.Q. Wilson, *Penalties and Opportunities, A Reader on Punishment* (1994), Duff, A. and Garland, D. (eds), p.186.
4. Rude, G., *Hanoverian London* (1971), p.86.

shop, but later discovered that the bundle contained a small silver mug and six spoons, some linen, a good smock, three handkerchiefs and 18s. 6d in money, a potentially very valuable haul. She would have had many ready female "role" models for an entry into such a life of crime. Women played an active role in London crime at this time. Of those accused of property offences in this period, in urban areas, just under 30 per cent were women.[5] Nevertheless, they do appear to have fared significantly better before the courts than their male counterparts. Of the 1,232 people hanged at Tyburn from 1703 to 1772 only 92 were women.[6]

Statistics notwithstanding, Flanders was not in any doubt as to the risks that she was running and feared that if she continued with such activity she would "be taken next time, and be carried to Newgate and tried for [her] life". However, in taking the goods she had embarked on what for her would turn out to be a slippery slope into a world of professional and habitual crime.

Theft of a Necklace

Because of these fears of capture and execution, Flanders did not become a hardened thief straight away. Nevertheless, she subsequently succumbed to yet another criminal "impulse", this time when going through Aldersgate Street. While walking there she saw a small child wearing a necklace of gold beads, with its shoes untied. As she pretended to tie up the child's clog, she surreptitiously stole the valuable necklace. Although tempted by the "devil" to "kill the child in the dark alley, so that it might not cry", and thus alert others to the crime, she speedily abandoned such a wicked notion.

That Flanders could even consider such a possibility might appear shocking. Similarly, later in the novel, she did not show much concern

---

5.   Beattie, J.M., *ibid.*, p.240.
6.   Gatrell, V.A.C., *The Hanging Tree* (1990), p.8.

at the shooting and killing of several countryfolk that were in pursuit of her Lancashire highwayman husband's gang. However, the era was, in comparison with the twentieth century, a violent one, albeit becoming markedly less so. As Lawrence Stone has observed, it is, perhaps, a mistake to assume that modern notions of emotional relationships were the "norm" before the mid-eighteenth century.

When it did occur, theft from small children in this period (especially of their clothes), and sometimes even their attendant murders, often does appear to have been the work of women. This may, partly, have been because they found it easier to get the trust of such infants. In 1713, according to *The Account* of the Newgate Ordinary, one Susan Perry, aged 22, had been condemned and executed for: "... stripping naked, robbing and murdering ... John Peirce, an infant of four years of age".[7] This case may have stayed in Defoe's mind when he was writing the novel.

Homicide in Seventeenth and Eighteenth Century England

At the start of the eighteenth century murder seems to have been more common than today (though the enormous improvements in medical treatment ought to be "factored" into the assessment when considering this, people could die as a result of much smaller wounds than today). It has been suggested, convincingly, that from being five times that of the late twentieth century in 1660, the homicide rate fell towards "modern" levels in the period up to 1800.[8] Thus, Defoe was writing in the middle of this period of transition. However, it was not a uniformly progressive process; there appears to have been something of a mini "crime wave" in the period 1720-50, as he wrote the novel; this was perhaps linked, at first, to the large numbers of discharged soldiers and sailors. However, the murder rate was falling again steadily by the mid-1700s. So much was

7.   Quoted, Faller, L.B., *Crime and Defoe* (1993), p.65.
8.   Stone, L., "Interpersonal Violence in English Society 1300-1980, Past and Present", no.101 (1983), p.22, supported on this point by Sharpe, J.A., in a reply at no.108 (1985), p.206.

this the case that it has been observed that from a viewing of the private judicial diaries from the mid-eighteenth century of the Common Pleas Judge, Sir Dudley Ryder, anyone accustomed to modern levels of homicide in, for example, America, would be surprised at how little murder appears to have occurred in what was then the largest city in the world (approaching 700,000 people by the 1750s). At the several Old Bailey Sessions he presided over (during his breaks from judicial work in the Royal Courts in Westminster Hall) only three homicides were prosecuted, all of them resulting in convictions for manslaughter rather than murder. Probably two of these resulted from conduct, essentially accidents, that would not have resulted in a prosecution at all in modern times.[9] This does not appear to have been a statistical "fluke". According to figures compiled by Stephen Janssen, a former Mayor of London, in the years 1749-1771 there had been slightly less than four convictions a year for murder, though these do not represent the manslaughter verdicts that were excessively lenient (and might today result in murder convictions); again, undoubtedly some murderers went undetected or arrested, then as now. Interestingly, the Murder Act of 1752 whose preamble noted that "the horrid crime of murder has of late been more frequently perpetrated than formerly and particularly in and near the Metropolis", would appear to suggest that the popular perception as to homicide rates and the reality had parted company at this time.

In any event, Flanders, some years before this gradual amelioration had fully taken effect, was certainly living in a more dangerous age than the present one, with a higher tolerance of inter-personal violence and a greater propensity towards killing. The eighteenth century was, in many other ways, also, a generally "rougher" age than the one that followed; it was one in which, as Lawrence Stone has pointed out, the constant presence of death made attitudes to life and sentiment different from those of the modern era. While, in many areas of the arts it may have been an

---

9.   "Shaping the Eighteenth Century Criminal Trial: a View from the Ryder Sources", *The University of Chicago Law Review*, vol.50, Number 1, Winter 1983. John H. Langbein, p.44.

"age of elegance", it was also the era portrayed by Hogarth; one of cruel animal sports, brawling, public drunkenness and duelling.

Indeed, to some extent there was a far greater toleration for some forms of violence than might be the case in the twentieth century; generally, a greater emphasis on the sanctity of property rather than the person was a characteristic of the period, allowing sentences such as that of John Dale, who "was fined 10 marks, and six months imprisonment, for attempting to ravish a young girl of about eight years old". This was especially noticeable with regard to the gentry and upper orders of society, who were perhaps the first social group to modify their manners significantly as the century progressed. Earlier in the century and in the previous one, even "respectable" men could be involved in public disturbances, as Henry Fielding's judicially important predecessor at Bow Street, the magistrate Thomas De Veil, was to discover to his cost; the *Monthly Intelligencer* for June 1731 noting that "Justice Webster and Mr Carleton were try'd before the Lord Chief Justice Raymond on an Indictment for Assaulting Justice De Veil and were both found guilty". A popular pamphlet published in London in 1684 had condemned the "gentlemen" "bullies and hectors" who murdered a lowly waterman who had bumped into one of their number in a dark alley. These men, it asserted, would respond with savage violence to the slightest affront to their dignity. However, in these situations, the victims themselves were not always blameless in their terrible fates at the hands of such gentlemen. A potential scenario for this type of confrontation might be that which was tried at the Old Bailey in 1679, and which arose, the court heard, when a gentleman had been challenged late at night (11 pm) by a footman who asked him "who came"? When the defendant replied "a gentleman" the footman swore and answered "with an oath, that he was none". This affront to his status prompted the defendant to strike the footman with his cane, in turn prompting the footman to "press so hard" that the prisoner was "forced to make use of his sword and the footman was kill'd." The jury, as was common in such cases where there had been some fault on both sides, took a sanguine view of the evidence and convicted of manslaughter only "this being found a sudden fray, and no premeditated malice between them".[10]

In the early 1700s there were also the "Mohocks" in London; these were essentially upper class hooligans, young men who regularly attacked passers-by in the streets and even sedan chairs and their carriers. In his *Journal to Stella* Jonathan Swift was to note the elaborate precautions he took to avoid them "I came home in a chair for fear of the Mohocks". When caught (itself quite rare) their social position normally ensured that they received only fairly small fines. Swift also recorded the very high social status of some of those involved "there is a proclamation out against the Mohocks, one of those that are taken is a baronet". Some very prominent men had, in their youth been involved with them. Thomas Burnet (born in 1694), whose father was the Bishop of Salisbury, and who was, quite late in life, to be called to the Bar and then rapidly to become a highly regarded Judge of Common Pleas, had a notably dissolute and licentious youth and was rumoured to be a prime mover amongst the Mohocks; according to a letter of 1712 by Swift to "Stella", "the Bishop of Salisbury's son is said to be of the gang".[11] Well-to-do women seem to have found such men quite exciting and often attractive, a letter in *The Spectator* in 1714 noting that "the Emperor of the Mohocks married a rich widow within three weeks after having rendered himself formidable in the Cities of London and Westminster". Another young "blade" reputedly won great fame by knocking down a constable.[12]

This Mohock activity was not merely a manifestation of youthful high spirits, an early modern equivalent of boat race night. Swift noted that the gang had savagely attacked a lady's maid during which: "they cut all her face, and beat her without any provocation". While other recorded attacks were also potentially lethal "Young D'Avenant was telling us at Court how he was set upon by the Mohocks; and how they ran his chair thro, with a sword. It is not safe being in the streets".[13] In 1712 the young John Gay also produced a short topical play, *The Mohocks*, concerning the exploits

10. OBSP, April 30 - May 2, 1679, p.4.
11. Foss, E., *The Judges of England* (1864), vol.8, p.106.
12. *The Spectator*, Monday October 4, 1714.
13. Swift, J., *Journal to Stella*, March 9, 1711 (Everyman, 1948 edn).

of this gang (they had named themselves after a supposedly fierce tribe of American Indians), in which he explored some of the themes that he would develop in his later works, and also captured the anarchic behaviour of these "gentlemen". In the play the members of the gang decide to "leave conscience's rules to women and fools", and resolve that "no laws shall restrain our libertine reign, we'll riot, drink on, and be free". Defoe himself was to be acutely aware of the low standards of elements of the upper orders of society, as graphically portrayed by him in the *Poor Man's Plea* (1701).

Nevertheless, despite this, generally, violence by a gentleman was felt to be less acceptable and was less common in 1750 than in 1550.[14] This can, in part, be seen as an aspect of a more long term and gradual change in social manners, going back to the late medieval period. It has been argued, with some degree of supporting evidence, that in the 1400s crime appears to have been committed by all social groups in roughly equal numbers, proportionate to the size of the respective classes to society, the nobility and gentry being just as likely to commit violence and felony as their inferiors, and with relatively few offences limited to one social group alone. It has also been asserted that there was in this late medieval period a much smaller social gulf between "honest" men and felons; as the opportunities presented themselves, a man might uphold or break the law.[15] The trend away from this situation was clearly underway by 1500 and was to continue markedly in the eighteenth century under the influence of the evangelical movement (and accelerated later by the advent of Methodism). It was also to be reinforced by the growing importance of the emerging urban middle classes, a group which had little time or tolerance for illicit activities. The new middle class "conscience" was to challenge the existing way of life of both the upper social orders as well as of those at the bottom of the hierarchy, being opposed to both rioting commoners and gambling, drinking and duelling aristocrats. It can thus

---

14.   Sharpe, J.A., *ibid.*, p.98.
15.   Bellamy, J., *Crime and Public Order in England in the Later Middle Ages* (1973), pp.29-30.

be said to have rejected much of the hierarchical moral order that still characterized the early 1700s, and was to set the tone of the later Victorian Age, with its emphasis on "respectability".

However, this "gentling" process, though already under-way, still lay very substantially in the future when Defoe was writing *Moll Flanders*, and perhaps explains Flanders' mental willingness even to entertain the possibility of such an appalling action as the murder of a child. In many ways it was still a very brutal age, in which life was, relatively cheap, as can be seen by numerous contemporary newspaper accounts, one even noting that one day "a female child, having a cord and a brick-bat about its neck, was drawn out of the canal in St James' Park by a spaniel dog". Against this it should also be noted, that even at this time, *premeditated* and calculated murder was a crime that people in England were never hardened to. It was probably already significantly rarer in England than on the continent and generally viewed very much as a "crime apart". The Frenchman, P.J. Grosley visiting in the second half of the eighteenth century wrote that "murder is, notwithstanding, looked upon in England as the most heinous of all crimes ... even highwaymen seldom go so far as to kill those whom they rob".[16]

An indication of contemporary "robustness", can be seen in the treatment of homicides who were not convicted of pre-meditated murder, but only of manslaughter (the legal distinction between the two, for much of the eighteenth century, was still in the process of being defined); normally they could expect to receive only a nominal sentence. The famous actor Charles Macklin killed a colleague in a fit of anger and walked from the Old Bailey, a free man, having been convicted of manslaughter, "to be branded on the hand and discharged". It is significant to note that in London and Middlesex between 1749 and 1771 only 72 of the 678 people executed were murderers.[17]

Juries appear to have been very willing, in most cases of homicide arising out of inter-personal disputes, to give any benefit of the doubt to

---

16.   Radzinowicz, L., *A History of English Criminal Law*, vol.1 (1948), p.708.
17.   Porter, R., *English Society in the Eighteenth Century* (1990), p.136.

the defendant in acquitting outright or returning a manslaughter verdict. The widespread presence of weapons, such as swords and knives, meant that such quarrels, often amongst friends who had been drinking, could often have fatal results. In this situation the court was usually concerned to establish if the defendant had deliberately engineered an unfair situation, when a murder verdict might be returned; normally, though, if there was wrongdoing on both sides the verdict would be manslaughter, with its modest attendant penalty, or even an outright acquittal. This can be seen repeatedly in the records of such cases from the Old Bailey, and the significance was something that potential witnesses were also well aware of. Thus when two friends quarrelled after playing dice for money, in 1725, and a "clashing of swords" ensued, in which one was mortally wounded, the man attending the dying victim made sure to make inquiry, "I asked the deceased on his death-bed, if he received the wound fairly"? To this he received the reply "I think I did - but - I don't know what might have happened". His assailant, giving evidence was also well aware that "if I had killed him [that] night, in the heat of passion, I should have had the law on my side", but that if he had done it any later this would not have been the case.[18] A strong and widespread sense of self-pride meant that even chance encounters could result in such incidents. John Hannoway received a not guilty verdict when accused of stabbing Thomas Hudson, a stranger he had met coming along "Lord Chinay's Walks at Chelsea". The killing occurred after there had been some "some justling and hard words".[19]

Theft of a Diamond Ring

Flanders found that the infant's gold beads were worth £12 or £14 (they had probably belonged to the child's mother). She left the child unharmed

---

18.   *Select Trials at the Sessions-house in the Old Bailey*, vol.II, 1724-1732 (printed 1735), pp.144-146.
19.   OBSP, December 8-11, 1697, p.4.

and escaped, and thus had made her "second sally into the world". The fresh success she had met with rapidly put out of her mind her earlier fears and shame at becoming a thief, while "poverty hardened [her] heart" to her new life. Shortly afterwards, while going through Lombard Street, she successfully retrieved the abandoned loot of a pair of thieves who were being closely pursued by the "hue and cry". This consisted of six or seven pieces of expensive silk, and involved her in almost no risk, and little self-reproach "how they came to get so many I could not tell; but as I had only robbed the thief, I made no scruple at taking these goods, and being very glad of them too". The next opportunity to present itself was the theft of a diamond and a gold ring from a house near Stepney, that had been left on view in the window by "some thoughtless lady that had more money than forecast". Her method of taking the rings would be recognized by any modern burglar. She walked past the house several times to see if anyone was in, and then tapped on the window to gain the attention of an occupant who might be inside but unseen. She planned to tell anybody who might come to the window that they should secure the rings as she had seen two dishonest looking men "take notice of them" (research indicates that modern burglars still often ring the doorbell to establish occupancy before entering). When no one came to the window Flanders "... thrust hard against the square of glass, and managed to break it with little resulting noise, and then took out the two rings". These were worth £3, and 9s., respectively.

At this time Stepney was a pleasant suburban village, close in to London, though there were already a few established pockets of criminals in the parish.[20] Samuel Pepys had been a frequent visitor in the 1660s. It was thus not surprising to find an apparently wealthy woman in this location at the time, though it might have been a century later. Indeed, Defoe had been of the opinion, expressed in his *Tour through England and Wales,* that such affluent types of people had increased in the nearby suburban villages of Stratford, Wanstead, Leyton and West Ham in the previous 20 or 30 years, it being an area that was "strangely increased"

---

20.   Specifically mentioned in a Parliamentary Statute of 1698.

not only in size (Stratford had doubled and was almost joined to Bow, and was indicative of London's general expansion) but also in the quality of the inhabitants and their residences "and this increase is generally speaking of handsome large houses" with substantial increases of carriages and excellent "conversation", but yet without "gaming houses and public foundations of vice and debauchery".[21] This was, in part, because the location was still popular with affluent city merchants who wanted to live a little way away from the financial centre of the Metropolis.

Flanders' Disposal of her Stolen Goods

At this stage in her criminal career Flanders confronted the perennial problem of the regular thief; she was at a loss for a "market" for her goods, and especially for the potentially valuable pieces of silk. She was "very loathe to dispose of them for a trifle", as the "poor unhappy thieves in general do, who after they have ventured their lives for perhaps a thing of value, are forced to sell it for a song when they have done". Having risked her life she wanted a just reward. She decided to go to her "governess" (who had earlier looked after her child by the Lancashire man) for advice. This woman had turned pawnbroker and was living fairly well. She agreed to sell the goods that were brought to her through her pawnbroking shop, which goods Flanders initially told her belonged to her (Flanders') late husband. She discovered that this type of outright selling (as opposed to lending money on the security of the goods) was quite common in the shop.

A Temporary Return to an Honest Life

Subsequently Flanders moved in and stayed with her "governess" and initially also returned to an honest life, doing some quilting work for

---

21. Everyman (edn) vol.1, p.6.

ladies' beds and petticoats. This was a pattern of behaviour for which there is good historical support. Even some hard core professional criminals drifted between legitimate and illegal activities. For example, one Cook, a shoemaker of Stratford (the village to the east of the City) was committed for trial in 1741 for what were thought to be more than 100 robberies in the Metropolis and its environs, carried out over a period of several years. Earlier, however, he had desisted for some considerable time from law-breaking and gone off to Birmingham where he worked as a shoemaker, quite legitimately, for several years before returning to his criminal activities.[22] This was an option that Flanders initially toyed with, with regard to her needlework. She worked hard at this honest employment but having been exposed to easy money temptation soon overcame her again.

The Theft of a Silver Tankard

One evening she took the chance opportunity to steal a silver tankard which had been left unattended by "the careless boys" serving in an ale house. These items being "much in use in public houses at that time"; silver tankards, whether from public or private houses, appear to have been regular items of stolen property, in part it seems because they were usually worth at least five pounds, and sometimes more. Thus, in a single Sessions at the Old Bailey, in 1689, there were two such cases, involving three women: Elinor Fluellin, who stole one worth five pounds and five shillings from the prosecutor's house, and Elizabeth Autley and her daughter who stole another worth five pounds from a tavern.[23] Similarly, in 1694 Merryman Hatley went into a tavern run by John Wellings with a friend, in Exchange Alley in the City, and "called for drink". However, in this case, unlike Flanders' ale house attendants, Wellings swiftly

---

22. G.M. 11 (1741), p.356, quoted Beattie, J.M., *Crime and the Courts in England 1660-1800* (1986), p.263.
23. OBSP, December 11-14, 1689, p.3. This series printed for Langley Curtis.

observed that "after they were gone, the tankard was missing".[24]

Flanders returned to her governess with the tankard and decided to make a clean breast as to the provenance of her goods. Her governess however, to her surprise, was not at all shocked and suggested that she should keep the tankard and sell it. She also remarked that she wished that she could "like on such a bargain" once a week in the future. At this point Flanders began to get a new "notion" of her governess' business, and observed that since she turned pawnbroker she had "... a sort of people about her that were none of the honest ones" that she had met with there before. This became even more apparent to her when she saw the numerous swords, spoons, forks and tankards which were brought in to the shop not to be pawned but to be sold outright to the governess. She bought them without asking any questions as to where they had originated. She also discovered that in following this trade, she (the governess) usually melted down the plate that she bought so that it might not be "challenged", and indeed this was the fate of the stolen silver tankard from the ale house. This was a regular phenomenon with stolen silver, even for quite small items, such as the spoon that Mary Lamb stole from her master in 1689, "broke into pieces" and offered to a goldsmith.[25] Thus also, James Mattocks, whose speciality was snatching gentlemen's swords from their sides (a frequent crime) noted, having turned King's evidence against his accomplice, that having "snatched away" a gentleman's sword outside a playhouse, as the victim "was delivering the ladies into a coach" he and the accused "broke it, and melted it down into a bar, in a three-cornered pot, with a charcoal fire, and the Prisoner sold it to a silver-smith by a pastry-cooks', near Fleet-ditch".[26] Even gold watches that were too individualized, and thus identifiable, might be melted for their bullion value in an emergency. This was well known to the general public; when John Gay's thief-taker, "Peachum", observed to the professional receiver, Mrs Tripes (while lamenting the fact that she had earlier purchased a

---

24.   OBSP, December 6-9, 1694, p.1.
25.   OBSP, December 11-14, 1689, p.2.
26.   OBSP, January 17-20, 1739, p.32.

"handsome" gold watch from him and his colleague for only seven guineas a substantial part of which they had kept for their own cut), "to a gentleman upon the road [a highwayman], a gold watch will be scarce worth the taking", she had immediately replied: "Consider, Mr Peachum, that watch was remarkable, and not of very safe sale".[27]

Flanders' governess was, of course, a habitual receiver of stolen goods, something that was not untypical of that occupation (pawnbroking). Fielding, in his *Inquiry* of 1751 was to say with regard to receiving that "it is impossible to find any means of regulating brokers and pawnbrokers". Some, he felt, might simply have been people who were none too particular about inquiries into the provenance of goods "clandestine dealers ... who satisfy their consciences with telling a ragged fellow, or wench, that they hope they came honestly by silver, and gold and diamonds". Others engaged quite openly in such criminal dealing. Over a century later dishonest pawnbrokers in London were still melting down plate, as can be seen in Mayhew and Binney's account of crime in London in the early 1860s, and of houses where "... the crucible or silver pot is kept ready on a slow fire to receive the silver plate, sometimes marked with the crest of the owner".[28]

A "Teacher" in Crime

As indigence threatened Flanders once more, her governess advised her to go out again, and take whatever she could find. Flanders, however, worried that as she had no skill in the criminal trade she "would be undone at once if she was taken". Consequently her governess initiated her into a more professional approach to crime by introducing her to a "schoolmistress" who "would make [Flanders] as dexterous as herself".

The "schoolmistress" was a very experienced professional criminal. Unlike most other parts of the country at this period, London had

---

27. Gay, J, *The Beggars' Opera*, Act 3, Scene vi.
28. *London Labour and the London Poor* (1862), vol.4, p.374.

significant numbers of such well established professional thieves. A school for pickpockets in the city was noted as early as 1585 in a report to Lord Burghley. Their training tool was a purse connected to bells to detect any movement, or as one city official put it "amongst our travels ... there was a schoolhouse set up to learn young boys to cut purses. The pocket had in it certain counters and was hung about eight hawks' bells and over the top did hang a little scaring bell".[29] This appears to have continued into the "Moll Flanders" period (and indeed Charles Dickens). Fagin, portrayed more than a century after "Moll Flanders" was written, was merely following a long line of professional criminal teachers, though young boys were more common as apprentices than women in their later years, having greater manual dexterity and lightness of touch. As the hero of *Colonel Jack* was to note, in pickpocketing "... the ingenuity of the trade consisted very much in sleight of hand, a good address, and being very nimble". However, the divisions between opportunist and professional criminal were probably quite fluid at this time. Most professionals would still usually have started life as occasional criminals learning by experience, rather than being specially trained individuals, as was the case with Flanders.

As a result of the school mistress's tuition, Flanders became "... as impudent a thief and as dexterous as ever Moll Cutpurse was".[30] Moll Cutpurse (she also went by the name Mary Frith) was a famous pickpocket turned fence of the seventeenth century. She gained a considerable degree of control over London thieving in the 1630s, establishing a warehouse for handling stolen property, which she would return to their losers at a fee.[31] The period in which *Moll Flanders* was written was also the heyday of Jonathan Wild who in fact merely perfected Moll Cutpurse's original system, to become both the self- styled "Thief Taker General" and also the most important receiver of stolen goods and organizer of crime in the Metropolis.[32] Defoe was to write a history of Jonathan Wild, after the

29. McMullen, J., *ibid.*, p.107 and see also Sharpe, J.A., *ibid.*, p.114.
30. Page 173.
31. McMullen, J., *The Canting Crew* (1984), p.113.
32. Tobias, J.J., *Crime and Industrial Society in the Nineteenth Century* (1967), p.34.

latter's fall, in 1725.[33] Flanders' choice of criminal comparison is thus very revealing as to the degree of skill she felt that she had attained.

Flanders' schoolmistress confederate helped her to master three sorts of crime: shoplifting, the stealing of shop books and pocket books, and the taking of gold watches "from the ladies' sides". It was to the last of these that Flanders was particularly attracted. That a self-respecting professional criminal would normally specialize in valuable goods like gold watches was a regular theme of Defoe's work, and probably the reality, in an era when theft from the person carried, in theory, a death sentence if goods to the value of 1s. were taken, even if no violence at all had been involved. Another of his creations, Colonel Jack, ignored things like handkerchiefs, he "... would not meddle with them, not caring to run the risk for small matters". In what was still overwhelmingly a cash economy rich people could walk the streets in possession of very large sums of money, as can be seen from a near contemporary newspaper report of a crime, "On Wednesday night a gentleman going home thro' Long Lane, near West Smithfield, was knock'd down and robbed of 300 guineas and his pocket book, in which was bills and bank notes to the value of £300 more".[34]

The most eminent people became the victims of pickpockets. Even, later in the century, King George III who allegedly (it could be apocryphal) had money taken while walking in Kensington Gardens, and certainly the Duke of Cumberland who had his sword stolen as he entered a theatre. Pickpockets could be quite shameless in the locations they chose for their crimes. In 1662, George Fox, while appearing before the Quarter Sessions in Leicester, noted in his *Journal* that "while we were standing where the thieves used to stand, a cut-purse had his hand in several friends' pockets", though, perhaps, a reflection of these Quakers' judicial unpopularity became evident as when the justices were informed of what had happened "they called him up before them, and upon examination he could not deny it; yet they set him at liberty". There was nothing new in

---

33.   Account of Jonathan Wild (1725).
34.   *The Original Half-penny London Journal*, Saturday March 6, 1725.

the audacity of such pickpockets in Flanders' time. Early in the seventeenth century, the pickpocket, John Selman had been caught at work in the Royal Chapel at Whitehall, stealing "even in the Kings Majesties presence, even in the Church of God, in the time of divine service". Despite being within earshot of a contrite speech by the condemned Selman at the scaffold at his own execution, in 1612, a speech in which he urged others not to follow his example "... one of his quality (a picke pocket, I meane) even at his execution, grew master of a true man's purse, who [the pickpocket] being presently taken, was imprisoned, and is like the next sessions to wander the long voyage after his grand Captaine, Mounsier John Selman".[35] The ruses used by thieves could be extraordinary; Tom Gerrard who was executed in 1711 was even supposed to have trained his dog to lift valuables from people's pockets![36] In 1694 Thomas Kerton allegedly carried out the theft of a trunk of shirts and linen from a domestic house in St Annes parish by telling the prosecutor, Abigail Hawthorne, that a rabbit that he owned had run up her stairs; while they were "busy about searching for this pretended rabbit, he made bold to take away the trunk". He was acquitted.[37]

At length Flanders' teacher put her to practise with the real theft of a gold watch from a young lady with a child. As the lady left church, she was jostled by Flanders' confederate who "... fell against the lady with so much violence as put her in a great fright", and Flanders swiftly took her watch, and managed to get it clean away. She received £20 from her governess for it, which she divided with her accomplice (her erstwhile "teacher"). This success resulted in her entering the life of a complete thief "hardened to a pitch above all the reflections of conscience or modesty", and she became a thorough and committed professional, "beyond the common rate". This was despite the fact that she had by then got enough work, as a seamstress, to have earned her bread honestly. She rapidly grew rich as she became more audacious and skilful, and ultimately had 21 gold

---

35. "The Arraignment of John Selman" (1612), printed by W.H. for Thomas Archer, p.16.
36. McLynn, F., *Crime and Punishment in Eighteenth Century England* (1991), p.7.
37. OBSP, February 21-23, 1694, p.1.

watches in her possession, simultaneously, and, fairly quickly, about £200 in cash. Despite this, she remained very cautious in her operations, something which worked to her benefit when her teacher, with another, was caught trying to steal from a linen drapers in Cheapside by a "hawk-eyed journeyman". They were taken to Newgate where they were condemned to die. However, they both "pleaded their bellies", and, though neither was pregnant, they were "... voted quick with child," and gained a temporary reprieve from execution as a consequence.[38] Flanders later visited them in Newgate but found the place so depressing that she ultimately desisted and "... left off going to see them". That she should feel melancholy after such a visit is not surprising.

Newgate Prison

Newgate prison was the principal prison for London and had been so for nearly 700 years, although there were other renowned prisons in the Metropolis. Defoe himself in his *Tour Through the Whole Island of Great Britain* (1724) was able to note that "there are in London more public and private prisons and houses of confinement than in any city in Europe". He went on to list 23 prisons of varying sizes and types as well as 100 sponging houses (for the initial detention of arrested debtors to see if they could satisfy their creditors before going to a debtor's prison such as the Fleet).[39] A barrister, William Leach, had estimated, in 1651, that in England there were between 12,000 and 20,000 people permanently in custody. Two other important prisons in London, that of the Marshalsea and the King's Bench prison, were south of the river in the borough of Southwark. Some prisons specialized in either criminals or in debtors, many others, like Newgate, were mixed. There had been sporadic but rather ineffectual attempts to keep debtors and criminals apart since an Act in 1670, and there was usually some rough segregation between the

---

38. And see below, p.166.
39. Imprisonment for debt was a regular phenomenon at the turn of the seventeenth century, and for much of the next century and more, though it was gradually ameliorated and restricted.

two classes of inmate though this was far from thorough, as was the case with regard to male/female separation.

In 1383 the Common Council of the city had ordered that Freemen in the city who committed minor offences should normally be held in Ludgate, reserving Newgate for more serious offenders alleged to have committed felonies (though it also had its complement of debtors). Daniel Defoe and William Penn had been held there, and the famous eighteenth century highwayman Jack Sheppard had escaped from it.[40] It had weathered internal attack by "jail fever" and in 1780 was to survive external attack from the "mob" in the Gordon Riots, who burnt most of it down, whilst also releasing the inmates (they did the same to the Fleet prison). Most people sent to Newgate were awaiting trial at the Bailey and their term of custody would be anything between a week and three months depending on the operation of the court, and the time in the cycle of hearings at which they were detained. This was often better however, than the amount of time that prisoners would have to spend in custody in the provinces while awaiting trial, where they might have to spend up to six months waiting for the twice yearly Assizes. If acquitted at the end of the sessions they would be released, if not, many would be remanded back to the prison pending further action (hanging, transportation, the payment of fines, the pillory and appeals against sentence). Newgate was a joint prison for both the city and urban Middlesex, though it was under the supervision (often not very effective) of the city authorities (ie, the Mayor, Sheriffs and Aldermen). In Flanders' period comparatively few convicts received sentences of imprisonment as a punishment for felonies (it only became a relatively frequent punishment, in its own right, in the latter half of the eighteenth century). As late as the early 1770s only 2.3 per cent of sentences passed at the Old Bailey were specifically for a term of imprisonment.

At this time, custody as a punishment in itself (as opposed to death, whipping, transportation, branding and fining) was most commonly confined to short periods, measured in weeks, or, at the most a few

---

40.   Priestly, V., *Victorian Prison Lives* (1985), p.3.

months, for minor offenders, often summarily convicted vagrants. These would be imprisoned in houses of correction or "Bridewells", where they could also be whipped; such institutions, at least originally, had a more "reformist" ethos than the prisons, they often also served effectively as workhouses for vagrants. This was at least in theory, though this practice started to wane at the end of the seventeenth century, because of changes in the general mode of poor relief. At this point, the idea of providing work for the inmates was commonly abandoned, instead of which deserving persons were given out-relief, or sometimes, especially after 1722, a place in a proper workhouse (parishes were first officially empowered to group together to create workhouses in that year). Colonel Jack's fellow, the juvenile "Captain Jack" for example, was given a sentence of three whippings at the local Bridewell for a minor role in crime (owing to his young age; there was a relative reluctance in the early years of the eighteenth century to pursue juveniles compared to the period from the 1790s onwards). The Vagrancy Act of 1744 was also to give the justices the power to imprison "all persons wand'ring abroad and lodging in barns or houses or the open air not giving a good account of themselves". These institutions (Bridewells) were themselves fairly grim and corrupting, albeit less so than the main prisons. Serious offenders, felons, were very rarely admitted to these prisons until at least the 1770s.[41]

However, many of those committed to Newgate were sent there for offences that were decidedly petty if not sometimes positively bucolic, albeit technically felonies. Thus from a newspaper of 1723, it can be learnt that "One William Jordan of Rotherhith was lately committed to Newgate, for robbing Mr Combs, gardener of Rotherhith, of great quantities of cucumbers, colly-flowers and other things".[42]

Newgate prison was a squalid and unhealthy place with a smell that sometimes forced nearby shops to close. A contemporary description captures the atmosphere at the time very well; "Newgate is a dismal prison ... a place of calamity", it was, "a habitation of misery, a confused chaos

---

41. Spierenburg, S., *The Prison Experience* (1991), p.264.
42. *The London Journal*, May 25, 1723.

... a bottomless pit of violence, a Tower of Babel where all are speakers and no hearers".[43] There were frequent outbreaks of the jail fever in the institution (a form of typhus, caused largely by poor hygiene and ventilation), usually amongst the prisoners but which threatened anyone who came into contact with them; on one famous occasion, in 1750, it spread to the Old Bailey sessions killing several Judges, jurors and even the Lord Mayor.[44] It was especially bad in the winter when clothes were changed and washed even less frequently than in the summer months (typhus afflicted ordinary Londoners as well, albeit to a smaller degree). In April of 1725 the prisoners were so weakened by the disease that none could leave their cells for chapel. In 1726, 21 people were hanged at Tyburn, but in the same year 83 men and women died of fever in Newgate. Some prison chaplains even took to carrying garlands of camphor while they did their rounds, in the belief that it would provide a degree of protection (something that the Bailey Judges did as well at times, strewing the dock with sweet smelling herbs and vinegar).[45] The efficacy of this precaution is doubtful. Dr Johnson was to estimate, as late as 1759, that one in four of the prison population died every year from fever or other causes. When explaining his motivation in initiating reform of the prisons and Bridewells towards the latter part of the century, John Howard was to say that "my attention was principally fixed by the fever and the smallpox, which I saw prevailing to the destruction of multitudes, not only of felons in their dungeons, but of debtors also".

The prison was also conveniently close to the Old Bailey, the main court for those accused of felony in the City of London. The Old Bailey Court was originally erected in 1539, in part to overcome the problems caused by the jail fever emanating from Newgate (where trials had formerly been held), and infecting the innocent. Many of the

43.	Smith, A., *A Complete History of the Lives and Robberies of the Most Notorious Highwaymen* (1719), vol.1, p.153, quoted Sheehan, W.J., *Crime in England 1550-1800*, p.229.
44.	Sheehan, W.J., *Finding Solace in Eighteenth-Century Newgate, Crime in England 1550-1800* (1977) (ed) J.S. Cockburn, p.230.
45.	Linebaugh, P., *The Ordinary of Newgate and His Account*, p.253.

developments in it (and the nearby prison) were thus aimed at improving the lot of the Judges, jurors and "turnkeys" rather than the prisoners themselves; an Act of 1666 had specifically noted, in its preamble, that the former often caught diseases from the latter.

However, the prisoners were able to make a contribution themselves to medical science; in the same year that Defoe was writing the novel, 1721, there was a serious outbreak of smallpox in London which claimed many lives. George I had two of his grandchildren inoculated against the disease but only after the new process had been tested on six inmates of Newgate prison, who volunteered to be guinea-pigs in exchange for having their death sentences commuted. Additionally, in the early eighteenth century some prisoners who were due to be hanged, but without having a Judge's order for their corpses to go after death to the surgeons, could sell their bodies in advance of execution to doctors who attended the prison. This presumably also made the crowd at Tyburn less likely to attempt to forcibly retrieve it. Thus it could be observed that "it is a superstition with some surgeons, who beg the bodies of condemn'd malefactors, to go to the gaol, and bargain for the carcass with the criminal himself".[46] Some prisoners would haggle quite hard, with even "little fellow(s)", with small and half-starved bodies refusing to accept 12 shillings and holding out for the normal 15.

To an extent, the squalor of Newgate was typical of many European prisons at the start of the eighteenth century. Though this was not universal, the Papal prison of San Michele, erected in 1704 by Pope Clement XI, was a little known precursor of later developments, providing, as it did, segregation, classification (of prisoners), separate cells and prison labour with a view to reforming inmates.

To try and deal with noxious smells and possibly disease-carrying fumes in the prison a windmill sail-operated ventilator, powered from the roof, was installed in 1753, though with only limited effect.[47] In Flanders' time the building dated from the fifteenth century, though much was

---

46.   *The Spectator*, no.504, Wednesday, October 8, 1712.
47.   Stockdale, E., *A Study of Bedford Prison 1660-1877*, p.70 (1977).

rebuilt after the Great Fire of 1666. It was razed and rebuilt again in 1767, a task which was to be repeated after it was largely burnt down by the rioters in 1780.

It was customary for the inmates who could afford it to pay for their lodging; fees were also commonly paid for both admission and release (at the time there were sometimes even fees for punishments inflicted as a result of a court order, 4s. 6d. for a whipping or a branding being not uncommon). Indeed, like much of contemporary English society (such as army regiments) the whole prison was run on a semi-private basis, with substantial opportunities to make money from the sale of liquor and the renting out of better accommodation.

Those in Newgate who were affluent could afford the "master side", while destitute prisoners would live free in the "charity" wards on the "common side". The common-wards at Newgate, especially for felons (as opposed to debtors), were particularly appalling. According to an account by one "B.L." of Twickenham, written in 1724, they were very overcrowded, with some prisoners, unable to find a place in a bunk, even being forced to sleep on the floor (often a stone floor), in rooms without proper fireplaces to heat them.[48] The regime between the two sides was radically different, with not only different accommodation, but also different diets and privileges. The rich were able to enjoy fine wines, foods and other amenities provided they could pay the enormous costs that such commodities fetched in the prison. The robber, John Hall, in his pre-execution memoirs of 1708 had much to say about the prison generally, and the exorbitant costs of the master-side in particular.[49] He observed that a man could take a palace at an "easier rent" than the cost of one "individual mansion [room] here to swing a cat in". Despite the price, however, he noted that there were always "... the miserable wrecks of several unfortunate gentlemen" willing to pay it, apparently these men were mostly imprisoned for treason, murder, rape, scandal and debt. This

48. Evans, R., *The Fabrication of Virtue, English Prison Architecture 1750-1840* (1982), p.39.
49. "Memoirs of the Right Villainous JOHN HALL, The Late Famous and Notorious Robber". Printed in London (1708) by Ben. Bragg, p.10.

bifurcated system of accommodation was not unique to Newgate. All of the main London prisons had different standards of accommodation, depending on how much a prisoner was able to pay. At the prison at Wood Street Compter, where he was imprisoned for debt, Jonathan Wild initially, according to Defoe, was also one who "suffered great hardship, having no friends to keep him out, or money to maintain him within, so that he was on the common side". He ultimately remedied this by running errands for the turnkeys and richer prisoners. At first, unable to pay 1s. 3d a week for a bed in a better part of the prison, he had been kept in a communal ward known as the "hold", which served as dormitory, kitchen and canteen, and where the prisoners slept on wooden shelves at night.

Occasionally, this difference in living conditions, led to friction between those who were in the common wards and those on the master side. In the Marshalsea prison, in 1639, there was even a riot amongst the former, in which they threw firebrands and stones, after the Under-Marshal of the prison ordered them not to abuse their wealthier colleagues. The irregular free bread allowance on the common side was also often necessarily supplemented by begging through the barred windows of the prisons. Another riot occurred in the King's Bench prison, in 1621, when the prison Marshal sealed up the main window through which this occurred, depriving the inmates of their sustenance.[50]

There was also permanent difficulty in the prisoners getting enough exercise. A physician visiting late in the eighteenth century noted the tendency of the prisoners' bodies to "turn to flab" as a result of the lack of healthy recreation. This was something that the prisoners themselves obviously appreciated. Early in that century they appear to have converted a large room on the second floor of the building into a makeshift gymnasium, allowing them to do exercises, until overcrowding made this use of the space untenable.[51]

The prison, especially when holding famous prisoners, was a popular

---

50. Jessica A. Browner, *Wrong Side of the River: London's Disreputable South Bank in the Sixteenth and Seventeenth Century, Essays in History* (University of Virginia), vol.36, 1994, p.47.
51. Sheehan, W.J., *Finding Solace in Eighteenth-Century Newgate, ibid.*, p.239.

and available "sight" in London, particularly for members of fashionable "society". For example, in the early 1720s, the highwayman, Jack Sheppard, when detained at Newgate was a source of widespread fascination; according to the *Newgate Calendar* "he was visited by great numbers of people of all ranks, and scarce any one left him without making him a present in money". People would also pay to see the condemned at chapel on the Sunday before an execution, those to be executed sitting together on a special pew (sometimes this pew was painted black). Forty years after Defoe was writing, James Boswell, having been disappointed in trying to see the radical John Wilkes, decided to seek an alternative source of amusement "I then thought I should see prisoners of one kind or other so went to Newgate". Once there he examined the condemned prisoners who included the highwayman Paul Lewis "... a genteel, spirited young fellow. He was just a MacHeath".[52] The presence of so many spectators could be distracting for the condemned prisoners. In a letter to the Lord Mayor in the same year that *Moll Flanders* was written, one Thomas Purney asked "whether it be proper that the chapel of Newgate should be crowded sometimes with a hundred or more strangers ... pointing and whispering, to the confusion of the wretched men to die".[53]

To modern penal notions, a remarkable degree of self-government was exercised by the prisoners. In 1725 Bernard de Mandeville was shocked at the freedom he found there on a visit "... they are debarred from nothing but going out. Their most serious hours they spend in mock tryals (*sic*)".[54] This latter point was supported earlier in the century (1708) by the inmate John Hall, who observed that their debates "run altogether upon law", with the prisoners vigorously disputing the finer points of the subject, such as the distinction between burglary and ordinary housebreaking. He felt that "the licentiousness of the place is abominable". Some pets were even kept by the prisoners, not contributing to the institution's already poor general

52.   Boswell's *London Diary*, May 3, 1763, Heineman 1950, p.250.
53.   Linebaugh, P., *The Ordinary of Newgate and His Account, ibid.*, p.251.
54.   Evans, R., *ibid.*, p.40.

hygiene (pigs were only banned in 1714). The prisoners themselves do appear to have felt that there were well established rights and customs to which they were entitled, even in the notorious Fleet prison, where in 1731 "they caused a riot and insulted the keepers, upon which the Warden procur'd from the tilt yard two files of musketeers consisting of 12 men. The prisoners alleged they were ill us'd and stood up for their rights and privileges".[55]

Jailers in eighteenth century prisons had only the loosest day-to-day influence over the lives of the inmates, the keeper and his turnkeys employing a very detached method of control. The "trustees", prisoners in some measure elected to preserve discipline and order, distributed charitable contributions and collected subscriptions from new prisoners to pay for candles and coal.[56] This indirect method of control inevitably facilitated periodic escapes, such as that of Jack Sheppard, and also disturbances in the prison itself. In 1726 one "Vulcan" Gates, a blacksmith, had been detained in Newgate on a relatively small matter, but foolishly mentioned to the prison barber that he was also wanted under the notorious "Black Act". The barber promptly informed on him (for the reward), and he was sentenced to death. On the day of his execution he and some other prisoners in the condemned cells "took it into their heads that they would not be hanged". They managed to obtain a crowbar, and, while other inmates smothered the noise by singing psalms, prised up the flagstones to make a barrier against the door. Eventually the Sheriff of London, Sir Jeremiah Morder, had to be fetched, and having established his identity by dangling his gold chain through a small hole in the ceiling "spoke seriously to them". This, or the hopelessness of their situation, appears to have been enough, for eventually they submitted to their appointed fate at Tyburn.[57] In 1748 another group of prisoners, seven smugglers, who had managed (significantly) to arm themselves while inside with pistols and clubs, rushed the main gate and got outside the

---

55. *The Monthly Intelligencer* (appended to *The Gentleman's Magazine*) June 1731, p.264.
56. Beattie, J.M., *Crime and the Courts in England 1660-1800* (1986), p.289.
57. Thompson, E.P., *Whigs and Hunters* (1977), p.174.

prison (five were swiftly recaught but the other two managed to evade capture).

Above all, financial resources, and practical help, from outside, could make life in Newgate more tolerable for the prisoners. Although there was a public and charitable bread allowance for poor convicts this was not always very reliable or adequate, usually consisting at most of a penny loaf a day. John Hall certainly felt sorry for "those poor prisoners who, for want of friends, have nothing else to subsist on but bread and water",[58] though, at least in Newgate, this was occasionally supplemented, as "charitable disposed persons" sent a consignment of free meat into the prison every Thursday. Cash, in particular, was valuable as those running the prison would sometimes deliberately interfere with inmates being supplied with food from outside (perhaps because it reduced their own sales to the inmates). This was despite Acts of 1670 and 1728 specifically allowing prisoners to send for provisions from outside the prison if they wished.

The House of Commons Inquiry of 1729, which focused particularly on the Fleet and Marshalsea prisons (and which resulted in the unsuccessful prosecutions of the corrupt jailers Banbridge and Huggins and their underlings), noted that jailers not only encouraged drunkenness but also "prevent the needy prisoners being supplied by his friends with the mere necessaries of life in order to increase an exorbitant gain to their tenants". There was nothing new in this in the 1720s. When imprisoned in the provinces in the 1670s the Quaker George Fox, on one occasion, was told that "the jailer would not suffer us to have any drink out of the town into the prison, but what beer we drank we must take of him" (this did not pose a problem for Fox as he drank only water).

As a result, as W.J. Sheehan has noted, for the inmates, cash was easily the greatest material solace to their circumstances.[59] For example at the very highest level, special, very comfortable, rooms (over and above the

---

58. *Ibid.,* p.24.
59. *Finding Solace in Eighteenth Century Newgate, Crime in England 1550-1800* (1977) (ed) J.S. Cockburn, p.245.

accommodation of the master side) were available in the "press yard" in Newgate to those that could afford them. Flanders' Lancashire husband, when imprisoned in Newgate later in the novel, had followed this path and "given money to the head-master of the prison, to be allow'd the liberty of that better part of the prison". Daniel Defoe himself appears to have been imprisoned in the press yard during his time in Newgate. The comforts that money could purchase in Newgate were touched on by Defoe again in *Street Robberies Consider'd,* by the narrator, who after being caught during his criminal career with his "Mawks" (a whore) and sent to Newgate managed to arrange comfortable non-sexually segregated accommodation "as I had money at command, we had a handsome room allow'd us and very comfortably lay together". Deciding to reduce her chances of testifying against him he even married her in the prison "with the assistance of the keepers" (that a wife could not be forced to testify against her husband was to become a firm principle of common law). Their superior accommodation, however, still did not protect them from prison diseases, "my wife got such a violent distemper in the prison, that our wedlock bonds were broke in less than a quarter of a year".[60] This ability to purchase comfort was a theme that recurred repeatedly in contemporary literature. Later, in *Amelia,* Henry Fielding notes how a wealthy woman having been brought into a London prison and being confronted by a surly keeper produced her money, whereupon "the keeper no sooner viewed the purse than his features became all softened in an instant".

As a former inmate, Defoe was well aware of the potentially destructive consequences of such an environment as Newgate, best illustrated perhaps earlier in the novel (during Flanders' first and voluntary sojourn in the American colonies), when Flanders' natural mother, told her daughter that "... we all know here that there are more thieves and rogues made by that one prison of Newgate than by all the clubs and societies of villains in the nation. Tis that cursed place, that half peoples this colony". Though this was certainly a gross exaggeration with regard

---

60. *Ibid.,* pp.47-48.

to the population of Virginia (mainly composed, as it was, by free emigrants). That prison, generally, could be a breeding ground for crime at this time was widely believed by contemporaries to be true, there being little faith in its reformatory value. The arch-criminal, Jonathan Wild, himself appears to have emerged from his four years in the debtors' section of the Wood Street Compter (a prison comparable for bad reputation to Newgate), in 1699, well set on his future life of crime and intimately associated with another prisoner, Mary Milliner, who was a professional thief and prostitute. In his third edition of *The State of the Prisons* in 1784, John Howard, who, later in the eighteenth century visited Newgate before and after the Gordon riots noted that: "of the 291 prisoners in 1782, 225 were men and 68 women, 110 transports, 89 fines, 21 death penalties and the remainder for trial", as well as there being a complement of debtors.[61] There was still beer for sale in the new post-1780 prison. Of the old prison he remarked "the rooms and cells were so close, as to be almost the constant seats of disease".[62] The new prison retained the old cells for the condemned, measuring only nine feet by six.

Inevitably, there was considerable scope for corruption in such an atmosphere. As John Gay's "Lockit" says to the newly arrived MacHeath at Newgate "you know the custom, Sir. Garnish, Captain, garnish" while threatening MacHeath with a particularly heavy set of fetters "we have them of all prices, from one guinea to 10". MacHeath pays up and is given an especially light set, wryly noting that "the fees here are so many, and so exorbitant, that few fortunes can bear the expense of getting off handsomely, or of dying like a gentleman". One contemporary prisoner, John Hall, noted that after the turnkeys had had their fill of a new inmate "they then forced him out to the convicts who hover about him (like so many crows about a piece of carrion) for garnish, ... which they from an old custom, claim by prescription". Later, when she was incarcerated there, Flanders "... knew one fellow ... was one of those they called night-flyers". A "nightflyer" was a prisoner who was deliberately let out at night

---

61. Everyman (edn), 1929, p.161.
62. *Ibid.*, p.170.

by dishonest turnkeys to raise money by stealing. In turn this prisoner provided work for "those honest people they call thief-catchers ... to restore for a reward what [he] had stolen the evening before".[63] This was, of course, also the *modus operandi* of Jonathan Wild.

The squalor and corruption of Newgate were not unique to that prison. The other London prisons were often equally bad. Thus, in 1691 one Moses Pitt revealed that he had been charged 8 shillings a week for a cell in the Fleet prison which was supposed to be only 2s. 4d. When his money was exhausted he was incarcerated in the communal dungeon where he slept on the floor with fellow inmates so infested and lousy that even their outer clothes swarmed with lice. It was this prison that had, as its keeper, Thomas Bambridge, who in 1729 was first acquitted and subsequently found guilty, of gross extortion and other crimes in the execution of his office. Perhaps not surprisingly, like Newgate, the Fleet was burnt down early on in the Gordon Riots of 1780. In the new prison in Clerkenwell things were so bad that in 1720 the Middlesex justices observed that many poor prisoners "wanting money, being destitute of friends, or falling sick, are in danger of perishing for want of help and succour". This was despite a special regulation in the prison that allowed a 12d. levy to be made of the richer prisoners to support the poorer ones. At the Gatehouse prison, near Westminster Abbey, one Mary Pitt alleged in 1711 that she had been thrown down a flight of stairs and forced to sleep next to a corpse because she could not afford to pay for a bed. In both of these smaller prisons (compared to Newgate or the Fleet) there were also regular complaints about the keepers' extortion and overcharging for commodities (including gin), by the inmates. In 1672 these, along with allegations of mistreatment, resulted in the keeper of the Gatehouse being fined and removed from office.[64]

At the end of the seventeenth century the newly formed SPCK formed a committee under Dr Thomas Bray to investigate conditions at Newgate and the Marshalsea prison, which body reported in 1702 and made a

---

63.   On thief-catchers or takers see above, p.32.
64.   Shoemaker, R.B., *ibid.*, p.119.

number of recommendations, such as the enforcement of segregation between the young and hardened criminals as well as the redress of other abuses. Little action, however, was taken as a result. There was an ineffectual attempt to limit the sale of prison offices in 1716. William Pitt, the keeper of the prison for much of Defoe's time, was, appropriately for someone in such a position to form profitable trading relationships with the inmates, a grocer. As the eighteenth century progressed there may have been some improvements in Newgate, especially after the end of Pitt's keepership, which had been a period of particularly serious abuses. Real reform, however, was to be delayed to the era of John Howard towards the end of the century, and even then was to be slow in progressing.[65]

Thus, it can probably be said that for a consistency of bad reputation Newgate was unrivalled. Flanders' dread of the place and reluctance to go there unnecessarily is quite understandable.

Benefit of Clergy

Flanders' teacher, having the "brand of an old offender", and thus presumably unable to claim benefit of clergy a second time, was executed after her conviction. Benefit of clergy was a relic of the Church-State struggles of the medieval period whereby originally clerics could escape temporal punishment by insisting on being handed over to the more lenient ecclesiastical courts after conviction (from the late medieval period "clergy" was claimed after conviction, not before). It was progressively extended, by a series of legal fictions to include most men, and, by statute in the sixteenth century, to also include women, even though of course they could not possibly have been priests at this time. In 1706 even the "neck verse" (the recitation of a set verse of scripture, usually from St Matthew's gospel, to establish clerical status by proving literacy) was dropped. This saved illiterate prisoners the trouble of memorizing it. That it should be extended is indicative of the fact that it played an important

---

65. See also *Imprisonment in England and Wales, A Concise History*, Harding C., *et al.* (1985).

function in the system rather than being purely an anachronism that had survived through inadvertence. Although a complete fiction it mitigated the normal requirement at common law that the commission of felonies be met by death. Initially this was without substituting an effective secondary punishment in its place, clergied offenders being simply branded and released. However, over time the courts acquired the powers to award alternative punishments to clergied offenders, for example short periods of imprisonment, whipping and very significantly, transportation, thereby gaining a much needed degree of flexibility (between the extremes of branding and release and execution). Clergy, of course, was more indiscriminate than some other selection mechanisms, and it was as a result of the urging of the London authorities that in 1706 clergied offenders could also be sentenced to a term of up to two years at hard labour in the house of correction, though this was comparatively rare.[66] As secondary punishments expanded, especially after the great growth in sentences of transportation after the 1718 Transportation Act came into force, benefit of clergy became progressively less important as there were other, more satisfactory, and sophisticated ways of achieving the same result. From 1489 laymen who "pleaded clergy" were limited to one occasion and to enforce this would have the brawn of their left thumb branded (with a T in the case of a thief, an M in the case of someone convicted of manslaughter), though the "one chance" provision was not always strictly followed. It appears to be this branding that Flanders' refers to when talking about the "mark of an old offender". However, in many cases the iron was heated so perfunctorily that it proved useless as a record (branding being completely abolished, as a result, in 1779 and replaced with whipping).[67] Additionally, as the seventeenth and eighteenth centuries advanced statute progressively withdrew existing offences from the ambit of benefit of clergy, (especially after transportation became readily available as an alternative punishment to execution). Thus, for example, after 1713 burglary in which more than 40s. was taken was not

---

66. Beattie, J.M., *ibid.*, p.624.
67. Baker, J.H., *An Introduction to English Legal History*, 3rd edn (1990), p.424.

clergyable. The legislative manner of effecting it can be seen in the Act 14 Geo.11 making the theft of a sheep a capital offence: "If any person or persons, after the first of May, 1714, shall feloniously drive away, or in any other manner feloniously steal, any sheep ... the person or persons so offending shall suffer death without benefit of clergy". As well as abolishing it for certain existing offences, from the end of the sixteenth century it had also become customary to create new offences specifically without benefit of clergy. As a result, the list of non-clergyable offences was extended throughout the seventeenth and eighteenth centuries until its remnants was finally totally abolished in 1827.[68]

One of Flanders' later grievances was that as she had never been convicted before she should not have faced the death penalty, albeit that she was a known habitual thief. By this she may have been suggesting that she felt she should have been allowed her clergy, although its refusal was something that she herself had forecast: "I consider'd that I began to be very well known by name at the Old Baily, tho' they did not know my face; and that if I should fall into their hands, I should be treated as an old offender". Alternatively, this may be another element of anachronism in the book. Writing in 1721 Defoe may have had in mind that since 1718 first offenders, except in serious cases, could often expect to have their capital punishment commuted to transportation.[69] In either case it is demonstrative of the system.

To a significant extent, the eighteenth century judicial process can be termed one of "negotiated" justice. There was no real intention on the part of the propertied class that all the property law in existence should be rigidly enforced. The system accepted that not all apprehended felons deserved to be executed, something that was evidenced by the decline from the early sixteenth to the early seventeenth centuries in the number of executions, despite the increase in offences which carried a potential death penalty. However, equally, all of them were subject to the process

68.   Kiralfy, A.K.R., *Potter's Historical Introduction to English Law*, 4th edn (1958), p.363.
69.   Baker, J.H., *An Introduction to English Legal History*, 3rd edn (1990), p.589.

of determination as to whether they might be amongst those that did.[70] The system allowed an enormous role for discretion, from the initial decision to prosecute to that to reprieve a condemned felon; everyone, victim, Judge and jury had a role to play in this process. To some "benefit of clergy" and reprieve was the mechanism by which they escaped being numbered amongst the executed. Character was a crucial factor in making this determination (as well, of course, as the magnitude and prevalence of the offence convicted of). Although not actually convicted until many years later, Flanders herself acknowledged the problems inherent in becoming "known" to the authorities. "I fell into some small broils, which tho' they could not affect me fatally, yet made me known, which was the worst thing next to being found guilty, that could befall me". The danger of a bad "name" can be seen, in a real case from the time, with regard to the "principal of those malefactors", who in 1676 burgled the Lord Chancellor; he was a man of whom it was expressly noted at his trial (contrary to modern practice) that he was a "person very well known in court, having been arraign'd at the same bar five or six several times before". Fortunately for Flanders, at this stage of her career, only her name and reputation, and not her face, had been identified by the authorities.

Fortunately as well, the teacher's younger accomplice was reprieved under a circuit pardon and escaped the gallows. Nevertheless as a result of the shock amonistered by the teacher's capture, Flanders temporarily stopped stealing.

A Fire in a Gentlewoman's House

However, one night, a fire in a domestic house, a gentlewoman's home, provided Flanders with the easy opportunity to seize a bundle of goods that was being saved from the blaze. In it was contained a veritable hoard of treasure: a gold chain, family plate, a gold watch, pieces of old lockets made of gold and £24 in old coins. This valuable prize reconfirmed

---

70.   Green, A.G., *Verdict According to Conscience* (1985), p.314.

Flanders in her criminal way of life, being thus "... the greatest and the worst prize" that she ever obtained.

Such fires and their attendant chaos provided obvious opportunities for thieves. On this occasion, Flanders, having obtained the bundle, met a "creature [who] in short was one of the same business with me" who was also after property under the pretext of helping in the rescue. The possibility of two thieves independently attending the same conflagration was a real one. The security problems involved in the regular fires of the period (a single fire in Wapping in 1715 destroyed 150 houses and killed 50 people) were a permanent issue for all levels of society. When the Earl of Cardigan's house was burnt down in a fire in Lincoln's Inn in 1725 and his wife's jewels lost, he was able to recover most of them from the ashes having arranged that "12 men being set to dig in the ruins of the said house, inspected by two proper persons". Sometimes it would appear that thieves even deliberately committed arson with a view to stealing the property that was thrown from burning houses into the street. Samuel Pepys, on a visit to watch trials at the Old Bailey in 1667, noted that one of the defendants there (a man called Gabriel Holmes) was a member of a gang involved in this activity "... there is a combination of rogues in the town, that do make it their business to set houses on fire, and that one house they did set on fire in Aldersgate Street", this being done, the gang's policy was "to take up what goods were flung into the streets out of the windows, when the houses were on fire". On Holmes' conviction for the Aldersgate blaze the Judge privately expressed an intention that he be hanged in "some conspicuous place in the town, for an example".[71] John Gay also referred, in 1728, in *The Beggar's Opera,* to the phenomenon of criminals profiting from the mayhem of a conflagration, even if they had not deliberately started it. "Polly", at one point observing that a fellow thief, "Nimming Ned" ("nimming" was a cant term for thieving) had "... brought in a damask window-curtain, a hoop-petticoat, a pair of silver candlesticks, and one silk stocking, from the fire that happen'd last

---

71.   *Diary of Samuel Pepys*, July 4, 1667, Everyman edn (1973), vol.3, p.2.

night".[72]

Flanders' governess was also initially very concerned at her teacher's arrest and subsequent hanging, not least of all because the teacher had enough information to send both the governess and Flanders to the gallows. She was consequently "in a very great fright" for some time afterwards. However, perhaps surprisingly, the teacher very honourably (and probably rather unusually) did not provide information against either of them, although "... it was in her power to have obtained a pardon at the expense of her friends".[73]

The teacher's misfortune, though, did lead Flanders to be exceptionally cautious in her fresh criminal ventures, especially with regard to shoplifting, and in particular such thefts from London's mercers and drapers "... who are a set of fellows that have their eyes very much about them", and who had been her instructor's downfall. As a result, she limited her shoplifting to taking pieces of bone lace from newcomers to the business who were "not bred to shops". Given that an Act of 1699 had made theft of more than 5s. from a shop a capital offence, this was not a surprising decision.[74] Her more cautious approach again led her to consider abandoning her commitment to crime. The governess, though, was not willing to lose such a valuable thief, and as a result, introduced her to fresh accomplices, a young man and woman who took her with them on three or four "adventures". However, fortunately for her, Flanders had early doubts about their competence and ultimately refused to take part in their planned theft, from a watchmaker, of three gold coins, which they had observed in his premises. The young man and woman, using a bunch of skeleton keys, referred to at the time as "pick-lock" keys (locks were not very sophisticated in this period, having been largely unchanged for centuries, and the widespread skill of picking them was known as "The Black Art"), broke into the watchmaker's house, something (house-breaking) that Flanders had rigidly refused to do at this point in her

---

72. *Beggar's Opera*, Act 1, Scene x.
73. On this, see below p.103.
74. 10 & 11 Will.3, c.23.

career.[75]

House-breaking and Burglary

It appears that robbery and pickpocketing were, at this time, the more widespread methods of instrumental crime (crime aimed at obtaining property and valuables), perhaps because they were easier and safer for the thieves. Householders would often have weapons readily to hand and their valuables well hidden. The typical terraced brown brick houses, with red dressing and stone cornicing and coping, three stories high, with flat street level entrances that characterized the residences of prosperous Londoners of the period, would have scored highly on modern notions of "defensible space" and design security, and presented considerable risks to burglars.[76] Their doors and locks were generally the main areas of weakness from outside. Indeed, with regard to burglary, one of the greatest threats came not from total outsiders, but from domestic servants "casing" the properties in which they worked. This was a recurrent problem, especially in London, where there was a fairly regular turnover of domestic staff, and in turn explaining the enormous importance of previous employer's references in obtaining future work. Defoe himself dealt with this aspect of crime in *Colonel Jack*; in the novel, Jack became involved with burglars "three of [whom] made it their business to get into gentlemen's services, and so to open doors in the night, and let other rogues in upon them to rob and destroy them".

The scale of this problem can also be seen from many of the contemporary advertisements of rewards published after the commission of serious thefts and burglaries, a typical one running "on the fifth instant, a young man about 20 years of age, his name Thomas Salkeld (formerly a servant to Mr Dimroad living in St James's Market, in Market-street, and lately received into his service again) went away with a considerable value of English and French gold, and watches; he was in a mixt-coloured serge suit ... if any one can discover this person and bring word to the

---

75.   On lock picking, see Linebaugh, P., *The London Hanged* (1991), p.365.
76.   *Cf.* Alice Colman, *Utopia on Trial* (1985).

gentlemans house aforesaid, or else apprehend and secure him, shall have five pounds".[77] Even lawyers were not immune from their depredations, thus an advertisement of 1692 sought the whereabouts of one: "Richard Fitzgerald, alias Gerald, aged about 20, middle sized, ... lank hair, or a short dark peruke, clerk to John Leigh of the Inner Temple Esq; [who] on Thursday, 19, instant stole out of his masters study, or desk, as is supposed, in which was great sums of gold and silver, jewels, rings, medals, seals and watches: whoever gives notice of him to his said master, or of the said goods, shall have £10 reward, or proportionable for any part".[78] In *A Warning to House-Keepers* (1728) Defoe's advice on how to reduce this risk was clearly stated, "I would advise all house-keepers never to take a maid servant without a good recommendation". Additionally, there was the suggestion that if the master of the house had many servants it was advisable to "let one whom you may confide in be watchful over the rest that may be last in Bed, and first up".

While the two young people (Flanders' erstwhile colleagues) made their escape from the scene of the crime, they were detected, pursued, caught and detained, and subsequently hanged as old offenders (and thus, depending on the period, either not able to plead benefit of clergy or not likely to be pardoned and transported). This prompted Flanders to even greater precautions, and she subsequently managed to make a substantial sum of money in a safer line of work.

Flanders and the Smuggled Lace

Having discovered the location of a large quantity of prohibited "Flanders" lace, from the Low Countries, hidden in a private house, Flanders informed a Customs House officer of its whereabouts, in exchange for a promise for her due share of the attendant reward for its seizure. Although highly prized for its quality, and thus much sought after

---

77. *London Gazette*, November 8, 1675.
78. *London Gazette*, January 23, 1692.

as a fashion accessory, Parliamentary Acts in the reign of Charles II, and later in that of William and Mary, had sought to protect domestic production by banning the importation of such lace. Despite this, it was a much smuggled item, and still widely sold, albeit illicitly, by drapers. Moll Flanders, with the customs officer and a constable, attended at the house, and she then directed the officer as to where to find the lace, concealed as it was in a "secret hiding hole". She herself went into the hole to take out the lace, and passed it to the customs officer, though "... taking care as [she] gave him some so to secure as much about [herself] as [she] could conveniently dispose of". The total value of the lace was £300 of which she managed to keep £50 worth back. In addition, she was entitled to a reward for providing the information, and by hard bargaining with the customs officer (she knew her legal entitlements), who initially offered her £20, she received from him £50 and a piece of the lace (itself worth about £8 or £9). She prudently made sure that he was unaware of her real name and address. Her governess, who had originally provided her with the information about the material, was given half of the spoils from this venture.

Flanders did run a few risks even in this activity, as informers were often widely hated figures amongst the general populace. Fielding was to note in his *Inquiry* that the "name of an informer", amongst some Londoners was "much worse [an] appellation in the opinion of the vulgar than that of thief". However, as lace was a luxury item for the wealthy it may be that providing such intelligence to the authorities would excite less concern than, for example, revealing the operations of an unlicensed gin shop (for which some informers were even lynched by the "mob" after the 1736 Act restricted its sale).

Customs and Excise Rewards

The Customs and Excise could provide substantial rewards under special statutes, and sometimes a share of seized goods as well (as in Flanders' case), to people who had provided valuable information about contraband.[79] Indeed it was in the enforcement of economic regulations that common informers and the rewards they received were probably most important and efficient. Though, it must also be said, that the marriage of justice with avarice did as much to discredit the informer system in this field as in any other aspect of criminal justice. Official statutory rewards to informers survived, in an attenuated form, the introduction of an official police force and publicly funded prosecutors (only to be totally abolished as late as 1951), though as far back as 1644 Sir Edward Coke in his famous *Institutes* had said that the informer "... doth vex and pauperise the subject and the community of the poorer sort, for malice or private ends and never for love of justice".[80] However, although continuing in existence, their importance was progressively reduced after the mid-eighteenth century.

Theft of a Gold Watch

Flanders' next criminal enterprise was a return to pickpocketing, and again an attempt to steal a gentlewoman's gold watch (her "speciality"). This occurred at a meeting house and placed Flanders at great risk. The watch initially failed to come away cleanly when she pulled at it, having first deliberately jostled the woman to distract her. This was (and is still today) a common technique for pickpockets. The problem of an item not coming free was a perpetual and well remarked risk in pickpocketing ventures. As John Gay's experienced thief "Filch" noted of an abortive attempt at theft of his own: "I had a fair Tug at a charming Gold Watch. Pox take the Tailors for making the Fobs [small pockets] so deep and narrow! It stuck by the way, and I was forc'd to make my Escape under a Coach".[81] Flanders, with great presence of mind, shouted out to the crowd that there were pickpockets about, and that someone had attempted to steal her

79.   Radzinowicz, *ibid.*, vol.2, p.66.
80.   Beresford, M.W., "The Common Informer, The Penal Statutes and Economic Regulation", *Economic History Review*, vol.10 (1957), p.221.
81.   *Beggar's Opera*, Act 1, Scene 12.

watch as well. The gentlewoman joined in the cry and an innocent man, a little further into the crowd was mistakenly picked out as the thief. This young man "this poor boy, was delivered up to the rage of the street, which is a cruelty I need not describe and which however, they were always glad of rather than be sent to Newgate, where they lie often long time and sometimes they are hanged, and at best are transported." The "hue and cry", the mass pursuit and detention of a fleeing felon was one of the most important aspects of policing (perhaps sometimes aided by the possibility of a reward). Of course the consequences of a mistake could be chaotic, hence the provision that "... if a man wantonly or maliciously raises a hue and cry, without cause, he shall be severely punished as a disturber of the public peace".[82]

Popular Justice

The genuine indignation of the crowds involved in apprehending street criminals should not be underestimated.[83] They could deal with extreme violence to those who had violated their community values, whether criminals or informers to the authorities. Much would depend on the criminal, the victim, the location, and the crime; pilloried prisoners could be virtually killed by stoning or have a collection taken up for them by the crowd, almost entirely depending on these circumstances.[84] For example, as the eighteenth century advanced the "mob" having gained a large degree of control of the environs of the public pillory would protect those who were exhibited for criticizing the government (as, arguably, Defoe himself had been) but would heavily pelt those criminals believed to have been involved in informing to the authorities (especially about breaches of the licensing laws), sodomy, assaulting children or any

---

82.   Blackstone, *ibid.*, vol.4, p.291. In strict law, "hue and cry" referred to formally organized popular pursuit of a fleeing criminal, but is often also used even where there had been no formal arrangement.
83.   Defoe deals with it in *Colonel Jack*, at p.19.
84.   Beattie, J.M., *ibid.*, p.133.

other strongly disapproved of crime.[85] When Charles Hitchin, the former City Marshal (and erstwhile thief taker and friend of Jonathan Wild) was convicted of *attempted* sodomy (the complete offence potentially carried a death sentence), as well as having to serve six months in Newgate, and being fined £20, he was also sentenced to be pilloried. He was removed after just 30 minutes of his hour-long sentence because of the threat to his life. This was despite the fact that, aware of what was in store, he had taken the precaution of paying the Under-Sheriff to blockade him from the "mob" with carts. Later, in 1732, one John Waller, pilloried for falsely accusing a man of being a highwayman, was stoned to death, and a woman who apparently had dressed as a man and three times "married" other women was blinded in both eyes by missiles thrown by an angry crowd.[86] As a contemporary journal noted laconically of one similarly unpopular man undergoing such a punishment "On Monday last Alexander Day, the sharper ... stood a second time in the pillory on Ludgate-Hill: none that were ever exalted to the wooden ruff could be more severely pelted than he was".[87]

In the case involving Flanders it is clear that the mistakenly taken young man was on the receiving end of a savage beating, though this was still preferable to going to prison. This theme, the risk of mistaken apprehension by the crowd, comes up again in Defoe's *Colonel Jack,* where, upon hearing the cry of "a pickpocket" the crowd mistakenly identified another innocent man "... who fell into the hands of the mob, but being known in the street, he got off with great difficulty". This preference for "popular justice", perhaps reflected the cost and problems of going through official channels, and was, at times, something that was also explicitly remarked on by foreign visitors to England. Thus Cesar de Saussure, a Swiss traveller in England writing between 1725 and 1730, noted that not only were there a surprising number of pickpockets and robbers in London, but also that there was a fairly widespread reluctance

---

85.   Cockburn, J.S., "Punishment and Brutalization", *Law and History Review*, vol.12, no.1, p.172.
86.   Crew, A., *The Old Bailey* (1933), p.12.
87.   *The London Journal*, May 25, 1723.

on the part of victims of the former to prosecute (he became one himself when his valuable and well concealed snuff-box was stolen). If caught in the act and given over to the crowd they were often swiftly "... dragged to the nearest fountain or well and dipped in the water till nearly drowned".[88] This was a practice that was also well supported by contemporary English sources. A pamphlet writer in 1718, who merely identified himself as "A Prisoner of Newgate" narrated a tale in which a countryman visited an inn that was also a well known thieves' house. During the proceedings a pickpocket suddenly burst into the house, pursued by the jeers of the crowd outside. He was soaking wet, having been ducked in a horse-pond seven times and then thrown into the river Thames.

Once again, the near reverse over this attempted theft provided a timely lesson. It prompted Flanders to special caution with regard to the stealing of gold watches, something, like her willingness to learn from all her other salutary shocks, that might have accounted for her unusually long career.

The Governess' Story

However, despite this reverse, Flanders' governess continued to be an inspiring force in her criminal life and a strong dissuader from returning to an honest life. This governess had originally herself been a natural pickpocket, until, having been caught, she was transported. However, on her way to America she succeeded in "jumping ship" in Ireland when the vessel briefly put in to port in which country "she practised her old trade for some years", as well as working as a midwife, an interesting combination of employments! It should perhaps be noted that in the early eighteenth century the qualification of midwives was still often rudimentary. Almost anybody could set themselves up as a midwife, though the medical profession was soon to begin extending its regulation

---

88.   "A Foreign View of England in the Reigns of George I and George II", p.130, Trans. London 1902, quoted Radzinowicz, L., *ibid.*, vol.1, p.707.

of the "craft". Flanders' governess was, however, particularly skilled in this legitimate profession, as Flanders herself could vouch from personal experience.

Subsequently she returned from Dublin to England and because at this point her time of transportation had not expired, she abandoned her former trade rather than risk being detected again (premature returnees facing death automatically, and there being significant state rewards available for their apprehension). Receiving was generally a much safer activity. Indeed, until 1691 it was only a misdemeanour, unless, as was sometimes the case with Flanders' governess, the receiver directly procured an offence. Flanders alludes to this when she says that the governess led her "into all the particulars" of her new "wicked" life.

Receivers

As well as "safe" houses, where thieves could hide, London provided easy access to receivers, both small-scale dealers such as pawnbrokers who might take in a watch or two, with "no questions asked", and some who were used to rather larger scales of handling. At the end of the eighteenth century, Patrick Colquhoun estimated the latter category at 50 or 60 people, of whom 10 were persons of very "substantial property", who could raise large amounts of money to purchase articles of value, though the sources for his amusingly precise figures are obscure. In the 1790s Colquhoun had identified twelve specific groups of handlers; as well as the "opulent" receivers, there were also inferior copemen, publicans, dealers in ships' stores, grocers and chandlers, rope spinners, female receivers who were often also keepers of brothels, covetous receivers, Jewish receivers, carters and "indiscriminate" receivers.[89] Colquhoun even estimated that there were 4,000 commercial receivers in the Metropolis at the end of the century (the figure must be seen as wildly speculative, and, as Thomas Wade was to note in 1829, like all his statistics the occasion of ridicule). However, inevitably a small number of them became disproportionately influential. The growing number of laws against

---

89.   Treatise, *ibid.*, p.197.

receiving at this time probably encouraged a more "professional" attitude amongst such people, discouraging some of the "amateurs", engaged in casual receiving, from the trade. In the 1680s it appears there were hundreds of houses in London where thieves could safely sell their stolen goods within minutes of taking them, at a price that was apparently fairly close to their real value. By the 1691 Act to combat receiving , according to Defoe in his pamphlet on Wild, "the receiving trade was spoiled at once. And when the poor adventurer had at the hazard of his neck gotten any purchase, he must run that hazard over again to turn it into money". Certainly Jonathan Wild seems to have felt that there was a need for a more careful approach to receiving. The account of Wild's preoccupations in the *Newgate Calendar* is in almost identical terms to Flanders' own concern at selling her stolen items to strangers "for a song".[90] Wild allegedly remarked to a group of thieves that if they sold to strangers they risked the law, additionally, "he observed that the most industrious thieves were now scarcely able to obtain a livelihood; and that they must either submit to be half starved, or be in great and continual danger of Tyburn". His solution to this problem was to set himself up as a commercial receiver of stolen goods who was also willing to return stolen items to their losers for a fee. He would arrange the return of the goods to their losers at a reasonable price, better usually than would be available to a thief or receiver from a resale in the "hidden economy". If he had problems with the thieves who worked at his behest, he would arrange for their arrest by the authorities (while also receiving the available rewards on their heads). In 15 years it is thought that he betrayed at least 120 criminals, including, according to Wild himself at his trial, 35 highway robbers and 22 housebreakers. One of them was the notorious Joseph Blake, alias "Blueskin", who tried to kill Wild with a knife when the latter visited him in prison, assuring him that although he could not secure his acquittal at trial he would make sure he did not go for dissection after death and would additionally arrange a good coffin and funeral! Where the goods were not returned to the owners but marketed he (Wild)

---

90. Wilkinson, G.T., *The Newgate Calendar 1816*, Cardinal edn (1991), p.139.

took particular care to disguise them; at Wild's first trial it was alleged "that he kept in pay several artists to make alterations and transform watches, seals, snuff-boxes, rings and other valuable things, that they might not be known".

It was frequently asserted that others of the biggest receivers were, like Wild, accessories "before the fact" as well as afterwards, by providing support, information and tools,[91] sometimes even running gangs of up to 15 men (though the normal maximum operating size was four to five men, and the larger gangs usually appear to have been loose amalgams of the smaller ones).[92] Although much receiving was local and small scale, some of the fences acquired very extensive influence over other aspects of crime and the lives of criminals. "Lifts" and cutpurses sometimes even "lived in" at the houses of notorious brokers and receivers, who "through their alluring speeches and their secret counsellings" stimulated the operations of thieving. In 1708, John Hall had also observed that "the fence and he [the thief], are like the devil and the doctor, they live by one another, and, like traitors, 'tis best [for them] to keep each other's counsel". "Fencing" stolen goods was a specialist form of crime, and carried fewer risks than the thefts themselves, even after the legislation to combat it had been passed. These fences often also provided much practical assistance to thieves, often accepting stolen merchandise as payment for lodgings and services.[93] This was certainly the case in the relationship between Flanders and her governess.

Flanders' governess appears to have been just below the top commercial receiving strata, certainly not doing it as a "sideline" to her legitimate business. For a woman to have pursued such an occupation is not surprising. As far back as the sixteenth and seventeenth centuries this crime was one that many women were associated with.[94] The women involved were often widows, perhaps attracted to receiving as a way of supplementing other incomes or to ward off indigence. Receivers played

---

91. Beattie, J.M., *ibid.*, p.256.
92. Sharpe, J.A., *Crime in Seventeenth Century England, A County Study* (1983), p.112.
93. McMullen, J., *ibid.*, p.106.
94. Beier, A.L., *Masterless Men* (1985), p.135.

a crucial role in London crime, and indeed were constantly identified as a major problem in the Metropolis. In criminal areas, such as the "sanctuaries" of the Mint, Alsatia and Thieves' Lane in Westminster, intermediaries such as "fences" promoted relations between the underworld and the wider society, reducing the personal risks to criminals themselves. The power of informing also gave some strength to fences who sometimes also colluded with the authorities and the judiciary and thus acquired a social usefulness that gave them, on occasion, a limited protection from prosecution.[95] Crime control, it appears, in many parts of London at this time was often essentially about a realistic effort to contain crime to certain discrete areas and levels rather than its total prevention (a practical impossibility).

A sophisticated system of fencing can thus be said to have been well established in London during the later seventeenth and early eighteenth centuries and was crucial to the high rates of London crime. Alehouses often appear to have acted as centres for receiving stolen goods (Jonathan Wild had begun a substantial involvement with crime while a tenant of an alehouse in Cock Alley, Cripplegate) and the authorities sometimes issued warrants against specific alehouse keepers who were believed to entertain criminals. There are numerous contemporary reported cases of such people being involved in receiving. However, pawnbrokers, because of the nature of their trade were even more associated with this occupation (and would continue to be so well into the Victorian period).[96] Defoe was to return to this theme in *Colonel Jack*, when "Jack" disposed of a pursued friend's booty in a pawnbroker's in Cloth-Fair. Once he had uttered the appropriate codephrase "the word" to the pawnbrokers "... without any words, they took the plate, weighed it, and paid me after the rate of two shillings per ounce for it". There is little evidence of such organized theft and receiving outside London in c.1700, that is crime where a receiver employed a team of professional thieves, again indicating the unusual nature of London crime. Receiving was also enormously facilitated by

---

95. McMullen, J., *Canting Crew, ibid.*, p.71.
96. Cf. Mayhew, H. and Binney B., *ibid.*, vol.4, p.374.

a still pre-industrial society that had a very high circulation of used or "second hand" goods, with the attendant shops to sell them. This would make selling stolen, but used goods, very much easier than today.

It should also be noted that in London, although the 1691 Act was followed by other more draconian statutes, sometimes making receiving a death penalty offence, the practical effect of the new legislation can be exaggerated. For example, Henry Fielding writing in 1751, still felt that "at present the thief disposes of his goods with almost as much safety as the honestest tradesman".

Thieves' "Sanctuaries"

The areas where thieves and fences particularly abounded were formerly termed "sanctuaries" because they were urban areas where, before the Reformation, fleeing felons could find, as the name suggests, "sanctuary", being ecclesiastical places where the King's writ did not fully run.[97] This was the subject of progressive legislative reform from the early Tudor period onwards, with most of the last vestiges of theoretical immunity being abolished in 1624. By 1712 the authorities had clamped down considerably on the remaining "bastard sanctuaries", only the Mint at Southwark, remaining as a sanctuary for debtors from the legal process, had retained any real legal privileges (which would linger until being finally abolished in 1723). However, even after the Restoration, these areas, although losing their theoretical immunity from criminal pursuit, continued as thieves' quarters and as places where debtors could escape court process, effectively often remaining as *de facto* if not *de jure* criminal and debtors' ghettos. Although the most famous of these was Alsatia, there were also many others; north of the river these included those in the Barbican area, Whitechapel and Covent Garden.

South of the Thames one of the most famous was the "Mint", located in the borough, near London Bridge. It was the target of special government legislation in 1696, the lack of success of which encouraged

---

97.   Baker, J.H., *An Introduction to English Legal History*, 3rd edn, (1990), p.585.

99

that of 1723 (in *The Beggars Opera*, "Mrs Tripes" laments the damage done to her receiving business five years earlier by the latter of these Acts). It was also the place that Moll Flanders first used the name "... Mrs Flanders, when [she] sheltered [herself] in the Mint". This was probably when she was trying to escape process for a debt after the bankruptcy of her second husband, though she may have also sought refuge there later in her criminal career. Some of the sanctuaries survived to become the "rookeries" of early Victorian London.

Also south of the river, in Southwark (perhaps the Metropolis' most lawless area in the late 1600s), serious social control problems arose from those other areas which had been specifically excluded from the Charter of the Borough of 1550 that had vested control of much of the area in the City of London. In particular, the areas of Paris Garden and the Clink posed special difficulties. These liberties were classic examples of "bastard sanctuaries". In the medieval period, they had been a mixture of lay and ecclesiastical franchises which by specific charter or prescription had established a degree of independence from royal justice and its administrators, and as such could provide shelter to fugitives and debtors. The Reformation had generally marked the end of the formal ecclesiastical jurisdictions, but did not automatically extinguish the immunities of all the former religious houses in these areas. When the post-Reformation purchasers and inhabitants of the houses in these locations claimed for themselves the immunities enjoyed by the former owners, it appears that the authorities were often prepared to allow them to do so, provided the right to collect taxes and raise troops there was retained by the City.[98] Even after these privileges were progressively abolished from the early 1600s onwards the areas' notorious reputations survived.

Thieves and receivers were, of course, not confined to these parts of London, most locations had a few dubious alleys close at hand, though there was a tendency for these to become more localized and concentrated

---

98.   See on this, Browner, J.A., *Wrong Side of the River: London's Disreputable South Bank in the Sixteenth and Seventeenth Century.* Essays in History (University of Virginia), vol.36, (1994), p.35.

after the Restoration. Additionally, there were smaller "notorious" streets such as Orchard Street and Petty France, too small to be considered as full sanctuaries, and juxtaposed with areas of relative respectability.

Flanders' Skill and Caution

Flanders, in her own estimation(!), became the greatest criminal artist of her time and worked "herself out of dangers with such dexterity" that she managed to practise for over five years without even being known at Newgate, when many of her colleagues in the "trade" were caught within six months of embarking on their criminal careers. She was thus clearly a degree above the normal run of criminal, something that she herself acknowledged when explaining her decision, later in her career, only to work alone. Flanders found that she was "best not entangled with the dull measures of other people, who had less forecast" than herself. In turn, these unsuccessful colleagues resented her success and several who were in Newgate vowed to "impeach" her if given the opportunity. This led Flanders to take even greater precautions, despite the injunctions of her governess not to lead such "... a useless unprofitable life". As a result, Flanders, with the assistance of the governess adopted ever more ingenious methods of operation to reduce the element of personal risk; she even dressed up as a man at one stage, and stole goods with a male colleague who was unaware of her true sex.

In the seventeenth century, women generally appear to have been less likely to work alone when engaged in burglary and theft than men. However, a considerable number also appear to have worked with other women rather than in mixed male/female groups. Men were often, it seems, fairly reluctant to work with members of the opposite sex. In Cheshire in the 1620s (obviously a considerable time before Flanders' period) fewer than 10 per cent of men were involved in burglary with women, though this is obviously of limited value as an indicator for

101

London in the period from 1660 to 1720.[99] Female burglars appear to have been more willing than men to steal ordinary household goods such as clothes and cooking utensils, perhaps not surprisingly, given that the onus would often seem to have been on them to provide such things for their families, and they would also have been more conscious of their importance and value. To that extent, Flanders was, it appears, a little "untypical" in her selection of smaller high value goods.

Strangely, there is some well documented evidence for the type of "cross-dressing" disguise adopted by Flanders. One famous highwayman of the period, Tom Rowland, who was executed in 1699, usually dressed as a woman when riding the roads and robbing (though presumably his victims eventually appreciated his real gender). The apparently bi-sexual Moll Cutpurse had dressed as a man and smoked a pipe. Further support for transvestism, probably from Defoe's own hand, can be seen in the account of Mary Read and Anne Bonny "the female pirates" in Charles Johnson's (almost certainly Defoe's alias) *Lives Of The Most Notorious Pirates.* They were apparently women of a "fierce and courageous temper", and habitually attired in the same way as their male counterparts. Anne Bonny had been captured in the Autumn of 1720, shortly before Defoe embarked on the novel.

Flanders and her new male accomplice's initial thefts were mainly from shopkeepers' counters. Eventually this alliance came to an end when they attempted to steal silk from a warehouse, despite Flanders' earlier advice to the young man not to attempt such a risky operation.[100] They were detected and pursued, parted company, and the man was caught, while Flanders, luckily, found sanctuary in her governess' house. Once there she quickly abandoned her male attire, so that the subsequent search of the house by her pursuers though from "... bottom to top, and then top to bottom", revealed nothing. After the search of the governess' house the pursuing "mob" insisted on carrying the governess before a justice who

---

99.   *Women, Crime and the Courts in Early Modern England*, Kemode, J., and Walker G. (eds) (1995), p.85.
100. Silk was one of most valuable and protected commodities, cf. Linebaugh, P., *London Hanged, ibid.*, p.256.

carried out a preliminary investigation into the matter before deciding that there was no case to answer "the Justice satisfied himself with giving her an oath, that she had not receiv'd or admitted any man into her house to conceal him, or protect or hide him from justice ... and so she was dismiss'd". Flanders noted that as she was not a man (though disguised as such) "this oath she might justly take"!

Her less fortunate male colleague, who had been captured, was carried away before the Lord Mayor (also an *ex officio* JP) and committed to Newgate, by "His Worship". The people who caught him were willing and able to prosecute him, and they offered themselves to enter into recognizances to appear at the sessions to pursue the charge against him (an indication of their seriousness and determination to pursue the matter). This man, however, managed to get "his indictment deferred" on a promise to "discover" his accomplice - Moll Flanders - whom he believed to be a man called Gabriel Spencer. Despite providing as much information as he could and having "... brought two or three families into trouble by his endeavours to find [her] out" he was unsuccessful, not surprisingly, given that Flanders had concealed the "... main circumstances of [her] sex" from him. This incident is highly illustrative of a fundamental feature of the eighteenth century criminal justice system, the extensive use of accomplice evidence and information.

Accomplice Evidence

However distasteful, and even in the eighteenth century there was nearly always concern at its use, it was felt to be crucial to admit accomplice evidence in order to prevent the collapse of the justice system. The use of such evidence was endemic. As Chitty was to note 100 years later, "the law confesses its weakness by calling in the assistance of those by whom it has been broken".[101] As Leon Radzinowicz also has observed it "... became a major instrument for bringing criminals to justice". Defoe himself was to note in his *Account of Jonathan Wild* (1725) that "all just

---

101. *A Practical Treatise on the Criminal Law*, 2nd edn, vol.1, p.769, quoted Radzinowicz, L., *ibid.*, vol.2, p.54.

governments discover a disposition to bring offenders to justice and on this account they not only receive and accept informations of the worst of crimes from the worst of criminals, ... but encourage such criminals to ... discover their accomplices".

This evidence was usually in two forms. Accomplices who still had their liberty could come forward and impeach their colleagues claiming a pardon as of right under a variety of statutes; for obvious reasons this was comparatively rare. More commonly, the situation would be one where an accomplice had already been captured and then attempted to make a "deal" with the authorities (as with Flanders' accomplice). Remorse, as with modern "supergrass" cases (such as that of the robber Bertie Smalls in the early 1970s), was rarely the motive. Later in the eighteenth century the magistrate Sir John Fielding was to observe that most accomplices who gave evidence in this situation subsequently returned to a life of crime.[102] An illustration of this can be seen in a typical newspaper report of the times: "Thomas Barton, who was one of the evidences in convicting the Blacks of Waltham we hear, was lately taken up for a robbery committed between Gosport and Fordham and was sent to Winchester Jail".[103] This form of "agreement" was termed the "equitable claim to the mercy of the Crown". Unlike the former situation, a pardon was not given as of right in this situation but was based on the practice of the court and amounted to a promise or an "implied confidence" of mercy.[104] The pardon would be given to those who "... behave fairly and disclose the whole truth and bring others to justice".[105] It amounted to the promise of a recommendation of mercy, if the accomplice fulfilled his part of the agreement, "... they are not entitled as of right to a pardon, yet the usage, the lenity, and the practice of the Court, is to stop the prosecution against them".[106] This had developed from the ancient common law

---

102. Radzinowicz, *ibid.*, Vol.2, p.54.
103. *The Original Half-Penny London Journal*, Saturday, February 23, 1725.
104. Baker, J.H., *Crime in England 1550-1800* (1977) ed, Cockburn, J.S., p.40.
105. Mansfield, C.J. in *R. v. Rudd* (1775) 1 Leach 120.
106. Mansfield, C.J. in *R. v. Rudd* (1775), quoted, Sir William Holdsworth, *A History of English Law*, vol.xii, p.514 (1938).

doctrine of approvement which in the early eighteenth century was still, at least technically, part of the criminal law, though about to undergo a decline to extinction as a result of the potential for abuse under the system. In theory the prerequisites for such a pardon (approvement) were that an offender would confess to the crime for which he had been apprehended and then offer to name an accomplice and prove his (or her) guilt. If the court accepted his offer the named accused was put on trial; if convicted, the approver was pardoned, if an acquittal followed, the accuser would normally be sentenced to death.[107]

Sometimes the informality of deals and "understandings", often based on the defendant's wishful thinking, was such that they could not be relied on. Thus in 1731, "William Maynee [a well educated and apparently industrious accountant], suffer'd for feloniously erasing two endorsements from Bank Notes [thousands of pounds were involved] ... Being suspected, he was stopped at the bank, January 2, and put in the computer from whence he sent to the Deputy Governor of the Bank, intimating that if he might be admitted to the mercy of transportation to Jamaica, he would make a full confession and discovery, and by the Answer brought back, conceiving some hopes, he made and sign'd his confession, impeached his accomplice, and pleaded guilty at his trial".[108] Despite his disappointment at going to Tyburn, "at the place of execution, he begg'd pardon of the court of directors, pray'd for the prosperity of the bank, and dy'd very penitent"!

Illustrative of a potential willingness to turn "King's Evidence" by even the most hardened of criminals was the case of Ralph Wilson of the notorious Hawkins gang, which specialized in the London area, and who impeached his colleagues John Hawkins and George Simpson. In fairness to him, it must be acknowledged that he had earlier warned them against committing a crime against the Royal Mail, saying that, "... their union would be dissolved when a promise of the King's pardon should be

---

107. Radzinowicz, *ibid.*, Vol.2, p.44.
108. *The Monthly Intelligencer*, March, 1731 at p.125. "An Account of the Malefactors executed at Tyburn".

published after such a robbery".[109] There was, it appears, often very little honour amongst thieves. John Wheeler in 1735, one amongst the famous group of highwaymen known as the "Gregory Gang" who included Dick Turpin amongst their number, also saved his own skin when he turned King's Evidence against the others.[110] Tom Sheppard, brother and accomplice of the famous Jack, even "impeached his brother" when apprehended "in the hope of being admitted an evidence", while the notorious criminal Joseph Blake, alias "Blueskin" (named after his swarthy countenance), who had worked for Wild, and who was executed at Tyburn in 1724 for housebreaking, had, earlier in his career, escaped conviction as a street robber by being admitted as an "evidence" against his erstwhile companions in crime. As he had only turned King's Evidence after he was captured, having made an "obstinate resistance" to the authorities, he was informed, to his chagrin, that he could not have the reward for their convictions![111] Later, Tom King, Dick Turpin's accomplice who was captured after being accidentally wounded by Turpin in a "shoot out" near the "Red Lion" tavern in Whitechapel, before dying from his injuries, "gave information that Turpin might be found at a house near Hackney Marsh". Though, in this case, it is possible that he had been deliberately shot by Turpin!

Thus, to an extent, the accomplice system does seem to have worked well, undermining the trust amongst criminals as well as securing numerous convictions, and with gang members often wanting to be the first to turn King's Evidence before one of their colleagues did so and precluded their own opportunity. Sometimes there would be chains of mutual incriminations. Certainly it was largely responsible for endemic distrust amongst criminals, their associates, and even relatives. As the appropriately named "Peachum" counsels Polly about her husband "the highwayman MacHeath, secure what he hath got, have him peached the next sessions, and then at once you are made a rich widow".[112] It was,

---

109. Beattie, J.M., *ibid.*, p.157.
110. Linebaugh, P., *The London Hanged, ibid.*, p.203.
111. Wilkinson, G., *Newgate Calendar 1816* (Cardinal edn, 1991), p.134.
112. *Beggar's Opera*, Gay, J., Act 1, Scene x.

however, a system that was very prone to abuse, as desperate criminals sought to save themselves at the expense of others.

Because of this potential for abuse, by the middle of the eighteenth century the courts had decided that accomplice evidence should normally be corroborated (the requirement for a mandatory warning to the jury to this effect was only finally abolished in England by the Criminal Justice and Public Order Act 1994). However, despite this, accomplice evidence remained quite routine as an important source of convictions. Thus, in July 1770, the *Universal Magazine* could still note, in passing, that Peter Conoway and Michael Richardson were executed for murder at Tyburn and then gibbeted, having been "... convicted on the evidence of one Jackson, an accomplice".[113] It was also a theme that recurred in Defoe's other work; in *Colonel Jack,* when one of Jack's friends was imperilled after a criminal colleague from his gang was apprehended, he quickly observed that "George has peached me and all the others, to save his life". It transpired that this individual had "upon promise of favour, and of saving him from the gallows, discovered his companions".

Financial rewards also, of course, encouraged criminals to break ranks and inform on their colleagues. Even thirty years later, Henry Fielding, who had campaigned against excessive rewards because they "had propagated the worst and wickedest perjuries" used some of the money from a treasury grant to capture a notorious gang of street robbers: "I was enabled to pay a fellow who had undertaken, for a small sum, to betray them into the hands of a set of thieftakers whom I had enlisted into the service".

This ongoing threat explains Flanders' and her governess' permanent concern at the possibility of being impeached by an associate, even a friend, such as the "teacher". Sometimes juries themselves were concerned at the way that accomplices who had been intimately involved in a crime might escape by turning King's evidence, and even on occasion expressed concern by asking which of those involved, the accused or the Crown's witness, had had the greater role in the crime, as happened in a case of

---

113. *Universal Magazine*, July 1770.

burglary at the Southwark Assizes in 1738.[114] The magistrate John Fielding (half-brother of Henry) was also of the opinion that it was "commonly the greatest rogue in the gang turns evidence".[115]

Trips to Dunstable

Flanders went to the country near Dunstable and decided to "lie low" until the pressure caused by her accomplice's efforts had worn off. From this point, Flanders firmly decided never to work in company again. Working with colleagues, as might be expected, appears to have been one of the common "hallmarks" of professional criminals at the time (and probably today as well). In the early seventeenth century, in Sussex, 62 per cent of defendants accused of more than one offence had been accompanied by another or were part of a group, compared to only 31 per cent of those accused of a single offence. Because of this the authorities probably tended to view felons who worked with others in a more serious light (as they always did when there was any suggestion of "professionalism" on the part of criminals).

Flanders subsequently learnt that her male colleague in the warehouse burglary, had been hanged "... which was the best news to [her] that [she] had had for a great while". By this stage in her career, Flanders had nearly £500 in cash saved up (an enormous sum at the time), but was totally committed to her criminal life, and did not have the least inclination to leave it. She noted that "from hence it is evident that once we are hardened in crime, no fear can affect us, no example give us any warning". Flanders' instinct of self-preservation, however, was kept finely honed by the capture of yet another earlier accomplice, one who had been involved with her in the theft of a piece of very good damask in a mercer's shop. Again, the accomplice's inability to identify Moll Flanders or her residence was

114. *Crime in England 1550-1800* (1970) ed, Cockburn, J.S., p.167.
115. Fielding, John, *A Plan for the Prevention of Robberies within 20 Miles of London,* (MDCCLV), p.11, London.

crucial to her safety. This woman, however, escaped the gallows and was transported to America instead.

Flanders' Adventure with a Gentleman

A safer source of income for Flanders was her subsequent, "adventure with a gentleman", whom she met at St Bartholomew Fair, a rowdy annual carnival held in Smithfield in August. In the eighteenth century many traditional celebrations, such as the May Fair in London, were progressively suppressed as constituting a nuisance (in 1720 in that case). Southwark's "Our Lady" Fair survived till 1763, leaving St Bartholomew Fair alone of the major historic fairs to survive in the Metropolis into the nineteenth century. It was probably only marginally more staid than the riotous proceedings at Southwark later portrayed by William Hogarth. A contemporary description of the May Fair also portrayed it as a scene of drunkenness and disorder "in all the multitudes that ever I beheld, I never, in my life, saw such a number of lazy lousie-loo'd rascals, and so hateful a throng of beggarly, sluttish strumpets".[116] Though popular with ordinary Londoners, in the seventeenth century, St Bartholomew Fair was also often frequented by richer ones (Samuel Pepys was a frequent attender), although the participation of patricians in such communal celebrations was on the wane by the 1690s in an increasingly socially stratified society. Thus Flanders' experience with the gentleman catches an older tradition, as from about 1700 the involvement of the elite in this aspect of popular culture became infrequent, and, when it did occur, increasingly patronizing, usually an attempt to court popular support rather than a genuine sharing in a common celebration. This process was to become progressively more marked as the upper classes and bourgeoisie produced an increasingly differentiated culture(s) to that of the ordinary people, a change that appears to have been almost complete by the early part of the

---

116. Burke T., *The Streets of London*, 4th edn, (1949) p.73.

109

nineteenth century.[117]

The gentleman was "extremely well dress'd, and very rich", perhaps again, evidence that at this time the "popular" culture and that of the upper class were not as hermetically sealed as was to be the case a century or more later. This man, having drunk a considerable amount at Knightsbridge, took Flanders to a house and attempted to seduce her. The drink got the better of him and he fell asleep, and Flanders took the opportunity to "search him to a nicety", taking a gold watch, a silk purse of gold, his periwig, silver-fringed gloves, a sword and snuff-box. While doing this Flanders took the time to reflect moralistically to herself on this drunkard's folly in associating himself with a whore, picked up in the worst of all holes "... among the dirt and filth of the town". Flanders even claimed to know some prostitutes who made a trade of robbing their clients, and who were so sophisticated in this that they kept a sham gold watch and a purse of base metal counters to be ready on such occasions, so that they could replace their victims' possessions, without the latter becoming suspicious.

In portraying this scene, Defoe was reproducing a scenario that was played out at almost every Old Bailey Sessions, so regularly that it appears to have often produced an almost "set" verdict on the part of jurors. Time and again the intoxicated victims of prostitutes would go through the public humiliation of explaining how they came to lose their valuables, often in a house of ill repute. For everyone that had the nerve to prosecute, there must have been many who feared discovery by their wives and took no action. Thus John Wilmar, in 1724, having sold seven horses in London (he was a "countryman") was walking the streets when he met Isabel Williams from St Martins in the Fields. He went to the private room of a tavern with her for a pint of wine "where instead of one pint, we had four or five, but after the second or third, I found myself weary and drowsy, and so I fell asleep". Fortunately for him, the attendant at the tavern "... saw enough in their behaviour to convince me that the prisoner was a woman of the town". He went in regularly to check on the victim,

117. Sharpe, J.A., *Early Modern England, A Social History 1550-1760* (1987), p.286.

and, when it was noticed that the countryman was missing 36 guineas and a diamond ring, sent for the beadle and watchmen, having also refused to be bribed to turn a "blind eye" by the defendant.[118] In the same year and Sessions, John Odell, having been "drinking part of two or three pints of wine, besides other liquor" at the Bull's Head in Tottenham Court was also the victim of such a crime, committed by a prostitute called Susan Edwards, in even more ludicrous circumstances. Having consumed so much alcohol he called on Edwards at her residence, and drank more brandy with her. At some point in the evening he felt her hand in his breeches upon which he questioned her "you are not going to pick my pocket are ye"? No says she and so I thought no more of the matter". He subsequently missed his silver watch and when he later returned to the scene of the crime, was told that he would have to pay a guinea to have it returned. At first, although threatening to "fetch a constable and send her to Newgate", he was reluctant to press the matter when she refused to return the timepiece "for fear my wife should hear of it". Unfortunately for the defendant, he eventually made a clean breast to the apparently very forgiving Mrs Odell (he promised to treat her with "much kindness" to make up for it), who even returned to the prostitute's residence with her husband, where they called a constable to the scene. As Susan Edwards was being taken to a justice she asked to stop at an inn where the watch was quietly returned in a bag to its owner. As in most such cases, while the jury convicted her (the evidence was clear), it was only for theft of an item worth 10d. (a non capital sum), rather than its real value, for which Edwards received sentence of transportation (instead of execution). Jurors in these cases clearly felt that if a man was fool enough to get himself into such a situation it would be quite wrong for the defendant to lose her life for it, and consequently committed "pious perjury" in down valuing the stolen goods. This was exercised whatever the class of the victim prosecuting; thus, in January 1725, one Ben Gofling, "bricklayers labourer by trade", who readily conceded in court that "I work hard for

---

118. Select Trials at The Sessions-House in the Old-Bailey, Vol II, 1724-1732, (1735), p.28.

my money, and therefore the more fool I, for taking no better care of it",
was robbed after meeting a woman in a ginshop where he drank "quartern
after quartern" of the spirit with her. The defendant was again convicted
only of theft of 10d. of money (she had taken much more) and also
transported.[119]

However, some apparently "loose" women had no intention of actually
sleeping with the men that they attracted. Another female criminal
speciality of the time was termed "Buttock and Twang".[120] In this case
a woman would walk the streets "to be pick'd up". When she met a man
she would take him to a lodging house, pick his pocket and then frighten
him with the supposed unexpected arrival of "her pretended husband"
(usually a friend). The victim would normally "turn gladly away without
his watch or money".

Flanders' governess, delighted at the haul from the gentleman,
subsequently identified the name and address of the man, a baronet no
less, who had been robbed. The governess then turned impromptu broker
with the gentleman, à la Moll Cutpurse and Jonathan Wild, and took the
watch to him, for which he gave her 30 guineas in exchange. This was
more than Flanders would have been able to realize for it by selling it to
a fence, or melting it down. Subsequently deals were struck over his
periwig, and his snuff-box (another 30 guineas worth). Generously,
Flanders sent him his sword free of charge. The governess explained her
knowledge of the goods to him as having been received in the course of
her profession as pawnbroker. She also reassured him as to the
unlikelihood of his having contracted venereal disease in the escapade,
giving him "... assurances that [Flanders was] ... a woman clear from any
such thing". Given that at this time gonorrhoea was ubiquitous (though
syphilis was rarer) the man's concern was understandable.[121] The subject
was a constant preoccupation with all classes, as can be seen in the many
contemporary newspaper advertisements offering supposed cures.

119. *Ibid.*, p.138.
120. Hall, J., *ibid.* (1708), p.9.
121. Stone, L., *The Family Sex and Marriage in England 1500-1800*, Harper Torchbooks
 edn (1979), p.379.

Typically, *The Daily Courant*, for April 24, 1704, carried an advertisement for "A True and Succinct Account of the Venereal Disease, Shewing its Nature, Crises, Various Ways of infecting, the easiness of its cure". Forty years later in the century, the philandering James Boswell was to live in dread of "Signor Gonorrhoea" a "foul fiend of the genitals" with its attendant "scalding heat and deep-tinged loathsome matter".

Flanders subsequently regretted that she did not blackmail the gentleman for an allowance, or in her words, "made some advantage of him", which, though a risky venture, would have been less dangerous than her ongoing life of theft.

In many ways the governess and Flanders were effectively producing a small version of Wild's "lost property" system, the latter being at his peak when Defoe wrote his novel, having survived the Act of 1717 specifically aimed at him (and popularly named after him). After his fall, three years later, he was also to have his biography written by Defoe. To the loser of stolen property it was cheaper to buy back the goods from the thief than to buy new ones, and in doing so he would usually be willing to pay significantly more than the proportion (sometimes less than a quarter) that would be obtained by the fence in an ordinary sale or by reducing the goods to bullion; this was especially so if the goods were of sentimental rather than commercial value or were important business documents, when their market value might be almost non-existent. This had been turned into a trade in the seventeenth century by Moll Cutpurse, whose system had then been enormously developed by Wild in the early eighteenth century, even though made illegal and a capital offence by Parliament in 1717.[122] As Fielding was to note in 1751, despite the demise of Wild, a thief was still almost certain to see the promise of a substantial reward with "no questions asked" for the return of stolen property. Such advertisements were a weekly feature of magazines such as *The Spectator*. Interestingly, it appears that these "deals" were usually honoured by all parties, the money being paid over and the authorities not involved. Subsequently, as a result of pressure, in part engendered by Fielding

122. Tobias, J.J., *ibid.*, p.34.

himself, placing such advertisements in a periodical was made punishable by a fine of £50, one that could be levied on the printer, publisher and advertiser alike. Such arrangements are also reflected elsewhere in Defoe's work. He returned to the theme again in *Colonel Jack;* when Jack had taken part in a theft of valuable bills of exchange, there was the rapid offer of a reward of "£30 to any one that had the bills, and would restore them, and would ask no questions". The promise not to ask questions, in this case of the identity of one of the thieves, as well as to pay the reward being faithfully kept by the loser, although he must have appreciated Jack's likely involvement.

Prostitute Again

Subsequently, however, at the robbed gentleman's insistence, she agreed to meet him again socially! On this occasion, Flanders consented to having further sexual intercourse with the man, who had been drinking once again. Despite the circumstances of their first meeting, he paid her five guineas for her services, which, as Flanders, observed was the first money she had gained "that way" for the many years since she had been a professional prostitute; she was by this time well over 50, but must have still had a certain allure! She subsequently saw him on several further occasions for sums of money. His visits ended after about a year.

Theft from a Coaching Inn

Flanders' versatility and eye for an opportunity also allowed her to take advantage of a servant maid waiting with a bundle for the Barnet coach outside an ale house, the "Three Cups Inn", in St John's Street. Flanders managed to convince the maid that she was employed at the inn and as a consequence the maid was persuaded to leave her bundle in the care of Flanders who promptly decamped with it, swiftly disguising herself as she went by taking off her apron and wrapping the stolen package up in it as it "was made up in a piece of painted Callico, and very remarkable".

114

Throughout the eighteenth century, coaching inns, with large numbers of people and goods rapidly passing through them, were popular places for thieves to congregate and operate. As Patrick Colquhoun was to note at the end of the century in his *Treatise on the Police of the Metropolis* "... many of these atrocious villains, are also constantly waiting at the inns, ... personating travellers, ... for the purpose of plundering everything that is portable".[123]

The stolen bundle contained a very good suit of Indian damask, a gown and petticoat, a laced head, and ruffles of very good Flanders' lace. Moll Flanders modestly admits in her narrative that this trick was not her own invention, but was given to her by one who "... practised it with great success". She subsequently tried the trick again, at different coach stations in London, for example in Whitechapel, by the corner of Petticoat Lane, where the coaches departed for the suburban villages of Stratford and Bow to the East.

Theft at a Warehouse

On another occasion the ever ingenious Flanders placed herself by a warehouse at the river's waterside, a point where coasting vessels from the north country came in, such as ships sailing from Sunderland. The huge quantity of goods arriving by sea in London and unloaded by hundreds of small boats and lighters mid-stream was almost impossible to police (the first enclosed docks still being 80 years away in 1721), and provided many lucrative opportunities for theft. The warehouse visited by Flanders was shut for some of the time, and when a young man came along with a letter containing the marks for a box and a hamper coming from Newcastle-upon-Tyne he was consequently unable to pick up his parcels. The boxes contained expensive linen and glass. Flanders, pretending to the man that she worked for the warehouse, read the letter and noted the sender's "name, and the marks", and other identifying

---

123. 6th edn, 1800, p.93, quoted Tobias, *ibid.*, p.39.

particulars of the parcels, and then told the messenger to come again in the morning when the warehouse keeper would be back. She then went away and wrote a letter in identical terms, containing the information that she had memorized and returned to the warehouse shortly afterwards (when it was open) where she took delivery of the box "... without any scruple" by the warehouseman (the value of the linen alone, contained in it, was £22).

Swindling like this was a well established and growing form of crime amongst those who had a "genteel exterior, a demeanour apparently artless, and a good address".[124] A classic illustration of this arose a year after the publication of *Moll Flanders*. In 1723 one Alexander Davenport hired a fine house in London and proceeded to order large quantities of "valuable goods", for example £48 of linen from a draper and also "... ordered a large quantity to be sent to his house on the following day, when he would pay for the whole. The first parcel was delivered, but the purchaser was decamped when the linen-draper went with the second".[125] Having successfully carried off a number of such deceptions he was eventually caught, convicted, pilloried (twice), sent to Newgate for two years and fined £200. According to the narrator of the account, at the time (1723) this mode of stealing "was not common, but now abounds". Flanders' ability to play the "Lady" would have greatly assisted her in this type of crime, just as Davenport's genteel airs had done in his operation. To this end, she made sure that "on these adventures we always went very well dress'd, and I had very good cloaths on, and a gold watch by my side, as like a Lady as other folks".

Flanders herself observed that she could fill up her whole narrative with an account of the "... variety of such adventures, which daily invention directed [her] to, and which [she] managed with the utmost dexterity, and always with success".

---

124. Wilkinson, G.T., *The Newgate Calendar* (1816), Cardinal edn (1991), p.100.
125. Wilkinson, G.T., *The Newgate Calendar* (1816), Cardinal edn (1991), p.109.

Flanders' First Experience of the London Magistrates

Ironically, for a professional thief, Flanders' first experience of the Metropolis' magistrates came when she was detained for a crime of which she was entirely innocent. While walking in Covent Garden she heard a cry of "stop thief" and found herself in the vicinity of a pursued thief who had dressed in the same way (as a widow) that Flanders had chosen to attire herself that day. Shoplifting, especially from mercers' premises, was a permanent concern for retailers. As a commercially minded man, Defoe was also well aware of the problems faced by these shopkeepers. In *The Complete English Tradesman* of 1725, he noted that "... such is the slippery dealings of this age, especially in mercers and drapers business, that the shop-keeper ought never to turn his back towards his customers". He also observed that this explained the large amount of expensive journeymen that such retailers had necessarily to employ, who "... were it not for the danger of shop-lifting would be a needless as it is a heavy expense for them".

There was a great range of differing methods for stealing from retailers. Some of these were extremely complicated, others very simple, many are still in use today. One sophisticated method, which produced ready cash rather than goods, that had been popular in the late seventeenth century (though, according to John Hall writing in 1708, "now gone something out of date") was to distract the owner with "excuses of seeing this thing and that thing" and, when he was not looking, "put a small whalebone, daub'd at the end with bird-lime, into the till of the counter, and draw up the money". People, often women, who employed this *modus operandi* were known as "till drivers". The lack of a Georgian equivalent of the modern self-service store did somewhat reduce the opportunities for theft in shops, though as the introduction of special penal provisions for it in the 1699 Shoplifting Act showed, there was still a considerable amount of it.

A common technique for such theft would be to pretend to barter over the price of a selection of goods "pretending to cheapen" them, till the shopkeeper was distracted, and then to secret some of them about the person. This was the case with Elleoner Davis and Ann Rye, "two notorious shoplifts", in 1680 (working together made it easier to distract the retailer's attention). Davis took three pieces of silk in such a manner, but unfortunately dropped one as she walked out of the shop; when this was pointed out to her by a passerby she thought (mistakenly) that she was detected and threw the others away as she fled "which raised a suspicion in some that they were stolen goods" and she was apprehended.[126]

Flanders, similarly, was detained by the pursuing "mob", some of whom mistakenly identified her as one of the thieves who had been chased from a nearby mercer's shop. She was then brought back to the shop where the owner initially denied that she was the woman he had seen on his premises earlier, and who was suspected of being the thief.

However, another man present insisted that she be detained and held under the supervision of a local parish constable, until a pursuing journeyman came back from chasing the other thieves. Foolishly, the mercer, despite his own initial doubts agreed to this course of action "they had called a constable and he stood in the shop as my jailer". At this point, Flanders prudently inquired of the constable, for future reference, as to where he lived and what "trade he was at" (constables then being the part-time, appointed holders of a parish office, responsible with the "watch" for local security and not to be confused with the post-1829 Metropolitan policeman). The mercer continued to refuse to let her go, despite the mounting evidence that she was not one of the thieves. When the constable began to have his own doubts the mercer taunted him by asking him whether he was a Justice of the Peace or a constable. In the light of the apparently fairly thin identification evidence in the mercer's case, the constable who had been "charged" with Flanders, in the shop, became progressively more nervous about detaining her further. Eventually the "true widow", who had been involved in the crime, was brought in by other pursuers. This is also indicative of the continuing role of the "hue and cry", the popular pursuit of a fleeing criminal (perhaps aided by an extensive system of rewards for their capture), and which explained both

126.   OBSP, April 26-28 (1680), p.4.

this woman's and Flanders' detention. At this point in the proceedings the mercer belatedly told the constable, who had now arrested the right woman, to let Flanders go. The constable, however, returned the mercer's earlier taunt by pointing out that as a constable and not a JP it was "... the law and the magistrate alone that can discharge" the prisoner once a constable had arrested and been charged with that person by a member of the public; which was, as a matter of strict law, correct, if often widely ignored in practice.

With the correct thief now brought back to the shop, the mercer apologized to Flanders for her arrest. Flanders, however, promptly demanded reparation for her detention. She insisted on going before a magistrate although the mercer no longer required it. The constable supported Flanders' insistence that she be brought before a justice, and, although the mercer sought forcibly to dissuade the constable from this course of action, he was unsuccessful. In Flanders' opinion this was because the constable happened not to be a hired officer but a "good substantial kind of man ... [Flanders thought] he was a corn chandler". By this Flanders meant that the man was fulfilling his parish office in person, rather than hiring an "inferior" person to stand in as a deputy, in his place.

Constables and Watchmen

The Anglican parish was the fundamental unit of local government, and still a very important one, with heavy responsibilities. Outside the City of London it was usually supervised by the JPs (often effectively the next tier of local government). There were onerous duties involved in being a middle-ranking householder in a London parish, being responsible as they were for law and order and also, at least in theory, for the care of the aged, disabled, sick and unemployed.

The parish constables, along with the night watchmen, were the basic unit of policing in London at this point (the Bow Street Runners, yet alone the horse and foot patrol, still being many decades away in 1721). The constables have been the subject of much ridicule because they were usually untrained and often portrayed as inefficient. Frequently, if they did not appoint deputies (a common practice), they came from the "tradesman" class in the towns, such as shopkeepers and small merchants. The courts themselves contributed to the process whereby people of standing and ability were removed from the ranks of the constables, by granting "Tyburn tickets", exemptions from having to carry out parish offices, as a reward for previously successfully prosecuting a felon to conviction.

The constables, even more than the magistrates, were the element of policing that had direct contact with the public. Not all of them appear to have been as inefficient or corrupt as is sometimes suggested in the propaganda of those later in the eighteenth and the early nineteenth centuries who were pressing for the introduction of a "regular" police force (it needs to be stressed that the Fieldings, and others like them, were actively campaigning for policing changes in the Metropolis). There were, however, often severe demarcation problems, as their scope of responsibility and the ambit of their duties was usually confined to the parish where they were appointed. Constables' areas of operation, especially in the heavily sub-divided City of London, with its myriad of small parishes were often very small. In theory, constables were possessed of great powers, as Blackstone was to note "they are armed with very large powers, of arresting, and imprisoning, of breaking open houses, and the like". So great were these that he also thought it was well that most of them were unaware of their full extent "considering what sort of men are for the most part put upon these offices". However, although their duties were extensive, ranging from whipping vagabonds and suppressing breaches of the Sabbath to raising the "hue and cry" they had little chance of being aided by a swift and effective mobilization of assistance if confronted by serious trouble, and had almost no bureaucratic support (or even a formal record-keeping body) behind them. As a result the effective reality of their power was often much more limited and they could often be defied by any sizeable grouping of criminals, especially in the sanctuaries. In an emergency they could, under a power given by the Law of Settlement of 1662, be supplemented by special constables, sworn in for the occasion, to defend a parish against "actual tumult, riot or felony". These special constables would be paid; in London, by the government, in the provinces from the county rate; this was usually up to five shillings a day.[127]

Although it is possible to exaggerate the level of corruption, widespread dishonesty in the policing and judicial agencies, whether constables, watchmen, informers, thieftakers or trading justices does appear to have been a feature of the late seventeenth and early to mid-eighteenth centuries. This was a phenomenon that was closely linked to the professional crime of the period, and which also contributed to the "blurring" of distinctions between legality and criminality, so manifest, for example, in Jonathan Wild's life. Some watchmen could be bribed to turn a "blind eye" to crime, some constables took illegal perks from office, some magistrates could be paid to dismiss cases against the evidence. This produced what has been termed a subterranean system of "bargain justice". Those who could afford it could gain protection to a significant, though not total, extent.[128]

Additionally, however, it must be noted that while the parish constables undoubtedly were, on occasion, rather ineffective their somewhat ambiguous local position did not help. They really were "community" policemen. As well as preserving the law they had to mediate between local people to preserve the "peace", something that a literal and non-discretionary application of the criminal law would have precluded. Probably, at least as damaging as corruption, for financial reasons, was the reluctance of some constables to suffer the permanent opprobrium (and thus danger) of some of the people in their own neighbourhoods by firmly enforcing the law during their year in office.

The constables were not a preventative or detective force, but largely charged with making arrests by injured parties, usually summoned or fetched after an incident had occurred. This also sometimes entailed considerable dangers. When Richard Probe was summonsed late at night in 1680 to attend a disturbance near the river involving seven drunk

---

127. Cornish, W.R., and Clark, G., *Law and Society in England: 1750-1950* (1989), p.556.
128. McMullan, J.L., "Crime, Law and Order in Early Modern England", p.261, *Brit.J.Criminol.*, vol.27, No.3 (1987).

"Scotchmen", some watermen and a damaged boat, because someone on the waterside "seeing some hurt might be done, went and called the deceased out of his bed to keep the peace", he was swiftly to be knocked down with an oar "and then mortally wounded by a boathook".[129]

Like the justices, the constables, and other parish officers, were not necessarily totally uninstructed in their duties, as can be seen from popular advertisements for appropriate instructive books and pamphlets. Thus one, in *The London Journal* of 1723, announced that there had been lately published the fifth edition of the "compleat constable", "directing constables, headboroughs, tythingmen, churchwardens, overseers of the poor and surveyors of the highways and scavengers, in the duty of their offices according to the power allowed them by the laws. Wherein the constables duty relating to the passing of rogues, vagabonds, and sturdy beggars is fully set forth".[130]

The next (indeed only) effective level of policing up from the constables would be the military, frequently used not just to suppress major riots in the Metropolis during the seventeenth and eighteenth centuries but also to bolster "routine" policing by backing up the civilian law officers. A classic example of this occurred in 1726 when the notorious Catherine Hayes' accomplice in murder was arrested for the vicious killing of Hayes' husband. A group of eight soldiers and a sergeant were necessary to escort him to prison (in large part because of the presence of angry crowds).

The use of paid stand-ins or deputies was not surprising. Those members of the parish chosen, in a variety of ways, to perform the duty of constable for a year would still have to conduct, simultaneously, their full-time employments or trades (constables only being entitled to basic expenses), a demanding regime unless they could hire someone in their place.[131] The latter (paid replacements) were much more notorious for corruption than those who fulfilled their offices in person, perhaps not

---

129. OBSP, April 26-28 (1680), p.2.
130. January 5, 1723.
131. Emsley, C., *Oxford Handbook of Criminology* (1994), p.158.

surprisingly, as even a century after Defoe was writing their pay was usually only between eight and £15 a year.[132] They did, however, accumulate a degree of practical experience which one year appointees could not match. This use of substitutes was not a new phenomenon in 1700; Shakespeare's "Elbow" in *Measure for Measure* had been doing the job for seven-and-a-half years because he did "it for some piece of money". Defoe himself had paid £10 in 1721 to be excused from such an allotted parish office. The experience also prompted him to write a diatribe against the "insupportable hardship" of serving in the office of constable in his *Parochial Tyranny* (1727).

Defoe was personally well aware of the many defects in contemporary urban policing, not just the constables but also the paid nightwatchmen beneath them (these men being under the constables' immediate supervision). The watch were the paid nighttime deputies of the constables; during the night hours they had "for the time being the authority of their principal".[133] They were appointed by the parish and paid a small sum for the service, and were considered to be markedly inferior even to the constables. In *Street Robberies Consider'd* (1728) the ex-criminal "narrator" expressly notes that "another reason of the frequency of street robberies, is the remissness or corruption of the watch, and as often want of vigour and youth; for you shall seldom see a man under 50 among them". The answer, he felt, was that "it ought to be the business of the heads of the parish to choose out young stout honest fellows for watchmen, who, for a little better allowance, would no doubt accept such an employment". Additionally, he felt that "The Kings of the Night", as the constables please to term themselves, should be a little more active in their employments; but all their business is to get to a watch house and guzzle till their time of going home comes.[134] The perceived low quality of the night watch also explains why the narrator felt they should not be armed with firearms as they could then commit more crimes themselves,

---

132. Radzinowicz, L., *ibid.*, vol.2, p.493.
133. Blackstone, W., *ibid.*, vol.1, p.345.
134. *Ibid.*, p.60.

or even insult "gentlemen that are coming home at an unseasonable hour". He felt that arming the watch in its then current condition was "a very dangerous way to cure the evil we are treating of, unless they were better regulated". The poor quality of the watch was a theme that Henry Fielding was also to retouch on, later in the century, in *Amelia* (1751) when noting that the "watchmen in our metropolis, who, being to guard our streets by night from thieves and robbers, an office which at least requires strength of body, are chosen out of those poor old decrepit people who are, from their want of bodily strength, rendered incapable of getting a livelihood by work". He noted that they were "armed only with a pole", which their feebleness meant they could barely lift![135] In this novel the improperly detained hero, Captain Booth, was initially offered his liberty by the watch after being wrongly and illegally arrested at night, in exchange for half a crown!

Even with regard to the watch, however, it would be wrong to over-exaggerate their low calibre. As Clive Emsley has noted, at least in some of the London parishes there were determined efforts a century before the advent of the Metropolitan Police to ensure that a competent and relatively able watch was in place.[136] This inevitably meant a willingness to spend greater amounts of money on the service. Even in the seventeenth century that at least some watchmen were conscientious about their duties, can be seen in a number of contemporary accounts. For example, Samuel Pepys in his *Diary* for September 11, 1663, noted that "this morning, about two or three o'clock, knocked up in our back yard, and rising to the window, being moonshine, I found it was the constable and his watch, who had found our back yard door open, and so came in to see what the matter was. So I desired them to shut the door, and bid them good night, and so to bed again".[137]

---

135. Volume 1, p.16, Barnes and Noble edn, vol.vi, (1967).
136. Emsley, C., *Crime and Society in England 1750-1900* (1987), p.175.
137. From *The Diary of Samuel Pepys, A New and Complete Transcription*, Robert Latham and William Matthews (eds). Berkeley: University of California Press (published 1970-1983).

Flanders' Visit to the Justice

The constable insisted that the mercer also accompany Flanders' party to the local magistrate, as he had "broken the peace" by his false arrest. The mercer and his journeyman initially refused to do so, and a fracas swiftly ensued, in which the constable was pushed by the mercer's journeyman (with the encouragement of the mercer himself), with the constable in turn knocking him down, calling for help, and having the master, journeyman and all his servants seized. During this disturbance, the woman who was really the thief, escaped, along with two other people who had been detained with her. The mercer then quietened down and with a mob of about 500 people at their heels, they went as a group to the local justice. When the mob were informed as to why they were going to the JP, they were "strangely pleased" at the explanation, and every now and then "... they [made] a good dab of dirt at the mercer," who was ultimately even forced to hire a coach to protect himself from the crowd and its missiles. In this passage, Defoe captures some of the volatility of the London "mob", as well as its potential speed of grouping, their ambiguous position towards authority, and perhaps a degree of latent class consciousness. A crowd of considerable numbers that had assembled so rapidly had to be treated with respect by the authorities, only the military would be capable of dealing with it if it were to become threatening.

The party containing Flanders and the mercer duly arrived at the nearest convenient magistrate "... which was an ancient gentleman in Bloomsbury". When he had heard the story the justice quickly went through the formality of discharging Flanders. He admonished the mercer for his behaviour and, very significantly, bound him over to keep the peace on pain of forfeiture of a sum of money. This was a "recognizance", a power gained by magistrates since the sixteenth century that had greatly enhanced the JPs' importance, and which appears to have been crucially significant in London in controlling low level disturbances and assaults (it was also used to ensure the attendance of witnesses at trial). Those bound over, often on condition that they "keep the peace" or be "of good behaviour", would normally be required to attend at the following Sessions, where they would often be discharged without any further formal action being taken against them (though in about 10 per cent of cases failure to appear or to keep the terms of the recognizance led to the sum involved being "estreated").[138]

However, the justice was compelled to point out to Flanders that he was not in a position to award reparation, though he reminded her of the possibility of a civil action for damages. The journeyman who had taken part in the fracas was ordered to Newgate (though then bailed by his master), for assaulting the constable and Flanders. As the mercer left the court (or magistrate's private room), Flanders again had "the satisfaction of seeing the Mob wait upon them both as they came out, hollowing, and throwing stones and Dirt at the coaches they rode in".

That the "mob" should not be respectful of the mercer's (relatively modest) status is not surprising. Ordinary people were not always quickly intimidated by those of even high social rank in London, let alone a tradesman, as can be seen from a case from 1731 at the Old Bailey. In this case Edward Stafford, the brother of Lord Stafford, was tried for the murder of Thomas Manwaring outside a Holborn coffee house. The victim made money by running errands for the customers and was sent by Stafford to fetch him snuff. When he failed to bring any he was pricked by Stafford with his sword but apparently without significant injury. Manwaring cried out and was taken to an apothecary for treatment from whence an officious porter hustled him back to the coffee house insisting that Stafford be charged before a constable. At this Stafford exclaimed "are you the scrub rascal that will have a constable charged with me"? Although the victim denied this, he was stabbed by Stafford, the latter declaring "I have not killed you but god damn you I will kill you"! He (Stafford) then walked back into the coffee-house where he was mobbed by other patrons before giving up his sword to them and being taken before a justice. Unlike the later case involving Lord Ferrers, Stafford received a special finding of "Lunacy" from the jury and was not

---

138. On this important power, see:, Shoemaker, R.B., *Prosecution and Punishment* (1991), p.95.

executed.[139]

Origins of JPs

The origins of the JPs lay in the fourteenth century, one of a number of royal experiments in the 1300s to deal with apparent widespread disorder.[140] They survived to become ever more important officials, with large numbers of statutes passed over the next few centuries adding to their already heavy burdens, and the office also coming to play a vital role in both law enforcement and county administration. By the late seventeenth century justices had significant powers of summary conviction for minor offences, as well as being able to hear misdemeanour trials, with a jury, at Quarter Sessions. In these situations one of the JPs (usually legally experienced) or a Recorder would have a presiding role as chairman, as can be seen from an account by George Fox of a contemporary trial before such a court: "many of the justices ... were moderate and civil; but Justice Strcct, who was the Judge of the Court, would not regard, but overruled all".[141] JPs also supervised a range of local government and administrative matters, from highway repair to the examination of Catholic recusants and a huge range of other functions.

As a result of statutes from Queen Mary's time (especially that of 1555) justices also had to take depositions from potential witnesses in cases of felony; prosecution witnesses would be entered into recognizances by them (essentially bound over) to ensure that they attended trial; justices would examine arrested suspects and commit suspected felons to prison, etc. In all criminal cases the JPs were the first judicial contact for those accused of crime (as they are today); during this

---

139. Walker, N., *Crime and Insanity in England*, vol.1 (1968), p.57.
140. Sharpe, J.A., *Crime in Early Modern England 1550-1750* (1983), p.28.
141. A fascinating account of many aspects of the Criminal Justice System of England in the 1650s, 1660s, and 1670s can be seen in the *Journal* of the leading Quaker: George Fox (1624-1691), who, in large part because as a Quaker he would not take an oath in court, the Oath of Allegiance to the King, or abide by the laws regulating public meetings was a regular visitor to prisons and courts up and down the land during this period.

process, weak cases could be thrown out and flaws in the case remedied, etc. This was an almost automatic process; when five men were arrested in London for the "audacious burglary" of the Lord Chancellor's Mace, they were first promptly "... carried before the Right Worshipful, Sir William Turner, who after examination (according to Justice) committed them to the common Gaol of Newgate".[142] In some (but not most), cases the arrested suspects would be examined in private, as was the case with the husband killer, Mary Hoby in 1677, "for fear of any unreasonable discovery of what she might declare". However, in this case the examining magistrate stressed that before he "put so much as one question to her" he gave her so full an account of the evidence against her that "she gave herself for lost", and without holding any "hope of either an acquittal or a pardon", made a clean breast of the matter, telling him "frankly from point to point" about the case as he recorded it.[143] Thus in many ways some of their work had a distinctly "inquisitorial" tenor.

The pre-trial examination was an important part of a conscientious JP's work. However, this procedure was apparently devoid of many of the features that marred the inquisitorial version of the investigative process in France, where the *instruction*, or preliminary investigation, was often accompanied by torture intended to obtain the names of accomplices, along with a brutal cross-examination of the suspect while he or she was seated on a low stool (*the sellette*). The accused was denied the right to any legal advice (not simply trial representation as in England), inspection of evidence and the confrontation of witnesses. The whole process was secret, written and non-confrontational.[144]

The justices would be assisted by the Clerk of the Peace, who, although not having any special qualifications at this time, would have an important

---

142. "A Perfect Narrative of the Apprehension, Tryal and Confession of the Five Several Persons that were Confederates in Stealing the Mace and the Two Privy Purses from the Lord High Chancellor of England" (1677), printed for E. Olivier, p.1.

143. *A Hellish Murder Committed by a French Midwife on the Body of her Husband.* Published by Randal Taylor (1688), p.38.

144. See Helen Trouille, "A Look at French Criminal Procedure", *Criminal Law Review* (1994), p.736.

administrative role and would also develop, by experience, a considerable degree of expertise. As with other such offices, there was a range of instructive manuals to assist the clerks in the execution of their duties, amongst them the important *Cabinet of the Clerk of the Justice of the Peace*, by W. Sheppard, published in 1641 and again in 1654 and 1660.[145] Nevertheless, despite this clerical support, in a city like London it needed considerable energy to carry out the function of a JP properly, something that Flanders' elderly justice may not have been fully up to. The dying Henry Fielding, on the trail of a particular and notorious gang of "villains and cutthroats" recorded that he had worked tirelessly to promote the case against them "in examining whom, and in taking the depositions against them, I have often spent whole days, nay, sometimes whole nights, especially when there was any difficulty in proving sufficient evidence to convict them, which is a common case in street-robberies".[146]

Pre-trial procedure in front of the JPs contributed to the efficient functioning later of the felony trial in the Assize court or the Old Bailey. In particular, the evidence of the defendant's examination by a JP, including any confessions made during the magistrate's questioning, would be adduced, being proved if necessary by the JP (or, probably more commonly, by the attendance of his clerk, who would normally have also acted as scribe during the examination). Indeed, the London police magistrates only lost their policing role (the supervision of the constabulary and investigations) in the 1830s. Flanders' decision to go to the local JP, once a case had been initiated was thus entirely correct legally, if not necessary, except to assist her to pursue a subsequent civil action against the mercer.

A Civil Action

Flanders quickly saw the potential opportunity for gain in the situation,

---

145. Skyrme, Sir Thomas, *History of the Justices of the Peace* (1994), p.349.
146. Fielding, H., *The Voyage to Lisbon* (1754), Everyman edn (1960), p.192.

and instructed an attorney to bring an action against the mercer. Although not mentioned explicitly in the novel, this can only be for the civil trespass of false imprisonment, as a result of her wrongful detention. An action for false imprisonment, which would often also be accompanied by one for assault and battery, was potentially lucrative because as a result of the tort, it was accepted law that the injured "... party shall recover damages for the injury he has received", while the defendant would also be potentially liable to pay a fine to the King for a violation of the public peace.[147] The risks of false imprisonment, in a society where so much legal redress was in the hands of individuals (such as commission-earning "bum bailiffs"), were well known, especially where the victim had the financial means to seek a legal remedy. In 1725 it was noted in a London paper that "two bailiffs, with an attorney of Furnival's Inn" while trying to execute a writ "against a gentleman from Africa" unfortunately "mistook the house and their man" and arrested an MP by mistake, "but being soon made sensible of the gross error they had committed, and of the penalties their zeal had made them liable to, they fell upon their knees, and with prayers and tears besought a remission of the trespass, assault, false imprisonment and breach of the privilege of parliament. We hear they will be prosecuted at law".[148] In theory Flanders could have brought actions under all these heads except the last!

Flanders' attorney, whose profession was becoming steadily more regulated in the early eighteenth century, with Acts of Parliament promoting this in 1605 and 1728 (he even promised to inform her "... if they offered him any bribe"), was obviously a highly competent lawyer. He managed to convince the mercer that Flanders was "a widow of fortune" who could afford any litigation costs that might arise in pursuing her action to a satisfactory conclusion.

---

147. Blackstone, *ibid.*, vol iii, p.138.
148. *The Original Half-Penny London Journal*, Saturday, April 10, 1725.

Attorneys and the Legal Profession in 1700

Attorneys, though often despised in this period, and ridiculed by pamphleteers because of their inferior education and social standing (compared to the increasingly elitist barristers), dealt directly with the public, giving legal advice and taking formal steps in litigation. They were, as a consequence vital to the nation's legal services and expressly cultivated by the barristers as a source of work, though, by this period, largely excluded from the Inns of Court.[149] In the late sixteenth and early seventeenth centuries the Bar had become not only more exclusive, but also firmer about demarcation lines between the work of the various legal professionals (something which had been very fluid in the late medieval period). By Defoe's time barristers would rarely work directly for the public. The attorneys tended to congregate in the Inns of Chancery, such as Staple's Inn, near the four great Inns of Court (Middle Temple, Gray's Inn, etc).

London had an overwhelming preponderance of the nation's attorneys, several times the combined totals for all of the provincial cities. As Doctor Johnson was to remark of the city later in the century "here the fell attorney prowls for prey". Around 1750 Sir John Fielding (a magistrate like his brother) also referred to the "vast multitude of attorneys, pettyfoggers, and understrappers of the law". London, as a legal honeypot, had 1,533 attorneys in 1729, approximately one for every 383 inhabitants. This was out of a national total of a little over 4,000 (4,600 according to the returns made to the House of Commons following the 1729 *Act for the Better Regulation of Attorneys and Solicitors*, which required each practising attorney, before 1730, to satisfy the Judges of the court to which they were admitted to practise, of their fitness to do so; though some of these would have been registered twice in different parts of the provinces). This was from a legal profession which numbered about 10,000 men altogether, if Gregory King's 1688 estimate is accepted as accurate (this figure, included everyone professionally connected with the law from

---

149. Lemmings, D., *Gentlemen and Barristers* (1990), p.113.

Judges to "hedge solicitors" not connected to any particular court, and sometimes even working out of coffee shops).[150]

Attorneys had developed after 1200 to spare their clients the trouble of attending drawn-out court procedures in person, in time being formally recognized by the courts.[151] They had always been distinct from the advocates in the courts. By the early eighteenth century they were slowly on their way to being replaced or swallowed up by the newer profession of solicitors, who were originally responsible for a variety of clerical duties for attorneys and landowners (the same person being often both solicitor and attorney), though this process was far from complete. The solicitors, like the attorneys, did the case preparation for barristers as well as doing routine work in non-contentious cases that attorneys might not wish to cover, drawing up deeds, marriage contracts and wills, managing property or other similar types of work. Unlike attorneys, they were not enrolled at a specific court. Until 1729 the solicitors were almost unregulated and indeed anyone involved in legal business could term themselves a "solicitor". These "pettyfoggers" (not representative of all solicitors of course) brought them an extremely bad reputation (much worse than that of attorneys), especially as lawyers who would stir up client's problems to gain extra work. This began to change after an apprenticeship of five years, in articles of clerkship, was required as the condition of the court-work monopoly granted in 1729.[152] In Fielding's version of *Jonathan Wild* (which drew heavily on Defoe's earlier version) one "Jack Swagger" was portrayed as "an Irish gentleman, who had been bred clerk to an attorney, afterwards whipped out of a regiment of dragoons, and was then a Newgate solicitor, and a bawdy house bully".

Top attorneys could match the earnings of the better barristers, while the lowest solicitors, working out of coffee shops might only earn a pittance. Barristers however, were from the upper orders of society while

---

150. Aylett, P., "A Profession in the Marketplace: The Distribution of Attorneys in England and Wales 1730-1800", *Law and History Review*, vol.5 (1987), p.1.
151. Baker, J.H., *ibid.*, p.24.
152. Cornish, W.R. and Clark, G.N., *Law and Society in England 1750-1950* (1989), p.51.

attorneys, whose educations and clerkships (normally five years) rarely cost more than £100 compared to an expenditure of £1,000 to £1,500 for the Bar, were more "middle ranking" members of society.[153]

Attorneys would be responsible for the inception and initial formal appearances, as well as negotiations, in a case. If the matter came to court for trial they would instruct counsel, either a barrister or a serjeant at law, depending on the court in which the action had been brought, to appear as advocate for the hearing. The Court of Common Pleas, at this time, was a monopoly of the serjeants (a historic but rapidly declining profession of advocates), the quickly growing court of King's Bench was open to barristers as well (the latter profession was very much in the ascendant at this time). Attorneys also often acted as bankers and political agents.

Settlement of the Action

Flanders' lawyer ultimately produced a fine settlement of the case and so had no need to brief counsel (probably, it would have been a barrister in the Court of King's Bench). She dropped her action for £150, costs, a suit of clothes, a supper and an apology. Then as now most civil actions settled in such a compromise. For a professional criminal to appear in court, with its attendant publicity, cannot have been a very attractive prospect, and Flanders' decision to accept the settlement was probably prudent. Flanders herself was well aware that her "name was so well known among the people at Hick's Hall,[154] the Old Bailey and such places" that she would get little in damages if she pursued the matter.

She also agreed not to press charges against the journeyman since, being poor "... there was nothing to be got by him". While they were at supper, provided by the mercer, the poor man was brought in to make his apology, which he did with great humility. Flanders quickly "abate(d) his

---

153. Earle, P., *The Making of the English Middle Class* (1985), p.61
154. This was the Sessions court for the county of Middlesex (including most of London outside the "City"), it was named after Sir Baptist Hicks and was located in Clerkenwell.

cringes" and told him that she forgave him. As a result of this success she now had over £700 in money, besides valuable clothes, rings, plate and two gold watches. This was a great fortune by the standards of the age.

Flanders' Adventure with a Horse

Ever willing to take her chances as they presented themselves, Flanders' next criminal venture was with a horse. Whilst standing near a tavern, a gentleman on horseback arrived, and, going into the tavern, handed the animal to a drawer. The drawer was summoned by his master and left the horse in the care of Flanders, who promptly, and rashly, led him away to her governess. Though it was very valuable, Flanders was totally at a loss as to what to do with the animal, as was her governess, who was "quite confounded" by the problem. They also knew that they could not leave the horse in a stable because a description of it was certain to be advertised quickly in the *Gazette*. The growth of the press at this period made the advertising of such thefts a practical possibility, greatly increasing the prospects of detection for those in possession of high value and identifiable goods (such as horses). The potential power of advertising was also well appreciated by the authorities. Later in the century, the magistrate Sir John Fielding suggested that there should be a daily fixture in the *Public Advertiser* specifically for the advertising of robberies of all kinds so that inn keepers could see the descriptions of highwaymen, stablekeepers that of their horses, and pawnbrokers their loot.[155]

Contemporary advertisements for the recovery of stolen horses were graphic and detailed. A typical one from 1704 can be seen in *The Post-Man*, "stole out of a stable at Wapping Well, London, on Thursday night, a large roan mare, about 14 hands and a half high, a brown nose, and a little heavy ey', comes seven years old, and had all her paces".[156] Perhaps

---

155. Fielding, John, *A Plan for the Prevention of Robberies within 20 miles of London*, p.18, 1755, London.
156. For January 6-8, 1704.

significantly, the chain of events that led to Dick Turpin's own downfall resulted from his theft of a horse; the owner, one Mr Major, printed and distributed handbills describing the animal, which was recognized by the landlord of the Red Lion in Whitechapel, where it had been stabled. The descriptions of stolen horses (or those ridden by highwaymen) in the *Gazette* were particularly detailed and often successful, explaining Flanders' fear of the periodical; as well as the reward they usually promised the bearer the costs involved in returning stolen animals. London was considered such a major market for stolen horses that even where their theft had occurred in the provinces advertisements in the journal were commonly placed. For an example can be considered two from the same edition of the paper in 1692, one announced "stolen or strayed out of the ground of Thomas Leatherland at Shacklewell, one bay gelding above 14 hands, a large blaze in his face, four white feet ... a guinea reward and reasonable charges for each". Another ran "taken away from Mr John West of Sarum in the County of Wilts, (by three highway men) on the 14 instant, about three, in the afternoon, a black gelding about 15 hands high, a pearl in his near eye, saddle spots, a little white about the fetterlocks on both legs behind: ... two guineas reward and charges".[157]

In the end Flanders and her governess had to abandon the horse at an inn and even sent a note by a porter to the owner's tavern giving its whereabouts. They decided not to wait until the owner had published and offered a reward and then claim it for themselves because of the risks attendant on this. They were not unique in this; Jenny Diver, who was a famous woman pickpocket in the 1730s, was nervous of returning even conventional stolen goods for the rewards that were offered on them, as she felt the injured parties were likely to use the opportunity to "take particular notice of your person". She much preferred using a regular commercial fence who was well known to her.[158] However, this option was not available for animals. Similarly, then as now, secret "lockups"

---

157. *London Gazette*, January 23, 1692.
158. McIntosh M., "Thieves and Fences: Markets and Power in Professional Crime", *Brit. J. Criminol.*, vol.16, no.3 (1976), p.258.

were frequently employed to hide the bulkier proceeds of crime, awaiting disposal; for example Sheppard and his partner, the infamous "Blueskin" hired a stable near the Horse Ferry, in Westminster, in which they deposited much of their stolen goods till they could dispose of them at a good price. They used this to store one hundred and eight yards of woollen cloth which they had stolen from one William Kneebone. However, these were obviously of no value in concealing a live horse.

Flanders problem was that though the horse was "booty to those that had understood it", disposing of stolen horses was a very difficult, and indeed professional business. It is, consequently, not surprising that she would have had trouble disposing of the animal. Horse theft was usually a specialist form of crime in the eighteenth century; it was often the province of gangs who operated over considerable distances using "safe" inns, stables and specialist receivers. For example, the notorious "Poulter" gang stole horses in the north of England for sale in the south and vice versa. The animals would also often be cleverly disguised, especially by gypsies, who were considered experts at this. Even horse colouring could be changed by experienced professionals (to an extent, it has been remarked, this was the eighteenth century equivalent of new number plates in modern car theft). Indeed, horse theft, along with "coining" was one type of crime which often seems to have necessarily produced a considerable degree of professionalism and organization amongst its adherents, wherever it occurred.

Although London was a popular market for stolen horses, casual thieves were likely to be detected because they attempted to sell the animals too close to home and too soon after they had stolen them.[159]. There was little popular or judicial sympathy for horse thieves, who would normally be sentenced to death, without having much prospect of a reprieve and transportation. The explanation for this attitude lay in the fact that such crime usually involved considerable sophistication and was often done for significant financial gain rather than out of any necessity, as well as being socially destructive in undermining the only method of

---

159. Beattie, J.M., *ibid.*, p.169.

long distance land transport.

Flanders' Involvement with Coiners

Flanders next became briefly involved with coiners of money. However, they wanted her to embark on the most dangerous part of the venture, namely, working the die, where "... detention or capture meant certain death, and that at a stake." Though they promised her "mountains of gold and silver" she refused to do it.

Flanders' awareness of the dreadful penalty for forgery fully explains her reluctance in this situation. Counterfeiting and forgery were viewed as high treason, and thus, like treason, subject to a special regime of execution. Unlike men, who would be hung, disembowelled and "quartered", females would experience the "mitigation" of being burnt alive at the stake. Throughout the century a number of women met this fate at Tyburn; for example, Barbara Spencer in 1721, whose widely publicized death in the year he wrote *Moll Flanders* may well have been on Defoe's mind.

Barbara Spencer had been foolish enough to progress from being the "utterer" of forged coins (that is the person who passed them on) for which she had been previously fined and imprisoned (presumably having been found in possession of only a small quantity) to being the actual "coiner" for which she was convicted, strangled and burnt. She initially showed little concern when sentenced to be burnt at Tyburn, on July 5, 1721, for the offence "... while under sentence of death, she behaved in the most indecent and turbulent manner; nor could she be convinced that she had been guilty of any crime in making a few shillings". At Tyburn however "... she was much interrupted by the mob throwing stones and dirt at her", perhaps itself a reflection of popular resentment at the possibility that they could be the losers if successfully passed a "silver" coin that was made of base metal.[160] As late as 1789 one Phoebe Harris was burnt in front of

---

160. Wilkinson, G.T., *The Newgate Calendar* (1816), Cardinal (1991), p.98.

20,000 people. Sometimes, as well as being surrounded by faggots the women would be smeared with tar to facilitate combustion. As the eighteenth century advanced the punishment was almost invariably mitigated by strangling the women with ropes before the flames reached them, though this was not always successful.[161] In 1726 the murderer (she had committed the "petty treason" of arranging her husband's killing) Catherine Hayes' executioner prematurely dropped the ropes that were fastened round her neck (to strangle her) when the flames reached his fingers, as a consequence she was burnt alive, screaming and kicking the faggots from around her as it occurred.[162] Even Blackstone, writing in 1768, thought that the punishment was rather extreme as the offence was not really motivated by antipathy to the Crown, "this method of reasoning is a little overstrained", forgery he felt being practised for private gain rather than out of "disaffection to the sovereign".[163]

Forgery and offences against the currency were, however, a major and ongoing social problem at the time, perhaps explaining the harshness of the punishment. At the end of the century, in 1795, the Duc de Brunswick could note that *les faux shilling et les faux pence courent d'une manière indécente, je n'ai presque jamais change une guinee sans en recevoir* (in *Promenade autour de la Grande-Bretagne)*.[164] By then, this had been going on for centuries. There were a great variety of different types of such crime, and manners of committing them. These could range, at the lowest level, from clipping the edges of gold coins to remove a small sliver of the metal or shaking them in a bag, to produce gold dust, up to more sophisticated techniques such as gilding low value coins with precious metal. In 1679, one man who was indicted for counterfeiting "... confessed that he had brass money of a friend of his to boyl for him, that

161. Radzinowicz, L., *ibid.*, vol.1, p.212 and Laurence, L., *A History of Capital Punishment* (1960), p.9.
162. She had committed the "petty treason" of murdering her husband, and then cutting his body up, with two male accomplices. One of these died of jail fever while awaiting execution and the other was hanged at Tyburn.
163. Blackstone, W., Commentaries (1765), vol.4, p.88.
164. Page 106, quoted Radzinowicz, *ibid.*, vol.1, p.707.

thereby it might be brought to a passable complexion". Given that he had not physically altered the coins, this posed considerable legal problems; however, after detailed "directions from the bench" the jury found that it fell under the appropriate statute and the man was condemned to be hung, drawn and quartered (like others going for this manner of execution he would also be drawn to Tyburn on a sledge rather than in a cart).[165] However, the technicalities of this area of the law (as with others), were usually respected by the courts if they favoured the defendant; in another case in the same sessions, where a man accused of counterfeiting the King's coins was found to have been forging Spanish "pistols" (the main Spanish gold coin), "... they not being proved against him as the coin of our King, the prisoner was brought in not guilty".

So dangerous and ruthless did Flanders consider the gang of coiners that had approached her to be, that she pretended to "relish" their proposals, and promised to meet them again, but did not attend any subsequent meetings with them because she felt that if she had seen them again, and then not complied with their proposals "though I had declined it with the greatest assurance of secrecy in the world, they would have gone near to have murdered me, to make sure work, and make themselves easy, as they call it".

Theft at St Katharine's

Flanders resolved that coining and horse stealing were not in her line of business. She also rejected several proposals to join a gang of specialist housebreakers. She was, however, willing to accompany a woman to St Katharine's, where they went "... on pretence to buy goods that were privately got on shore by some Dutch people". There were many Dutchmen, mostly quite poor, in this area of London at the turn of the seventeenth century. As previously mentioned, the port area of the Thames near to, and in, Wapping was, and continued to be for many years,

---

165. OBSP, April 30 - May 2, 1679, p.7.

a thieves' paradise as huge quantities of goods were unloaded in the world's busiest port (in 1705 almost 160,000 tons from abroad alone). This problem became more serious as the expansion of trade continued and was only to be partially resolved by the new enclosed docks built at the start of the nineteenth century (surrounded by a ditch and a high wall), and the advent of Patrick Colquhoun's River Police in 1800 (the first proper centralized police force in London).

On two or three occasions Flanders visited a warehouse at this location, where she saw a large quantity of prohibited goods (probably similar to the Flanders' lace, that she disclosed to the Customs officer), and with her companion managed to steal three pieces of Dutch black silk. She was subsequently unsuccessful when she went there alone, and ceased to visit because the owners began to suspect something was "amiss".

Theft in the Strand

Another opportunity presented itself to Flanders when the Queen passed by, in procession, in the Strand, distracting a shopkeeper and her maid, who were in the process of showing some lace to a group of ladies. Flanders swiftly slipped the paper of lace into her pocket and quickly walked away "... so the lady milliner paid dear enough for her gaping after the Queen". She used a coach to make good her escape from the scene. This was as well, because shortly afterwards the milliner's maid and five or six others, came running down the street, shouting "robbed" and "lace" (rather than "stop thief" because nobody was identified running away). Luckily the coachman had already set off and she was safe with her £20 worth of stolen fabric. If the 1718 pamphlet of *A Prisoner in Newgate* is to be believed, pickpockets, or "street files" would take great care to establish the times and dates of events, such as a royal procession or an execution in advance, being greatly assisted in this by the growing number of media announcements of these occasions. Crowds always provided large numbers of prospective targets and an ideal environment in which to operate and escape.

Theft from a Young Woman

The next day, Flanders spotted a well-to-do girl of 12 or 13 years old, and a young woman escorting her that she thought was her sister; the former was wearing a particularly fine gold watch and a necklace of pearls. She spoke to their footman, who was nearby, ascertained their identities, and learnt that the young lady was governess to the whole family. Flanders approached this woman and pretended, on the basis of the knowledge that she had apprised from the footman, to be a family acquaintance herself, something which her graces, as well as the fact that she "was well dressed, and had [her] gold watch as well as she [the `target']" facilitated. Luckily for her, on this same day the King was passing by to the Parliament House. The young ladies ran to watch this and Flanders helped them up onto the edge of the boards beside the Mall, and simultaneously helped herself to the gold watch. She made her escape by running with the crowd while pretending to watch the King, though she had some regrets about not taking the necklace of pearls as well. She thus safely avoided the "... great outbreak in the park" which the girl made as soon as she missed her watch. Such outbursts were a real danger to thieves and regularly successful in attracting help, especially if a fleeing man could be identified. Much more, it appears, than today, many bystanders in large (and respectable) parts of the city were willing to "have a go" and become involved in catching felons. This was something that John Jones and John Lloyd discovered to their cost in 1724 when, with two others, they robbed a servant man of his wig (they were initially disappointed that he was almost devoid of money "what a plague signifies these half pence? Let's take the Cull's wig"). The victim called out a fellow servant and pursued them to Leather Lane, with the assistance of a local watchman. There he "knock'd down Lloyd and seized Jones by the Collar". When the former managed to run off he was quickly re-arrested "... being followed by an outcry of stop thief! he was quickly taken".[166]

---

166. *Select Trials at the Sessions-House in the Old Bailey*, vol.II, 1724-1732 (printed 1735) for J. Wilford, p.20.

London, especially the City, was a labyrinthine warren of streets at this time, which facilitated escape for street criminals like Flanders, provided they could put a small amount of distance between themselves and the scene of the crime. Behind the main streets were "inner areas, where alleys, courts, yards, and closes meet each other in an inscrutable topographical jigsaw".[167] In any period this would present enormous policing problems. With the rather limited policing available in the early eighteenth century they were almost insuperable at times. Later in the century, Henry Fielding expressed the view that parts of London could have been purpose built for concealing criminals, because of the "... vast addition of their suburbs, the great irregularity of their buildings, the immense number of lanes, alleys, courts and bye-places".[168] As the inherently rather disorganized and uncontrolled popular "hue and cry" was the basic mode of pursuit of fleeing criminals at the time, the potential problems are obvious.

A Gaming House

Ever willing to try new pastures, Flanders next ventured into a completely new field. She visited a gaming house at Covent Garden, and placed wagers on behalf of a gentleman there whose eye she had caught. Her luck was "in" and she made a considerable amount of money at this, the bulk of which she returned to the gentleman, but every now and then she surreptitiously "conveyed some [of the stock] into [her] own pocket". Additionally, the man rewarded her with half of the profits that were made, his generosity making her sorry for her earlier theft and giving her a total of 73 guineas. However, she subsequently took her governess' prudent advice not to play again as she appreciated that were she to do so she might quickly lose "... all the rest of what [she] had got".

Gambling was a popular diversion for all social classes in late

167. Summerson, J., *Georgian London* (1978), p.25.
168. *Inquiry, ibid.*, p.83.

seventeenth and eighteenth century England; the wealthy favouring lotteries, stocks (very volatile at the time) and cards (in this case it may have been "Hazard"), the poor often "Crown and Anchor".[169] Blackstone was later to note that it was almost a mania and that while there were numerous laws forbidding or regulating it, these were little enforced, because those "... against gaming are not so deficient, as ourselves and our magistrates in putting those laws in execution".[170] Occasionally some gamblers were unlucky, especially if they were from the lower "orders" of society and were too public about their gaming, and were punished for it, but this was very rare.[171] The sums involved could be enormous, literally thousands of pounds, especially at the new gentlemen's clubs of the time, such as Whites. Government measures to combat the evil were not helped by the state running its own lottery, which was adopted by Parliament to raise revenue in 1709 (in 1713 a fortunate ticket-holder won £36,000).[172]

Flanders' Excursion to the Provinces

Faced with her criminal "trade" having fallen off during the "rambling time" of year in the summer, Flanders reconsidered her options. The reason for this being necessary was that "the gentlemen being most of them gone out of town" to Tunbridge and Epsom (then highly fashionable resorts for the gentry), and the population of prosperous people in the city

---

169. Plumb, J.H., *England in the Eighteenth Century* (1950), p.13.
170. Blackstone, *ibid.*, vol.iv, p.173.
171. Henry Fielding in his *Inquiry*, s.iii, felt that gambling was "a school which most highwaymen of great eminence have been bred" but prudently, as always in his study, ignored the habits of the upper classes, "I have only the inferior part of mankind under my consideration". He appreciated that with "the great who are beyond the reach of any unless capital offences" it would be wasted effort. He also felt that upper class vice was less dangerous to society than its spread to "the useful part of mankind".
172. Rude, G., *ibid.*, p.71.

being as a result, rather thin, so were lucrative possible targets for theft from the person. This reduction in potential victims during the high summer season was a theme covered by Defoe elsewhere in his work; in *Street Robberies Consider'd*, for example, the narrator noted that "one summer in particular, I found trading [stealing] very bad in town, for all the world had followed the Queen to the Bath".

Flanders decided to go out to the provinces with a "gang" of other criminals, in particular to Bury Fair in Suffolk (a popular annual carnival). However, she was disappointed to find that except for "mere picking of pockets, there was little worth meddling in", and also appreciated that were something to go wrong, escape was significantly harder in such a small town, when compared to the ease with which pursuit could be shaken off in London's warren of streets. All that she profited from this trip, was a gold watch from the fair and a small parcel of linen from Cambridge. Her method of obtaining this latter material was an "old bite", which she felt would not have worked with a sophisticated London shopkeeper, but was worth attempting on a country one.[173]

An "Old Bite"

To obtain the material Flanders ordered £7 of fine Holland linen and some other goods at a linen draper's shop, and asked for them to be sent to an inn where she pretended to being lodged for the night. She agreed with the draper to pay cash on delivery. The draper sent the goods, via a messenger, to the named inn, where one of Flanders' gang, pretending to be her servant, informed him that she was asleep but would be awake in half an hour, and that if he left the goods there and returned later he would have his money. When he did so they immediately decamped with the fabric and goods.

Defoe was well aware not only of the ploys of shoplifters but also of those who would abuse the credit of shopkeepers. In *A Caveat for*

---

173. A "bite" was a contemporary expression for any kind of confidence trick.

Shopkeepers (1728), he attempted to summarize a number of basic precautions that could be taken to combat the mischief, though, like much of his other practical advice, most was mundane and common sense, "beware of all persons in riding hoods and great coats, or cloaks for sometimes thieves have the appearance of gentlemen". This was especially "if more than one comes together". With regard to goods, the obvious advice with customers was to "shew them but one piece". Additionally, he opined that it was necessary to "be cautious how you send goods home unpaid for" advice that the provincial draper appears not to have been aware of.

A Trip to Harwich

From Cambridge, Flanders went to Ipswich and then on to Harwich, taking up in an inn and pretending that she had recently arrived from Holland (then as now the port handled a considerable Dutch trade). She intended to prey on prosperous foreigners that came ashore there. However, "pickings" were thin, though she succeeded in stealing a portmanteau from the room of a gentleman when the footman guarding it was drunk and asleep on the bed. Flanders was concerned that she would not be able to escape with such a heavy case, and was intending to return it to the room and leave it where she found it, when she noticed that the Ipswich ferry was about to leave. She quickly took her clothes and things from the inn, along with the case, and took the boat. At Ipswich the customs officers insisted on opening and searching the trunk for possible contraband. Flanders consented, having first explained that it belonged to her husband, as, although she had not had a chance to find out what was inside it, she knew that it must be a man's possessions. The portmanteau contained Dutch ducatoons (coins), periwigs, razors, washballs (scented soaps), perfumes, and some French pistolets (also coins), a very valuable haul. At this point in her travels, Flanders decided to return to London and her governess. Having "taken the substance" out of the trunk (probably mainly the foreign coins and perfumes) she abandoned the "lumber" in an inn like any modern bag thief. She then

hired a horse to take her to Colchester, where her early life had been
passed, and then took passage in a wagon to London, as she "would not
venture being seen in the Harwich coaches", for fear of meeting the
Dutchman from whom she had stolen the trunk. Although the theft from
this man had been lucrative, Flanders resolved that the provinces were
not for her and that she would not go on any more "country rambles".

Flanders' Narrow Escape

On the Christmas day following her return, Flanders went out looking for
"work" (Christmas had only been reinstated as a festival, following its
banning during the interregnum, after the Restoration in 1660; it was not
unusual for people to be "abroad" on such a day). When passing a
silversmith's in Forster Lane (a street where many silver and goldsmiths
congregated at this time) she saw a tempting target - an apparently empty
shop and a good deal of loose silver plate in the window. Flanders' first
legitimate arrest came when, flushed by her previous "success
unparalleled", she entered the silversmith's and was about to attempt to
steal some of the plate at which point she was noticed by the smith's
neighbour and subsequently detained by him. Shopkeepers do appear to
have exhibited considerable solidarity in "looking out" for each other. The
records frequently narrate how thieves were arrested by such people. Thus,
when Anne Smith, Mary Roly and Elizabeth Wolf, three "notorious shoplifts" were apprehended in 1681 while stealing silk, it was because they
had been "observed by an opposite neighbour", who had raised the alarm
as a result of which they were "persued, and apprehended all three".[174]

Flanders showed her customary aplomb in trying to talk her way out
of the situation as she had "... always most courage when [she] was most
in danger." Fortunately, at this difficult point "Sir T.B., an Alderman of
the City, and Justice of the Peace" came by and the smith invited him to
decide the issue.

---

174. OBSP, July 6-9, 1681, p.2.

The Social and Educational Background of the Justices

The Lord Mayor of London and 22 of his 24 Aldermen (effectively the government of the Square Mile) also acted, *ex officio,* as JPs for the City, providing a comparatively efficient service compared to the rest of the "Metropolis", and helping to meet some of the increasing problems of inadequate judicial provision in London. From as early as 1737, they were taking turns to sit at the Guildhall from 11.00 am to 2.00 pm to deal with judicial business. However, from a much earlier date they were already heavily involved in judicial matters. Thus, in 1670 George Fox noted in his *Journal* that he had been brought in front of the Lord Mayor, Sir Samuel Starling, in his official house, for investigation as to possible involvement in seditious meetings, though "after some more discourse he took our names and the places where we lodged, and at length set us at liberty".

The judicial (as opposed to administrative) function of JPs, sitting without a jury, in "petty sessions" (that is the power to try criminals and to sentence them), is largely the result of developments over the past 300 years. JPs' powers in this area were extended gradually from Tudor times onwards, these changes slowly accelerating in the eighteenth century.[175] Throughout much of the early history of this expansion, however, the complexion of the Bench and the legal climate in which their proceedings were conducted meant that their status as laymen judging not only issues of fact but also points of law presented relatively few problems.

Of course, lay justices, especially those in London, have always been subject to a degree of criticism and even ridicule. In literary form this has been illustrated in novels by, for example, Henry Fielding in *Tom Jones* or *Amelia*, in which work he would say of one JP that "to speak the truth plainly the justice was never indifferent in a cause but when he could get nothing on either side". This same fictional magistrate was also somewhat prejudiced: "Sirrah, your tongue betrays your guilt. You are an Irishman, and that is always sufficient evidence with me". Additionally, some dramatic characters, such as Shakespeare's "Justice Shallow" have

---

175. Baker, J.H., *English Legal History*, 3rd edn (1990), p.584.

147

received a similar degree of ridicule from playwrights. At a more serious level, there have been the parliamentary criticisms of men like Edmund Burke, who was to allege in the late eighteenth century that the JPs of Middlesex (effectively at this point, the bulk of London), were "the scum of the earth, carpenters, brickmakers ... some ... of infamous characters". Also in this vein, Henry Brougham was later to say in Parliament, in 1828, that "there is not a worse constituted tribunal on the face of the earth than that at which summary convictions on the Game Laws take place". However, this attitude is a little severe if applied to all JPs active in the country around 1700.

In the early modern period it should be remembered that their lay status was certainly not as genuine as it is today. For example, the widespread prevalence of the habit of spending a period at the Inns of Court amongst the gentry (from whom the justices were largely drawn) meant that in Kent, in the 1680s, 40 per cent had attended one of the Inns, even if not called to the Bar. Even in 1761 the figure was still 18 per cent.[176] However, this was probably much less likely to apply in London, for social reasons, perhaps explaining Fielding's lament in *Amelia* that "I own I have been sometimes inclined to think that this office of a Justice of Peace requires some knowledge of the law". Interestingly, this novel suggests that even then "unlearned" JPs were heavily dependent on their court clerks to advise them as to the law. More importantly, however, the cultural and legal environment of summary courts was totally different to that of today.

The JPs were historically local gentry of some importance and "substance". In 1774 the justices Qualification Act formalized the long established principle that JPs should be men of property, by requiring possession of an estate to the yearly value of £400. The following year another Act amended this to include occupation of a house rated at £100 (the property qualification was only fully abolished in 1906).[177] This meant, in practice, that in the eighteenth century only three per cent of

176. Landau, N., *The Justice of the Peace*, p.379.
177. Page, Leo, *Justice of the Peace*, 2nd edn (1947), p.23.

the adult male population could, even in theory, become JPs.[178] In rural areas (most of the country) this was undoubtedly also the reality. However, to accuse these JPs of being inherently "unfair" at this time would be harsh. Even radical historians accept that the JP in this period often emerges, on close scrutiny, as a paternalist, though he was also someone who, where necessary, was sometimes willing to collude with fellow landowners and manufacturers to effect convictions of those deemed to be "trouble makers".[179]

However, while the higher courts, such as the Assizes and even the Quarter Sessions administered by JPs with a jury, were less arbitrary, and had, even at this time fairly well established court procedures, the whole tenor of petty sessions was relatively informal. It is probably true that the JPs at this time were fairly "robust" in their judicial functioning, doing justice according to their lights, and not always excessively concerned with legal niceties. However, after 1670 this was remedied to some extent when it became common to provide an appeal from some of their decisions to the courts of Quarter Sessions (which kept the matter in the county, and allowed for the correction of obvious mistakes); additionally, the court of King's Bench exercised some supervisory functions over these inferior courts.

Against the periodic criticism of the JPs, it should also be remembered that the justices played a crucial, and sometimes demanding, role in English society, and that there were already a considerable variety of instructive books published, and widely purchased, in Defoe's day to assist the JPs in their work (one of the earliest, Dalton's *Country Justice,* had come out in 1618 and run through numerous editions since that time). There were also risks in the office, mistakes by poor justices could be personally very expensive for them. A 1730 manual even expressly warned JPs in London who were not rich that they could be sued heavily for some types of error, while the magistrate, Sir Thomas de Veil, was able to note that the large numbers of attorneys around the Old Bailey

---

178. Hay, D., *Crime and Justice in Eighteenth and Nineteenth Century England*, p.46.
179. Hay, D., *Albion's Fatal Tree* (1977), p.53.

were always eager to "entangle" a justice so that he could later be sued before the "Judges" (in the Royal courts).[180] It is also important to remember that the JPs had a huge range of heavy responsibilities for non-criminal matters as well; Burns' *The Justice of the Peace and Parish Officer*, a classic eighteenth century work on their responsibilities, and one which also ran to numerous editions, listed over 200 headings, ranging from supervision of the Highways and Herring Fisheries to Hackney coaches and chairs, Fires in London, Bread Prices and the Militia. Their duties brought them into contact with issues concerning crime, local government, revenue collection, licensing, the military , religion, property, food supply, employment and marriage.[181] England could not have functioned without their work.

The Trading Justices

However, although in theory JPs were men of substantial property, local standing, reputation, and, ideally, education, in some parts of the Metropolis, outside the City of London itself, and North of the river (ie, Middlesex and the City of Westminster), as well as in the "borough" south of the Thames, problems in finding suitable JPs, willing to undertake such a demanding and thankless task, were to lead to the infamous "trading justices", men of relatively low social status who made their incomes from the court fees that they collected for providing judicial services.[182] This was not surprising given that the position had become one which in 1780 the Duke of Newcastle was able to describe as an "exceeding troublesome office" which it was "impossible to persuade gentlemen of family and fortune to undertake". Areas like Tower Hamlets with few resident men of "quality" even in the early 1700s, were entirely in the provenance of such magistrates. Even in some parts of the provinces there were potential

---

180. Landau, *ibid.*, p.355.
181. Holdsworth, Sir William, *A History of English Law* (1938), vol.x, p.162.
182. Not all JPs taking fees were corrupt. However, it should also be remembered that Sir Thomas de Veil, the reforming Bow Street magistrate before the Fieldings, lived largely on his court fees.

recruitment problems despite the power and prestige involved. A shortage of other suitable candidates during the eighteenth century may have encouraged the increasing numbers of clerical JPs (though the unprecedented move into the Church of upper class men in the century, who would always have been likely JPs, no doubt also explains this). This was not a realistic source of recruitment in the Metropolis.

Trading justices were frequently accused of taking bribes to license alehouses and to ignore the presence of gaming establishments in their area. They were also accused of encouraging quarrels amongst local people so that they could bind them over and exact the appropriate fee for doing so. It appears that four of the seven justices who returned the highest amount of recognizances (binding witnesses to appear) at Middlesex Quarter Sessions in 1737 were trading justices (they received special fees for this work).[183] However, it should be remembered that these men also provided a much needed legal service, and not all of them were totally corrupt in their dealings. Henry Fielding's predecessor, Sir Thomas de Veil, was effectively a "trading justice", albeit a relatively honest one; he wrote in this connexion "as to justices' fees or perquisites, the best rule is to observe strictly the oath of office; which tells you what you may safely take yourself or suffer your clerk to receive for you".

De Veil, who was the leading Metropolitan magistrate from 1729 to 1747, was also a justice in four neighbouring counties and enjoyed significant treasury grants from the government. In many ways he laid the judicial groundwork that was later built upon by Henry Fielding. Fielding also continued to receive court fees for legal services, after his appointment, as well as treasury grants, though he felt that he lost considerable amounts of money "by composing, instead of inflaming, the quarrels of porters and beggars ... and refusing to take a shilling from a man who most undoubtedly would not have had another left".[184] Despite this personal restraint he readily admitted that some contemporary urban JPs regularly did all of those things (he was writing in 1754). Fielding was

---

183. Landau, N., *ibid.*, p.185.
184. Fielding, H., *The Voyage to Lisbon* (1754), Everyman edn (1960), p.192.

certainly considerably more careful in what fees he accepted than Thomas de Veil had been (the latter had had a taste for luxury as well as four wives in succession and 25 legitimate children to support).[185]

As a consequence of these Metropolitan problems, Edmund Burke was only slightly exaggerating the judicial problems in London when he made his scathing comments while speaking in Parliament towards the end of the century (he was also heavily influenced by the JPs' apparently dilatory performance during the five days of the "Gordon Riots" of 1780, effectively only brought to an end by extensive recourse to the military who had been ordered not to wait on their commands). However, problems with the JPs were by no means totally new in Burke's day.

At the start of the century, Defoe himself had identified the Middlesex justices as being one area and group of JPs whose conduct was "especially bad", for a variety of reasons, along with those of Essex and some other locations. He felt, perhaps with some exaggeration, that generally the "conduct of the justices in most parts is intolerably scandalous" with consequent deleterious social effects, as "wherever there happens to be moderate justices the people live easy".[186] In 1709, Jonathan Swift had also joined the chorus of criticism of the justices in the Metropolis when claiming that "... such men are often put into the Commission of the Peace whose interest it is that virtue should be utterly banished from among us ... these worthy magistrates, instead of lessening enormities, are the occasions of twice as much as there would be without them".[187]

The eventual cure for this problem, based on the developments initiated at Bow Street in 1739 by Thomas de Veil, and built on subsequently by his successors, Henry and John Fielding, from 1748, lay in establishing the Metropolitan stipendiary magistrates, professional magistrates supported by subventions from the government. This was especially so after 1792, when police offices were established at half a dozen locations in the Metropolis, with a salaried justice permanently

---

185. Ascoli, D., *The Queen's Peace: the Origins and Development of the Metropolitan Police 1829-1979* (1979), p.33.
186. Letter to Robert Harley, November 6, 1705, Harris, G.H., *ibid.*, p.113.
187. *A Project for the Advancement of Religion and the Reformation of Manners*, p.15.

available (there were usually three at each), effectively bringing the trading justices to an end. Even today the concentration of stipendiary magistrates in inner London and the big cities suggest that the "normal" system of lay JPs does not work totally satisfactorily in such an environment.

Other Courts with Jurisdiction over Petty Crime

It should also be observed that even in the late 1600s and early 1700s, as well as the JPs' judicial work (whether in petty or Quarter Sessions), there were still the relics of other court systems possessing some types of petty quasi-criminal jurisdiction, and running in parallel with the petty Sessions, Quarter Sessions and Assizes courts in the provinces, or their London equivalents. In rural and suburban areas, there could still be found the survivors of the local manorial and leet courts, though these were of much reduced significance, having lost power steadily since the 1500s. Even in some urban areas, as late as the early eighteenth century, some of their equivalents, such as the Court Leet of the urban manor of the Liberty of the Savoy or the Westminster Court of Burgesses heard cases involving bawdy houses, disorderly alehouses and selling using false measures. There were also, still in existence, the ecclesiastical courts such as the Arch Deaconry courts or the higher Diocesan courts, which had a jurisdiction over many offences of immorality and church observance. These religious courts had never recovered from their prolonged abolition during the English Civil War and were only a shadow of their former selves after the 1660s.[188] They were further damaged by the Toleration Act of 1689. The most important of the London ones, such as the Consistory court, were centred round Doctors' Commons, which had also been the home since 1511 of the small number of English "civilians" (those lawyers learned in ecclesiastical law and those other branches of

---

188. Ingram, M., *Church Courts, Sex and Marriage in England, 1570-1640* (1987), p.374.

law, such as Admiralty, which drew heavily on a Roman Law tradition).[189] At least till 1689 some types of offence involving immorality, such as keeping disorderly alehouses and allowing tippling or the opening of shops on the Sabbath were prosecuted in the Consistory court, though its process was considered slow and inefficient and its penal sanctions weak.[190] However, by the time Defoe was writing his novels, their control of even minor types of "conventional crime" was very small and of almost no significance, the field having been largely left to the justices.[191]

Sir T.B.'s Decision

Although the formal Sessions of the Peace for the City of London were heard at Newgate or the Guildhall, Sir "T.B." agreed to hold an informal, impromptu, in situ but nevertheless "full hearing" of Flanders' case. He decided that she was innocent and the neighbour labouring under a mistake.

JPs did, in very limited circumstances, have the legal power to dispose of some very minor cases "on the spot" in the seventeenth and eighteenth centuries. If they heard someone swearing a profane oath or saw someone drunk on the highway they could impose a modest penalty (usually a fine or short period in the stocks) summarily, though the exercise of this power must have often been impractical in London. In theory, JPs were supposed to report such convictions at the next Quarter Sessions or their equivalents, but in practice this was rare.[192] Certainly though, a JP had no power to hear a theft case in such circumstances; had he decided that there was a case to answer, Flanders would have had to be brought before a

---

189. Manchester, M., "The Reform of the Ecclesiastical Courts", *American Journal of Legal History* (1966), vol.10, p.53.
190. Shoemaker, R.B., *ibid.*, (1991), p.20.
191. In the sixteenth century they were an important part of the criminal justice system, ignored by historians of the secular courts at their peril.
192. Sir Thomas Skyrme, *History of the Justices of the Peace* (1994), p.484.

sitting magistrate.[193] However, it is not surprising that the shopkeeper and the assembled crowd sought the decision of the Alderman. While it may seem strange that a justice should be asked to mediate in the street in such an informal situation, it appears that this was by no means an unusual occurrence (except with regard to the gravity of the offence with which Flanders was accused). Many misdemeanours, particularly in rural areas, but also it appears in towns, were dealt with informally by JPs exercising their offices and status to resolve disputes, especially assaults and public order offences, without there being recourse to formal court proceedings. According to law, in some circumstances dealing with felonies in this way, arranging a "settlement" between parties, was strictly forbidden (being termed the "compounding of felonies"), however it still probably occurred on occasion, and such regular mediation provided the social background in which the incident between Flanders and the silversmith could be dealt with in such a way.[194] Contemporary popular songs also indicate the widespread willingness to have recourse to the justices when there was a legal dispute, whatever its nature. For example, a popular one concerned that between a vintner and a fruit girl from Islington to whom he refused to pay five pounds rent, as previously promised, after he had slept with her:

> "This maid she made no more ado,
> But to a justice went;
> And unto him she made her moan,
> Who did her case lament."[195]

Flanders was released once she had made a purchase of silver spoons (her pretended explanation for entering the silversmiths). This was an explanation borne out by the fact that Flanders was carrying more than 20 guineas when stopped, her normal custom. She was by no means

---

193. The word "magistrate" as an alternative for "justice" was an eighteenth century innovation.
194. Shoemaker, R.B., *Prosecution and Punishment* (1991), p.42.
195. Songs from Thomas D'Urfey, "Pills to Purge Melancholy", edition of 1719.

unique in her apparent affluence and elegant "style" of operations, several other well spoken women thieves employed it; Mary Jones, who was hanged in 1691 for stealing considerable quantities of fine lace from shops, usually arrived at the retailers' premises dressed as a lady, and carried in a Sedan chair![196] The danger of carrying or going after valuable items that could not be justified by apparent social status (as well as the success of advertisements for stolen goods) was also alluded to by Defoe's fictional narrator in *Street Robberies Consider'd* (1728) who noted that his mother having stolen a watch "but going to dispose of it, the goldsmith suspecting her, secured her; put an advertisement in the news papers, and the right owner soon prov'd it down right thieving". As a consequence his mother went "to St Tyburn where she made a very comfortable-end".[197] This was a well documented contemporary situation; in 1680, one Walter Gilman had broken into a house using a "picklock key", stealing a gold watch. Unfortunately for him, he was slow in disposing of the time-piece, and by the time he tried to do so, the victim had "put out bills for the staying of such goods". As a result he was detained when he tried to sell it, the loser having had "notice from a watchmaker that the watch was bought to be sold or pawned and that he had stopt the party".[198] Honest tradesmen would be put on their guard by someone who obviously did not have the resources to justify the possession of so valuable an item. However, Flanders' luck was finally about to run out.

---

196. Beattie, J.M., *ibid.*, p.65.
197. Page 24.
198. OBSP, April 26-28, 1680, p.2.

Chapter 5

Arrest and Conviction

"The hungry Judges soon the sentence sign,
And wretches hang that jury-men may dine."
Alexander Pope, The Rape of the Lock (1714).

An Attempt at Housebreaking

Only three days after the incident at the silversmith's, and nothing chastened by her close escape or, as she phrased it, "not at all made cautious by my former danger as I us'd to be", Moll Flanders attempted to enter a private dwelling house, with a view to stealing two pieces of flowery brocaded silk, which she had seen on display. She was arrested by two ferocious female servants "two fiery dragons cou'd not have been more furious than they were" who speedily summoned a constable to the scene.

As previously mentioned, one potential explanation, that has been advanced for the expanding significance of burglary as a crime in the eighteenth (and even more so in the nineteenth) century, is the existence of greater opportunity structures based on the ever wider availability of valuable consumer goods. While as a general theory there are deficiencies in this, as an explanation for increased burglary in the houses of middle ranking people it does have significant strengths. The apparent greater general wealth was well remarked by contemporaries. For example, Bishop Berkeley was to note in the eighteenth century, householders of middling status were increasingly purchasing goods that had hitherto been the province of the rich and upper orders of society, for example: valuable prints, pewter, Spode or Royal Derby china, silverware, expensive fabrics, etc. This belief in a greater general prosperity and possession of material goods had been present from at least the late seventeenth century, and was founded on economic reality. One commentator of that time even confidently asserting that "... we have more wealth now, than ever we had at any time before the restauration (*sic*) of his sacred Majestie".[1] The anonymous writer went on to claim that increasingly "our houses be built like palaces, over what they were in the last age, and abound with plenty of costly furniture; and rich jewels to be very common". This was certainly the situation in Flanders' case, as the house was clearly that of a person of middle status (a weaver's broker), someone who two centuries earlier might well not have been in possession of the valuable fabric she attempted to steal.

The records appear to indicate that many, if not most, property cases, like that involving Flanders in this instance, came to court because a thief had been caught red-handed and immediately delivered to a local constable who had been called from his place of abode or work (being the part-time holder of a parish office and not to be confused with later, post-1829, patrolling police officers), and then taken by him before a nearby magistrate. This was important, not least of all because it meant that one traditional, highly effective and commonly used avenue of defence, a false alibi sworn by perjured witnesses, was not open to them; as Henry Fielding noted in his *Inquiry* that "the usual defence of a thief, especially at the Old Bailey, is an alibi".

The justice to whom the apprehended person was brought investigated the matter, took statements and then decided whether to commit the arrested person for trial, before then considering questions of bail. Despite her entreaties to the householder to be released Flanders was taken in front of a justice (within three days of any arrest a prisoner had to be examined

---

1.   "England's Great Happiness", anonymous pamphlet, published in 1677. Printed by "J.M." for Edward Crof.

before a magistrate) and remanded in custody to Newgate prison (the main London prison).

Flanders' pleading with the householder was not necessarily totally pointless. There was a growing reluctance on the part of victims of minor but capital property crimes to prosecute those offences by the middle of the eighteenth century, and even sometimes before. This was something that Henry Fielding in his *Inquiry* identified as a particular problem in the 1750s, attributing it to sentimentality, people being "tender hearted" (as well as to the financial burden of prosecution). Flanders herself alluded to this when speaking to the master of the house and pointing out that "it would be cruel to pursue me to death, and have my blood for the bare attempt". In this case though, although the wife of the broker was "mov'd with compassion and inclined to let me go", and the master was himself weakening, it was to no avail for Flanders. This was despite the fact that she offered to pay the value of the goods that she had unsuccessfully attempted to steal (this would have been "compounding the felony" but appears to have occurred quite widely). The constable's arrival had set matters into motion and led the master to fear that he would be in trouble himself if he did not pursue the matter.

Although the Tudor period had seen the start of a process of extension of JPs' powers, including that to try minor (often rural) offenders, either sitting alone or with one or more other JPs, this process was still in its early stages in the seventeenth and eighteenth centuries. These new summary offences included the embezzlement of materials by employees, wood theft and hedge breaking, as well as offences under the various vagrancy laws. Flanders, however, accused of a serious felony, was certain to go for a jury trial at the Old Bailey.

Efforts on Behalf of Flanders by the Governess

The same night that Flanders went to Newgate she managed to inform her governess of what had happened. Her governess (also, of course, her professional receiver) then attempted to subvert the course of justice by endeavouring to interfere with the prospective evidence. She found the whereabouts of the two fierce servant women who had accosted Flanders, approached them, and proposed to bribe them, even offering £100 to one of them to go away from her mistress. But, perhaps surprisingly, though one weakened temporarily, they were ultimately resolute, although only on wages of three pounds a year as servant maids. It is possible they were incorruptible, or did not trust her to keep her promise, or they may simply have been motivated by the possibility of a reward (there were considerable state and private rewards for the successful prosecution of burglars). As Blackstone later noted "by statute 5 Anne c.31 any person for apprehending and prosecuting a burglar, or felonious housebreaker (or, if killed in the attempt, his executors) shall be entitled to a reward of £40".[2] This possibility may, in part, explain the tremendous dedication to their master's interests displayed by the two maids.

The governess then again approached the master of the house with a view to getting him to drop the prosecution out of pity and compassion "but the man alleged that he was bound to prosecute, and that he should forfeit his recognizance" otherwise. Even the governess' offer to find influential friends that would have this removed from the file did not allay his concerns.

Contemporary System of Private Prosecution

The approach to the master is indicative of the way in which the English system of criminal prosecution at this time was, essentially, based on private initiatives. Indeed it was only in the 1750s that provision was even made, by Parliament, to financially reimburse poor prosecutors who had brought about successful prosecutions. Only in the rarest cases did local constables actively prosecute themselves (though frequently called as witnesses), when such prosecutions did occur it was frequently for "victimless" crimes such as sedition. Similarly in homicide cases, the victim being dead, prosecutions were usually instigated by the coroners and their ancient courts. Generally, however, the victim was the central agent in the criminal process, responsible for instituting the case, and

---

2.   Blackstone, W., *ibid.*, vol.iv, p.292.

carrying it through its various initial stages, deciding whether to report it, whether to value the goods stolen at a capital (usually over 40s. from a house, much less from the person) or non-capital rate, and eventually whether to appear to give evidence, or not.[3] The costs of prosecution were considerable. These would begin as soon as the victim took his complaint to a magistrate. He might have to pay for subpoenas to have witnesses summonsed, and a warrant to have the accused brought in to be examined if he had not already been detained by the victim or a constable (as in Flanders' case). Additionally he (or she) would have to pay fees for the recognizances, in which he and his witnesses would be bound over to give evidence if the magistrate committed the accused to trial (these would be estreated if they failed to appear to give evidence at the trial hearing), and which were introduced as an attempt by the magistrates to prevent prosecutions that would "fold" at trial, something that still remained very common (33 per cent in seventeenth century Essex according to one study).[4] Further fees would be payable to the clerk of the court for drawing up the indictment, as well as to the doorkeeper, the crier and the bailiff. The total cost would be likely to be *at least* 10 shillings to £1 in the eighteenth century, and sometimes significantly more. For this reason Henry Fielding in his *Inquiry* felt that the costs involved were a major deterrent to combating crime. This was partly because many people were so "avaricious" that even if they could afford the money involved they were reluctant to spend it, while others were "necessitous" people who "cannot really afford the cost, however small, together with the loss of time which attends it". As this comment indicates, the basic cost did not include the time, inconvenience and trouble involved in prosecuting, which were considerable, especially for busy tradesmen (many of whom would have recovered their property undamaged if they had also detained a suspect).

Furthermore, as Henry Fielding also appreciated, any system of

3. Interestingly there has, in the past two centuries, been a shift in view as to relative severity of crimes from the person or from houses (not involving violence).
4. Beattie, J.M., *ibid.*, p.41.

criminal justice, that is so reliant on individual initiative is open to illegal pressuring or bribing of prosecutors and witnesses. A clear illustration can be seen in a contemporary note delivered to a weaver in East London who had had his silk destroyed in the loom in a dispute between rival journeymen, and whose wife (significantly) had issued warrants for their (the journeymen's) arrest "if you don't make your wife discharge the warrants your house shall be pul'd down and you all murdered and dead people". Not only could this system lead to honest prosecutors being pressured not to give evidence, but dishonest people could "frame" those against whom they harboured enmity. This was something the magistrates themselves were well aware of; a pamphlet from 1672 recounts how, when a group of men went before a justice in London to lay an information to the effect that one Jonathan Frost had threatened to set the "Jamaica" public house in Wapping on fire, "that design took not" and the justice bid them "go about their business for he perceived it was but malice".[5] Bribery of witnesses was probably even more common. There are frequent references to this in contemporary accounts. Thus, when in 1691 a Mrs Johnson was asked to sell stolen silver and silk on behalf of Nicholas Chappel and another thief, and was brought to court as a witness against them (she herself had successfully denied knowing that the goods were stolen), her evidence was that she was told by them, after their arrest that "if she did swear against them, they were dead men and [they] offered her money to be silent".[6]

Availability of Bail

Flanders was committed to prison. Generally, bail was available for misdemeanours, such as assault, trespass, most forms of cheating and extortion. This is not surprising given that the normal penalties for misdemeanours were relatively small, usually involving fines and corporal punishment, or sometimes small sentences in houses of correction. A

---

5.   "Jonathan Frost, Close Prisoner in the King's Bench, His Case" (1672), anonymous pamphlet, but almost certainly the work of Jonathan Frost.
6.   OBSP, December 6-9, 1694, p.1.

fairly common combined penalty of the period, for a range of different misdemeanour crimes, was the pillory and a short period of imprisonment. Defoe himself had received such a sentence in 1703 for publishing the *Shortest Way with Dissenters* (not a misdemeanour), much the same sentence as Francis Kyte was to receive when convicted of a misdemeanour, namely "uttering a bank note eras'd and altere'd", for which he received sentence to "stand once in the pillory on Tower Hill, to suffer six months imprisonment and to find security for his good behaviour (*sic*) for 12 months". More than 20 years earlier, Defoe had also been fined.[7]

For those accused of felony, where the normal punishment (even if later reprieved) was death, it was very different. Bail was only allowed in extremely restricted circumstances. Justices were encouraged to be very cautious in the granting of it, and a single justice could not do so (to discourage bribery and corruption of magistrates). The distinction between the two main divisions of crimes (not always a very logical one) was crucial.[8] The potential technicality of a bail decision that turned on this difference was later well caught by Henry Fielding in his novel *Amelia*, when Captain Booth, incarcerated in a London prison, noticed a young woman with her aged father. She was inside for the theft of a small loaf, and he was there for receiving the bread. When Booth asked why they had not been bailed, while a notorious perjurer nearby was about to be released on bail, he received the reply that "the offence of the daughter, being felony, is held not to be bailable, whereas perjury is a misdemeanour only". As well as considering the question of bail, the justice(s) before whom Flanders was taken would also have carried out the preliminary examination of her.

Not surprisingly, in Flanders' case, given that she was accused of two serious offences, she was remanded in custody to Newgate prison. Despite Blackstone's belief that an unbailed prisoner, awaiting trial, ought "to be used with the utmost humanity", this was always theory rather than reality,

---

7.   *The Original Half-Penny London Journal*, Tuesday 2, March 1725.
8.   Treason was a numerically much less important third classification.

and she appears to have secured no extra privileges at all.[9] Given the proportion of inmates at Newgate who were on remand pending trial (probably the great majority of non-debtors) it would have been totally impractical to give any such privileges.

Newgate Again

Newgate was the place of Flanders' birth, and also a place of special horror to her, "my very blood chills at the mention of its name". The other inmates, jealous of her long run of success, "triumphed" over her now that she had "come at last" to the "college".[10] They called for brandy and drank to her, but put it all up to her "score", believing that because she had just come to the prison she must have money in her pocket. Additionally, there appears to have been a well established custom called "garnish" whereby new prisoners would purchase drinks or tip older established inmates as well as the turnkeys. In John Gay's satirical portrayal of London's criminal aspects, the *Beggars' Opera,* of 1728, the highwayman MacHeath observes, on his arrival at Newgate, that "the fees here are so many, and so exorbitant, that few fortunes can bear the expense of getting off handsomely, or of dying like a gentleman", while Fielding's Captain Booth in *Amelia* has his coat stripped from his back in another prison because he has no money to pay a crowd of inmates who surround him on his arrival "demanding garnish". John Hall, an inmate of the prison 40 years earlier, confirmed this latter detail. He recorded that the turnkeys, "truncheon officers", first claimed, from the "ordinary" prisoners "six pence apiece, as a privilege belonging to their offices, then they turn him out to the convicts". These established inmates, "like so many crows about a piece of carrion", then also claimed their share of garnish, usually, according to Hall, a total sum of six shillings and six pence, which they

---

9.   Blackstone, *ibid.*, vol.v, p.297.
10.   College was a widespread, and indicative, name for Newgate amongst criminals. It is used by numerous contemporary authors.

claimed by "prescription, time out of mind for entering in the society". Failure or inability to pay would result in the "poor wretch" being stripped of his clothes.[11] This was not just a Newgate tradition. When Mary Hall, in the smaller Gatehouse prison was unable to pay her garnish money at that jail, in 1711, she recorded that the turnkeys and other prisoners "took off her gown and threatened her". Flanders' reception may well have been a reflection of this old prison custom.

The women's section of Newgate was, in many ways, particularly unpleasant. In the common side for female felons a visitor to (and future inmate of) the prison, John Hall saw a troop of hell-cats, lying head and tail together, in a dismal nasty room; "... vollies of oaths are discharged through their detestable throats ... the licentiousness of the women on this side is so detestable, that it is an unpardonable crime to describe their lewdness".[12] That female inmates of the more hardened sort could be particularly terrifying, was also caught by Fielding in *Amelia*, "Blear eyed Moll, and several of her companions, having got possession of a man who was committed for certain odious unmanlike practices [sodomy], not fit to be named, were giving him various kinds of discipline, and would probably have put an end to him had he not been rescued out of their hands by authority".

Excessive drinking in Newgate prison (as in London itself) was endemic. The taphouse was the centre of prison life.[13] This institution was a perquisite of the keeper's office, though its administration was delegated to a full time tapster who also sold candles, soap, tobacco and other luxuries, making a large profit of up to £400 a year.[14] However, there were regular complaints about the quality of the beer, which many prisoners

---

11. Pamphlet, "Memoirs of the Right Villainous John Hall, The Late Famous and Notorious Robber", London (1708), printed by Ben. Bragg, p.24.
12. Hall, J., *Hell upon Earth; or, the Most Pleasant and Delectable History of Whittington's College, otherwise (vulgarly) called Newgate* (London 1703). It is not clear, though it appears very likely, that this is the same John Hall executed for robbery in 1708.
13. Cockburn, J.S., ed, *Crime in England 1550-1800* (1977), p.239.
14. *Ibid.*, p.240.

felt to be expensive and watered down "hogwash". As a result, a lot of prisoners would have alcohol, including spirits, brought into the prison by outsiders (indeed in 1737 the inmates even set up their own still in the prison). A visitor to Newgate in 1725 noted that "great fear is overcome by greater drinking". The guards, even when from the military, as, in the seventeenth century, occurred in some provincial prisons, did not set a good example. George Fox when imprisoned in Scarborough prison noted in his *Journal* that "there were, amongst the prisoners, two very bad men, that often sate drinking with the officers and soldiers; and because I would not sit and drink with them too, it made them the worse against me".

Several of Flanders' colleagues in custody were "pleading their bellies", though not truly pregnant (unlike genuine cases such as Flanders' transported mother). This was a common ploy amongst younger female prisoners. If a woman was proved to be pregnant after "pleading her belly", she would secure a temporary reprieve, until the delivery of the child, when in theory she would be hanged (though a considerable proportion were not).[15] In those days this (pregnancy) could be difficult to establish, and was determined in a traditional fashion; as Blackstone was to note "... the Judge must direct a jury of 12 matrons or discreet women to try the fact".[16] According to the jurist Mathew Hale the jury of matrons normally gave the benefit of any doubt to the defendant, and the Judge was then bound to respite judgment of death till after her delivery or it becoming apparent that she was not genuinely pregnant. Certainly, however, for some women, a false claim to pregnancy was only a temporary reprieve before death, especially if they had been "shamming". This was the case in 1703 with Moll Hawkins, who "having been repriev'd for nine months, upon account of her being then found to be quick with child, tho' she was not, she was now called down to her former judgment".[17] This was a common theme in Defoe's work. In *Street*

---

15.   Beattie, J.M., *ibid.*, p.431.
16.   Blackstone, W., *ibid.*, vol.iv, p.388.
17.   Captain Alexander Smith, *The History of the Lives of the Most Noted Highway-Men, Foot-Pads, House-Breakers, Shoplifts, and Cheats of Both Sexes ... for above 50 Years Last Past* (London 2, edn, 1714).

Robberies Consider'd the (fictional) narrator's mother had allegedly been condemned for shoplifting and consequently decided to get pregnant inside the prison to avoid her fate. Having unsuccessfully propositioned the Ordinary (the prison chaplain) she was in a difficult situation, "but some pirates happening to stop at Newgate, on their way to Wapping [where pirates were normally executed] took pity of my poor mother" before they "all lovingly swung together at execution-dock". The narrator was unable to say which was his father![18]

Flanders, when she had settled in somewhat, noted that her fellow Newgate inmates often took a philosophical attitude to the fact that they believed they would be hanged once their guilt had been established, and some were as "impudently cheerful and merry in their misery" as they were when they were out of it; she observed from this that hell came by degrees to be "natural and not only tolerable but even agreeable" to some. One inmate she observed, who was confident that she would be executed, even nonchalantly sang a well known Newgate ditty "if I swing by the string I will hear the bell ring, and then there's an end of poor Jenny". (Bell being the bell at nearby St Sepulchre's church which tolled upon execution day).

A Visit from the Ordinary

The Ordinary of Newgate came to visit Flanders, as was customary, and talked "a little in his way", unfortunately "all of his divinity" ran upon encouraging her to confess to her crimes. Later, Flanders was so demoralized to find that the same Ordinary who preached confession and repentance to her in the morning was totally drunk with brandy by noon that she "... began to nauseate the man, and his works too by degrees". She asked him not to trouble her any further.

The Newgate "Ordinary" was the official Anglican chaplain to

---

18. Defoe, D., *Street Robberies Consider'd: The Reason of their Being so Frequent* (1728), Geoffrey Sill edn (1973), p.6.

Newgate prison, responsible for ministering to the spiritual needs of the inmates, especially as they approached execution, "the Ordinary is their dry nurse and gives' em constant attendance in this their visitation".[19] It was a fairly secure but not rich living, and was certainly not normally a prestigious stepping stone to higher office in the Church. As well as his religious duties the Ordinary had acquired some other lucrative occupations and "side-lines". In 1620 the Reverend Henry Goodcole had been the first Ordinary of Newgate to publish a popular account of the prisoners' crimes.[20] At first it was looked down on (at the start of the century the court of Aldermen had even regarded the *Account* as an "undue practice"), then tolerated, and eventually received semi-official status, its sale becoming a major perquisite of the Ordinary's office. The Ordinary, however, would often have to pry to get the requisite details of their lives and transgressions from the prisoners. Most prisoners appear to have assisted him as he went about his task of compiling accounts of their careers, but would often need some close questioning to volunteer all the details. Only, it appears, a few dozen inquiries out of over a thousand led to an outright refusal of biographical details. Additionally, from the policing aspect, one benefit of the questioning was that more information about other criminals still at large might be obtained by getting these "accounts". Thus the Newgate Ordinary would have at least two purposes in getting his story from the inmates, the money available by their subsequent sale to the public and the judicial discovery of accomplices.

The mixed motivations of this prison cleric can be clearly seen in the words of Flanders' new Minister from outside the prison, who was specially arranged by her governess, and who ultimately effected Flanders' own religious conversion, "he told me he did not come as Ordinary of the place, whose business it is to exact confessions from prisoners for private ends, or for the further detecting of other offenders". Given that the Ordinary lived in what has been termed an "ecclesiastical and literary

---

19.   *Memoirs of the Right Villainous John Hall, ibid.* (1708), p.35.
20.   Sharpe, J.A., *ibid.*, p.115.

oblivion", the quality of clergyman recruited to the office was inevitably very mixed.[21] Some were undoubtedly drunkards, while the Reverend John Allen, who held the office early in the eighteenth century was even dismissed for extortion and "undue practices"; others, however, were quite dedicated, working in very difficult circumstances. It should also be remembered that Defoe had a personal antipathy towards the Reverend Paul Lorrain, who was Ordinary at the turn of the seventeenth century. Certainly some of the prisoners do appear to have sought spiritual counsel from the Ordinary. Jonathan Wild, in the evening before his execution in 1725, and just prior to taking an unsuccessful overdose of laudanum specifically sought the religious advice of the Ordinary as to the morality of suicide (advice he evidently did not follow).

However, the speed of the success of the early Methodists in preaching to the Newgate prisoners from the late 1730s, men of whom, in a way, Flanders' good Minister was a precursor, suggests that the Ordinary could normally give only limited religious comfort to the inmates.

It was, generally, a less devout age than the one that had gone before. On the religious front the lessening faith of the era, especially in the established Church, or at least the decline of "enthusiasm" (compared to the previous century) was not assisted in London by the failure of the Anglican church to keep up with the changes in the size and population of the Metropolis. That this was recognized by the authorities can be seen in the 1711 Act providing for the construction of 50 new churches (though only half of these were actually built). These included a few that were targeted at the burgeoning parishes to the east of the City, areas that were already occasioning some concern, such as Stepney and its adjacent parishes and offshoots (including Hawksmoor's St Anne's Limehouse, Christ Church in Spitalfields and St George in the East, the average cost being £19,000 per church). These steps, though, were inadequate to bolster faith in the Established Church of the time, especially in an increasingly cynical city like London; it is, perhaps, not surprising that

---

21.   Linebaugh, P., *The Ordinary of Newgate and his Account, Crime in England 1550-1800*, ed, J.S. Cockburn, p.269.

Flanders found little comfort in the prison chaplain, but sought her religious advice elsewhere.

The Grand Jury

The governess did succeed, by her "indefatigable application" in preventing a Bill being preferred against Flanders for the first Session to the Grand Jury sitting at the Guildhall, consequently she had an extra five weeks in Newgate to consider her life, though at this point, as she herself noted, she "... had few signs of repentance about [her]".[22] However, Flanders was subsequently informed that at the very next Sessions a Bill would be preferred against her.

The Grand Jury had started life as a result of the Assize of Clarendon in 1166. Originally its duty was to "present" local people suspected of crime to the King's itinerant justices. As this duty gradually passed to the Justices of the Peace in the fourteenth century, its function became a supervisory one, sitting at the start of Quarter Sessions and Assizes to decide whether a prima facie case had been made to the court. By the sixteenth century this was largely based on the depositions taken by the justices in their preliminary examination, though the Grand Jury, deliberating in secret, also had the power to interview a witness itself. Although only finally formally abolished in England in 1933, the advent of a modern police force, after 1829, meant that the justices were free to turn their own hearing more purely into a committal proceedings, examining the strength of the evidence (especially after reforms in 1848) and rendering the Grand Jury redundant (though it has actively survived, to this day, in America). Even before the advent of the new police, however, it had been gradually undermined by the increasingly judicial nature of the initial magistrate's inquiry.

---

22.   Birkenhead, Lord, *Famous Trials of History* (1926), p.157. In the 1760s, for Old Bailey Sessions, the Middlesex Grand Jury met in Hick's Hall in St Johns Street, while that for the City of London met in the Old Bailey itself.

However, at this point (Flanders' time) its function was still unquestioned. The magistrates committed the accused to trial, the Grand Jury decided whether they should be indicted to stand that trial. It decided by a majority (unlike the trial, or "petty" jury which had to be unanimous) so that an odd number was favoured, with 23 being a common complement. As the preliminary examination by justices became more thorough so the number of "true Bills" found by this body became predominant (over 90 per cent by the mid-eighteenth century). If the Grand Jury found no case to answer it would return a finding of "ignoramus". In the 1700s its membership (especially the Assize Grand Jury) was characterized by an increase in social status, compared to the middle-ranking trial jury, and thus increasingly included many JPs.[23] The Grand Jury that was sworn, at the Old Bailey Sessions in December 1681, for the county of Middlesex was made up of "17 substantial freeholders, Sir John Knight being foreman". In London, in the seventeenth century, this body sometimes appears to have met in the Old Bailey itself though more often it was in the Sessions House at Hick's Hall; thus, when Sir John Reresby noted in his memoirs the fates of three men accused of murdering a Mr Thynne in 1682 he observed that "the Bills against the three murderers of Mr Thynne had been found against them as principals ... at the Sessions at Hicks Hall ... On the 28th they were tried at the Old Bailey".[24]

Despite her friend's vigorous attempts to approach the members of this body and to persuade them not to find a "true Bill" (something that the secrecy of their deliberations facilitated), "... the jury found the Bill for robbery and housebreaking" and Flanders was set to stand trial on both counts.

That the criminal justice process could be interfered with even after it was under way was a recurring theme of contemporary literature and

---

23.   Beattie, *ibid.*, p.326.
24.   *Memoirs*, February 22, 1682. The men were all convicted and executed after an unusually long trial (9 am to 5 pm), the dead man's family not sparing expense or effort in supporting the prosecution, there being a "very strict prosecution by the relations of Mr Thynne".

probably also the reality. Gay's *The Beggars' Opera* opens with "Filch" telling "Peachum", a thief taker, that "Black Moll hath sent word her trial comes on in the afternoon, and she hopes you will order matters so as to bring her off". There are numerous other accounts and allusions to this happening, though as "Blueskin" found when Wild could only promise him a good coffin while he awaited execution, it had its limits.[25]

Flanders Meets her Highwayman Husband

In the middle of this terrible period of her life, another surprise occurred. One night three highwaymen were brought into the male section of Newgate. These men, having committed a robbery on Hounslow Heath, had been pursued to Uxbridge and captured "... after a gallant resistance in which many of the country people were wounded, and some killed" by the highwaymen. Amongst the three was Flanders' Lancashire husband (who was also a committed highway robber). Some of the anachronism in the supposed date of the writing of Flanders' memoirs (1683) can be seen in her reference to this man; at one point he was compared by her to other famous highwaymen of the seventeenth century because he "committed so many robberies that Hind, or Witney or the Golden Farmer were fools to him". Of these, Witney was only executed in 1694, some years after the alleged date of Flanders' authorship.

London was surrounded by heaths and woodlands in the early eighteenth century, places that still came close in to the confines of the Metropolis, providing excellent cover for highwaymen. In particular they used the heaths along and adjacent to the main routes of travel into the City; thus, Newmarket Heath, Shooters Hill and Hampstead Heath all had an unhealthy reputation,[26] as did Hounslow Heath, a particularly dangerous area.[27] The celebrated William Parsons, when he turned

---

25.   Herrup, Cynthia, *Law and Morality in England, Past and Present*, no.106 (1985), p.123.
26.   McMullen, J.L., *The Canting Crew* (1990), p.63.
27.   Beier, A.L., *Masterless Men* (1985), p.137.

highwayman in England, later in the century, in 1750, operated largely from Hounslow Heath, robbing an assorted collection of farmers and gentlemen on the local roads. London was the national centre of consumption and there were consequently plenty of tempting targets to be sought in its vicinities. Farmers and drovers returning from market were especially popular, carrying, as they often would be, large sums of money in cash from the sale of their animals and crops. This is alluded to by Defoe as well, when Flanders refers to her husband's more lucrative robberies "he gave me a long account of some of his adventures, and particularly one, when he robb'd the West Chester Coaches, near Lichfield, ... and after that, how he robb'd five grasiers, in the west, going to Burford Fair in Wiltshire to buy sheep".

This late seventeenth and early eighteenth century flourishing of the highwayman was closely linked to the emerging market orientated society of the era, at a time when the sophistication of banking and the ability to police the roads, had not sufficiently developed to prevent large amounts of cash still having to move at risk.[28] The mounted highwayman targeted the rapidly increasing number of travellers on the roads of a newly mobile England, especially those near the Metropolis. This was something that Defoe himself considered in detail elsewhere in his writings. In his important work *An Essay on Projects* (1697) he realistically suggested that the best way to ameliorate the problem was for a system of "county" or provincial banking to be established whereby "... all loss of money carri'd upon the road, to the encouragement of robbers, and ruining of the country, who are su'd for those robberies, wou'd be more effectually prevented, than by all the statutes against highway-men that are or can be made".[29] From the early eighteenth century the increasing numbers of mail coaches were also a popular target, conviction inevitably leading to the highwaymen who had perpetrated such attacks being tarred (to preserve their bodies) and then publicly gibbetted after execution as a

---

28. Such as John Fielding's later Bow Street Horse patrol which policed the environs of, and entries to, London, in the 1750s, and made a significant impact on such crime.
29. Quoted Linebaugh, P., *ibid.*, p.211.

deterrent. For a period in the early 1720s there was also an increasing degree of concern at the apparent ability of highwaymen to operate quite close in to the centre of the Metropolis, in places such as High Holborn and Whitechapel, rather than simply the outskirts of the city.

The advent of effective firearms, especially the flintlock pistol in the seventeenth century (replacing the unreliable wheel lock and matchlock), was also a necessary prerequisite of the highwayman's flourishing. They allowed effective control of the "target" without requiring the robber to get into the range at which even unarmed men could effect resistance (unlike a sword or dagger). It should also be remembered that the average highwayman might set out to rob with as many as half a dozen such pistols (easily carried given his mounted status), allowing a considerable discharge of firepower in an emergency.[30]

Footpads, unlike their mounted colleagues, often tried physically to disable their victims to avoid pursuit (at least by stunning them with a blow to the head), before effecting an escape. Typically, when one Christopher Pratt was attacked on Finchley Common by two footpads he was much "beat and wounded" by the robbers before they departed. Footpads were also necessarily quick to use their firearms when occasion demanded it. When, in 1764, John Fielding sent a foot patrol of four men into the fields near Tyburn and Tottenham Court road, "to search the ditches where footpads have lately infested", before the patrol had even managed to get out of their coach "they narrowly escaped being murdered, by three footpads, who without giving them the least notice fired two pistols immediately into the coach".[31]

However, as John Beattie has observed, highwaymen, while able, to an extent, to behave differently to footpads (whom they often despised as being of lower social status, in part because they were unable to afford a horse), and who nearly always had to use some violence to effect a safe escape unlike a mounted man, still regularly showed violence themselves to their victims, and were occasionally, in their turn, seriously wounded

---

30.   McLynn, F., *Crime and Punishment in Eighteenth Century England* (1991) p.70.
31.   Letter from Sir John Fielding to Mr Jenkinson, June 2, 1764.

by them (many travellers being armed and willing to put up resistance).[32] A typical newspaper report in 1723 could note in passing that a highwayman "Joseph Rice ... was shot in attempting to rob Governor Chudleigh's Lady". Frequently those who were attacked could show spirited defiance, especially if not alone. In 1707 the notorious Captain Richard Dudley and his gang robbed a nobleman of £1,500 on Hounslow Heath "... after a severe engagement with his [the nobleman's] servants, three of whom were wounded, and two had their horses shot under them". This explains why Flanders could also note of her highwayman husband that "he had one or two very terrible wounds indeed, as particularly one by a pistol bullet which broke his arm; and another with a sword, which ran him quite thro' the body". In one case he had had to ride over 70 miles to find a doctor far enough away from the scene of the crime to receive treatment without risk of detection (he pretended to having been the victim himself of such a robbery).

Any traveller was potentially at risk. Defoe himself remarked in a letter that he had specially purchased a pair of saddle pistols to take with him on a journey to Newcastle, in 1706, to protect himself against such robbers. He also examined some of the "mechanics" of highway robbery in *A Warning for Travellers* (1728), again allegedly the work of a criminal (in this case an escaped inmate of Newgate) who was also the son of a parson! In some respects this was an early illustration of a situational approach to crime prevention and "target hardening". Defoe provides useful advice as to how to reduce the risk of highwaymen. Much is little more than common sense, "if you travel, never admit of any stranger in your company". If a traveller did meet a stranger on the road he should tell him that he had heard of a hue and cry in the last town that he had gone through and then "observe his countenance" for guilty signs. The danger of inns and their keepers was stressed: "When you come into an Inn, don't be too readily acquainted with your Landlord" some of them "intrigue with the highwaymen". However, highwaymen, like modern muggers were probably primarily concerned with "easy pickings". This

---

32.   Beattie, J.M., *ibid.,* p.154.

might explain the robust advice provided by Defoe to travellers if they still had the misfortune to be attacked, "if you can muster up so much courage, tell them boldly you will sooner part with your life than your money, and tis 10 to one if they don't leave you upon an instant". Alternatively the attacked traveller could say he had been robbed already and offer to be searched for "thieves have but little time to lose".[33]

Despite well documented accounts of their frequent gallantry, outright brutality by highwaymen was also fairly widespread. The famous Dick Turpin, for example, was willing to torture servants and other victims by roasting them over fires to exact information, even telling one old woman who would not divulge where her valuables were hidden "God damn your blood, you old bitch, if you won't tell us I'l set your arse on the gate".[34] In 1722 a gruesome case was reported where three highwaymen had allegedly been identified by a poor woman who witnessed the incident and who foolishly cried out that she knew the men involved. The highwaymen then supposedly returned to the scene to cut out her tongue. Another victim, in 1739, observed how his attacker had used extremely coarse words towards him "damn your blood - you're a dead man - I'll shoot you through the head, etc, was the language he made use of".[35] Nevertheless, some did attempt to live up to the title of "gentlemen of the road", in conduct, and, more commonly, in their flamboyant lifestyle. During the disturbances after the English Civil War, a number of former gentlemen who had lost their lands in the conflict, and subsequently failed to recover them, do appear to have had recourse to this form of crime to survive in a manner fitting to their stations in life, perhaps also promoting such a tradition. In the following century, Thomas Butler, who was tried for robbery (of a gold watch on the highway) at the Old Bailey in January 1720, and who had allegedly committed a "vast number" of robberies in Kent and Essex, can be seen to have been an extreme example of this. Ensuring, as he did, that he "lived generously upon what we got with so

33.   Defoe, D., *A Warning for Travellers* (1728), pp.62-67.
34.   Haining, P., *The English Highwayman*, p.99.
35.   OBSP, January 17-20, 1723.

much hazard", taking lodgings that were "genteelly furnished", and making sure that his companion, Jack, at the proper times "wore a livery, and attended me in quality of a footman". As the report of his trial made clear, there could be few cases of highwaymen living lives of such "apparent gaiety" as Butler, "yet it ended in an infamous death at Tyburn".[36] Although there were some large gangs of highwaymen, most, like Flanders' husband, worked in groups of two or three, and sometimes even alone.[37]

The decline of the highwayman towards the end of the century can be attributed to many causes, increased urbanization of their "haunts", better policing such as the "horse patrol" operating out of London to combat them, more sophisticated banking reducing the value of available targets, greater control of those public houses that had harboured them, by refusing them licences (something that George Borrow had thought was especially important in their decline when writing about it in 1857), better general policing and intelligence, greater numbers of people on the roads, etc. The "social status" of highwaymen certainly fell as the century advanced, and it became less common for the more handsome of them to be attended in prison by crowds of well to do young women in the way that Jack Sheppard had been.

Once highwaymen were detained or under suspicion, there were sometimes attempts by the authorities to clear up other outstanding robberies that they might have committed during their careers, if only to bolster potentially weak cases on the "holding" charge. In one typical advertisement, from 1692, a Joseph Harpur from Southwark, who stated that he had been robbed on August 17, 1689 on Shooters Hill in Kent, by three men "one being upon a light dapple gray nag, well forehanded, about 14 hands high" (the animals were usually harder to disguise than the men) gave notice that if anybody "... was, or were robbed about that time on that road, or in Hartfordshire, or upon Kennington Common near

---

36.   *Select Trials at the Sessions House in the Old-Bailey*, vol.I, 1720-1723, printed
       for J. Applebee (M.DCC.XCII), p.13.
37.   Beier, *ibid.*, p.138.

Newington in Surrey; if they, or any of them will repair to the said Joseph Harpur, he will shew them the person, who rid the said horse, as also the horse, of which (as to his said robbery) he hath made oath".[38]

Flanders' Indictment

Flanders was ultimately indicted for feloniously stealing two pieces of brocaded silk (the value being £46), and for burglary (by allegedly breaking open the doors of the house), though in reality, the doors had been open when she entered the building. Both were capital offences. The indictment document, even at this time, had to be quite precise as to the charge against the defendant. This common law insistence on technical correctness could sometimes work in a defendant's favour. George Fox appears to have escaped trial at two Assize courts in the provinces (at least in his own rather vain opinion) because he cleverly spotted flaws in the indictments "look at the indictment, and ye may see that ye have left out the word *subject*". While his companion, Margaret Fell also "had counsel to plead [on a point of law as was permitted], who found many errors in her indictment". There were many other instances of defendants being released on a procedural technicality. These points of course often required either native wit or a lawyer to spot them. The day after the indictment, a Friday, Flanders was brought to her trial (very long periods on remand in the eighteenth century were, by modern standards, rare).

Criminal Courts in London and England

The bulk of serious felonies in the provinces (those cases likely to result in a sentence of death if proved) and that were considered too serious for jury trial in front of the justices at Quarter Sessions would be heard in front of the Assize courts. These survived until 1971 (when they were replaced by the modern Crown Court). They were not permanent courts but bi-annual events, held with great pomp, in Lent and the Long Vacation. The country was divided into six circuits and the Assizes

---

38.   *London Gazette*, January 23, 1692.

Judges, most of whom were also Judges of the superior courts in London (such as that of King's Bench), would ride their "circuits", when the Royal courts were not sitting, dispensing justice under two commissions, that of *oyer and terminer* and that of *gaol delivery*. The itinerant Royal Judges would "deliver" the local jail by presiding over the jury trials of those in custody. The inferior courts of Quarter Sessions, held, as the name suggests four times a year (usually at Epiphany, Easter, Michaelmas and around the Feast of St Thomas), in which benches of JPs, some of whom would normally be legally qualified having trained at the Inns of Court (often the "presiding" justice would be in this category), presided over the jury trials of misdemeanours and occasionally lesser felonies (though originally, and theoretically, they had a more extensive jurisdiction, able to try any case other than treason).

However, criminal courts in the Metropolis differed markedly from those outside London and Middlesex. In the City of London, the Old Bailey sat eight times a year (and roughly approximated to an Assize court in status) dealing with felony trials (and occasionally serious misdemeanours) for the city and the county of Middlesex (it was a joint court); in Westminster, the court of King's Bench sometimes also sat to hear criminal cases from Middlesex or cases with political overtones, such as treason.

The Court of King's Bench

Although there was generally considerable overlap between their civil jurisdictions in the late sixteenth and early seventeenth centuries, the court of King's Bench was the only one of the central law courts to have any criminal jurisdiction (as well as its important civil one), the other two courts, Common Pleas and Exchequer being purely civil. Since the fourteenth century the Crown side of this court (ie, the criminal side) had had an unlimited jurisdiction for criminal matters in England, either for first instance trials, or as a court into which indictments could be removed from other criminal courts for the discussion of a point of law that had arisen. The court of King's Bench had the supervisory power by order of *certiorari* to insist that cases be removed before trial from other courts into its jurisdiction, though this was very rarely allowed in respect of cases that were to be heard in front of the Assizes or the Old Bailey Judges (as opposed to cases being heard at Quarter Sessions where it was more frequently exercised).[39] However, there are a few recorded instances of this occurring even in the Assizes courts, such as that in 1629, when one John Eve stabbed James Remmington in a dispute over a gambling game in the Blue Boar tavern in Maldon, Essex. George Fox also had quite a lot to be thankful for to this court in its supervisory role of the many provincial courts he fell foul of. When one Anne Curtis interceded on his behalf with Charles II in 1660, when Fox was due to be tried by a provincial Assizes, an order of *habeas corpus* was granted from the King's Bench, removing the case to that court's jurisdiction, though its execution was delayed as the Chancellor and Sheriff of Lancaster were "enemies to truth" or at least jealous of the power of the local Assizes and initially found ingenious technical faults in the writ (which apparently said "George Fox in prison under *your* custody" when addressed to the Chancellor, although Fox was actually in the custody of the Sheriff and so it should have said *his* custody).[40] Fortunately, when produced in court two of the three Judges present were well disposed towards him and he was released (the exception was Sir Thomas Twisden who Fox was to meet again at a provincial Assize court when the latter was on circuit). In 1673, George Fox was again able to get a writ of *habeas corpus* from the court of King's Bench against the Worcester justices "the Judges who were three, were all very moderate, not casting any reflecting words at me". He was told that if the court "found any error in the record, or in the justice's proceedings, I should be set at liberty". Though subsequently "... some of my other adversaries moved the court that I might be sent back to Worcester. Whereupon another day was appointed for another hearing, and they had four counsellors that pleaded against me".

In addition to this supervisory role, King's Bench, as a court of first instance, could try criminal cases from Middlesex, found before it by a

---

39.   Baker, J.H., in *Crime in England 1550-1800*, at p.27.
40.   *The London Journal*, 1660, Everyman edn (1948), p.188.

Grand Jury for that county, though most routine Middlesex cases were heard by the Middlesex Sessions, or, if more serious felonies, at the Old Bailey. Jack Sheppard's final judicial appearance, in 1724, was at King's Bench, rather than the Old Bailey.

Additionally, King's Bench dealt with many political cases. In the seventeenth century (until its abolition in 1641), the Court of Star Chamber had heard many criminal matters with a political import, such as sedition cases, where the Crown found advantages in a court where proceedings were begun by information and tried summarily, without either a Grand Jury or a trial jury (which might not be so co-operative as the Judges). When it was abolished many of these types of case, were transferred to the criminal jurisdiction of the court of King's Bench (where they were tried in front of a jury).[41] Thus as well as dealing with some Middlesex cases it was the forum for many state trials as well, such as that of the Jacobite Christopher Layer, for treason, in 1722.

Hick's Hall

In addition to this court, there was the Sessions court for Middlesex, held at Hick's Hall in St John's Street (often mentioned by Flanders, and named after its founder) and which was normally presided over by justices (and roughly approximated to a provincial court of Quarter Sessions, though with a greater number of more serious cases, there was also its equivalent for Westminster and the City). As most of its cases were misdemeanours the characteristics of the trial process was significantly different to that at the Old Bailey. As with the provincial Quarter Sessions many administrative or quasi-administrative matters were also dealt with by this court. For example, in a celebrated trial in this court, in September 1684, parish constables for the hamlets of Spitalfields and Bethnal Green were convicted and fined for failing, at the behest of the justices, to suppress 16 "great and public" Dissenters' conventicles, and other Dissenter meeting places (Dissent was especially common in the sometimes unruly

---

41.   Baker, J.H., *ibid.*, p.137.

parishes to the East of the City). When 15 of the constables refused to give undertakings to do this in future and also to find sureties to appear at the Sessions to answer for their "contempt", they were imprisoned in the New prison (used for those awaiting the Middlesex Sessions at Hick's Hall; it was also in Clerkenwell) where they initially refused to "apply to any of the Justices of the Peace to be bailed" for their misdemeanour (they were subsequently bailed by order of a King's Bench Judge). At their trial "by a commission of *oyer* and *terminer*" they appear to have been represented by counsel (as was permissible in misdemeanour cases), but still convicted. Those who "confessed the said indictment" were fined relatively modest sums (five marks), those who denied the accusation and had it proved against them up to a hundred pounds, while the most senior of their number, John Child, the Head-Beadle of Spittalfields was further ordered to "... be set twice in the pillory". This was clearly, and avowedly, "exemplary justice", designed to prevent a breakdown of law and order in those parishes, a situation in which it was feared by the justices that they "... would have been in danger to have been knocked o'th'head by the mobile".[42] Nevertheless, the great bulk of serious crimes in London and Middlesex were tried at the Old Bailey.

The Old Bailey

At first there was no regular court for the trial of prisoners held in Newgate, the trials being conducted in the prison itself. The first "sessions house" was erected in 1539 and was built "over against Flete lane in the old bayly". Initially, the building did not even have a proper roof, though this was soon remedied, and the premises extended in 1726. This rather primitive court at the Old Bailey survived, with improvements, till 1774 when it was replaced by the New Sessions House, built on rather grander lines (which in turn was replaced by the present building in 1907).

---

42.   "Mob" appears to have been a shortening of this word; the account is taken from that of the proceedings in Hicks' Hall on September 6, 1684 printed by one "R.R." and sold by Randall Taylor that year.

From the start this court was closely linked to the adjacent prison.[43] Additionally, unlike the Assizes courts with their differing Judges going on circuit from London to exercise the general gaol delivery, there was a considerable continuity of membership on the part of at least some of the "bench" of the Old Bailey, that gave a special quality to the court's trials. Although many of the Judges at the Old Bailey would be taken from the Royal courts, sitting in Westminster Hall, in the same way that the provincial Assizes Judges were, often during the Westminster court's breaks and vacations (because of geographical proximity, some of these would be very regular attenders), in the case of the Recorder and Serjeant, the judicial positions were permanent ones, the same Judges sitting from month to month and year to year. Furthermore, while Assize Judges would normally preside over cases alone (or very occasionally with their brother itinerant judge), it was not unusual for those at the Bailey to sit in panels, though with one Judge, normally the Recorder if present (or the Common Serjeant if not), presiding, and being directly responsible for most of the legal decisions. Thus, at the trial of the pirate, Captain Kidd, in 1701, the bench consisted of Lord Chief Baron Ward, the Recorder, Sir Salathiel Lovell and three other Judges, while in 1777 three Judges presided over the trial of Dr Dodd.[44] The numbers of the judiciary sitting could be even greater; at the Sessions in October 1681, there were 10 Judges, including the two Lord Chief Justices (from the two main central courts in Westminster Hall) present! For this reason Flanders correctly talks of "Judges" (in the plural) being at her trial. Theoretically, if Flanders' chronology were accepted, it would be possible that one of these Judges might have been the notorious, George Jeffreys (1648-89), a former Lincoln's Inn barrister, and infamous for his conduct of the "Bloody Assizes" on the western circuit after Monmouth's defeat in 1685. He had been Common Serjeant of London in 1671 and Recorder of the City of London in 1678, before becoming a Lord Chief Justice and then Lord Chancellor until his demise after the Glorious Revolution.

---

43.   Crew, A., The Old Bailey (1933), p.8.
44.   Birkenhead, Lord, Famous Trials of History (1926), p.109.

These criminal courts were, by modern standards, flawed in many respects in the quality of the justice they administered. However, it should also be remembered that at this time pre-trial judicial torture was a regular, if sometimes exaggerated, feature of many seventeenth and eighteenth century, Western European criminal justice systems (though its use in many countries started to decline from the mid-seventeenth century onwards). It was frequently used on women as well as men (though again, sometimes the torturers would first apply it with "kindness" by allowing the suspect sight of the torture instruments that would be used to extract a confession, before actually applying them for real with "pain".)[45] Englishmen in the seventeenth and eighteenth centuries genuinely were right to believe that by comparison with much of Europe there was a real prospect of "due process" and a fair trial before their courts.

Flanders' Trial

As, because of her previous skill, it was Flanders' first formal appearance in a court, it is not surprising that she was not very familiar with the procedure of the Old Bailey. When the trial began and the indictment was read, she initially wanted to speak but was informed "... that the witnesses would be heard first, and then she would have time to be heard". Her lack of comprehension would not have been helped by the fact that until 1731 the indictment was normally drawn up in Latin, though it was nearly always read aloud in English when the prisoner was arraigned; as the Act which abolished this stated, no doubt "many and great mischiefs do frequently happen to the subjects of this kingdom, from the proceedings in courts of justice being in an unknown language". At this point in the trial, at least in the 1670s, the "custom of England" was for the prisoners to be "... told to hold up their hands, and ask'd whether guilty or not guilty".

---

45.   Boes, M.A., "Women and the Penal System in Frankfurt am Main, 1562-1696", *Criminal Justice History*, vol.13 (1992), p.65.

Nearly all trials in this period began with the prosecutor (who was also usually the victim), directly telling his version of events to the jury.[46] The prisoner could not give sworn evidence in his own defence, a situation that persisted till 1898, and reflected the common law's fear of the possibility of facilitating perjured evidence by allowing those who had an "axe to grind" to give evidence on oath. However his (or her) speech to the jury served the same purpose and, in the minds of the jurors, was probably little distinguished from those of the prosecution witnesses (it survived as the unsworn "dock statement" till 1980). Trials were brief, often only minutes and very rarely more than a few hours,[47] (compared, for example, to the two days, or seven-and-a-half hours of court time that the average modern Crown Court trial lasts).[48] It was not even fully established till the end of the eighteenth century that a felony jury could adjourn over-night to hear the remainder of the evidence in the case in the morning.[49] Hearsay evidence was still often admitted at the start of the century, and witness testimony was largely ungoverned by rules of admissibility. Rules of evidence appear to have started in civil cases and moved into criminal ones at the end of the seventeenth century. However, they were still very flexible in the early eighteenth century.[50] Indeed, they were only to harden into relatively rigid rules towards the end of the century, partly it seems under the influence of the advent of lawyers to the criminal trial process (interestingly, at Christopher Layer's trial for treason in 1722, where, as was normal in such cases he was allowed legal representation, a significant amount of prosecution evidence was rejected). Jurors, trying batches of prisoners, had to keep verdicts in their heads.[51] So fast were the proceedings that the unrepresented defendants often had

---

46.   Beattie, J.M., *ibid.*, p.342.
47.   Beattie, J.M., *ibid.*, p.376.
48.   Ingman, T., *The English Legal Process*, 5th edn (1994), ch.7.
49.   Baker, J.H., p.38, *Crime in England 1550-1800* (1977) ed, J.S. Cockburn. However, such adjournments had always been allowed in treason cases (with misdemeanour and felony, one of the three main criminal classifications).
50.   *Ibid.*, p.39.
51.   Beattie, J.M., *ibid.*, p.147.

little idea as to what had occurred, and many of their theoretical rights, for example, peremptory challenge to jurors, were rarely exercised in practice as a consequence. Although the clerk always advised the defendants that they should "look to their challenges" examination of the Sessions Papers reveals that in practice this potentially important way of influencing jury composition (by rejecting jurors who appeared potentially hostile) was very rare.

At the conclusion of the prosecution case the Judge usually directly asked the defendants what they had to say about the evidence brought against them, allowing them to begin their own account of events (Flanders had been premature in this).[52] In most early eighteenth century trials counsel was acting for neither the prosecution nor the defence, and the trial Judge had to take a very active, almost inquisitorial, role by modern standards in his conduct of the process to ensure the smooth running of the court. He would exhibit considerable involvement in the questioning of witnesses and other evidence, and remained a very dominant presence throughout the trial. Indeed, at this time, as Blackstone himself was to later note, it was one of a trial Judge's obligations to "... be counsel for the prisoner; that is, shall see that the proceedings against him are legal and strictly regular".[53] In part as a consequence of this, in the early eighteenth century, the burden of proof in a trial was not clearly fixed on the Crown (something that only changed towards the end of the 1700s). Once a *prima facie* case had been made by the prosecution (something that was almost inevitable, if the witnesses came up to "proof" given that by the trial stage the case would have survived scrutiny by both a magistrate and the Grand Jury) the reality was that it was normally for the defendant to prove that he was not involved in the commission of a crime. It was even doubtful if the "presumption of innocence", in any modern sense, properly existed. Indeed in James I's time, in the early seventeenth century, one legal writer had felt that the defendant could be convicted without any Crown witnesses giving testimony at all, the

---

52.   Beattie, J.M., *ibid.*, p.343.
53.   Blackstone, *Commentaries, ibid.*, vol.iv, p.349.

evidence of the indictment being sufficient![54] In reality, a failure to give an account in these circumstances, via the defendant's statement to the jury (albeit unsworn at this stage) would have been almost tantamount to an admission. An examination of Old Bailey Session papers from c.1700 reveals that this virtually never happened.[55] The effective reality of the "right to silence" arrived only towards the end of the eighteenth century along with the regular presence of counsel in the criminal trial (such lawyers then being able to conduct the case on behalf of the defendant, and allowing the accused greater freedom to refuse to give evidence via a speech to the jury).

However, Defoe was writing on the cusp of a time of change in English criminal procedure. It has been observed that some of the most fundamental characteristics of modern Anglo-American criminal trial procedure emerged or developed during the eighteenth century. Amongst them was the modern law of evidence, the fully adversarial nature of the criminal trial and the rules regulating the relationship between Judge and jury.[56] Additionally there was to be the advent of lawyers to the process. By the 1730s, counsel were being allowed to act for defendants in felony trials where, previously, in such cases, they had been limited to arguing points of pure law on the rare occasions that they came up (strangely they had always had rights of audience on behalf of defendants at the less serious misdemeanour trials held at Quarter Sessions).[57] Counsel acting for the prosecution (not previously forbidden, unlike the case with defendants, but in practice normally only found in treason trials), have also been found in a handful of cases at the Old Bailey in the 1720s, and in greater numbers in the following decade. Initially, these tended to be sedition offences (or similar types of case), where there was no obvious victim to take the "lead" in the courtroom process.

A number of somewhat fanciful explanations were advanced by

---

54.   Baker, *ibid.*, p.37.
55.   Langbein, J.H., "The Criminal Trial Before the Lawyers", *The University of Chicago Law Review*, vol.25, no.2 (1978), p.283.
56.   Langbein, J., *A View from the Ryder Sources, ibid.*, p.2.
57.   Beattie, J.M., *ibid.*, p.356.

contemporary commentators as to why counsel should normally be absent in the more serious felony trials; for example, that the evidence should be so overwhelming that it could not be questioned. Against this, there were also many published justifications for the existence of defence counsel in felony trials from the late seventeenth century onwards. For example, Sir Robert Atkins, who had been a Judge in Charles II's reign, and was Chief Baron in 1689, thought that it was a "severity" in our law that a prisoner on trial for his life was "not allowed the assistance of a grave and prudent lawyer". An important precedent for the following century was set by the 1696 Act for Regulating of Trials in Cases of Treason which allowed those accused of this crime a right to legal representation.[58] The use of counsel for defendants who could afford them was quite widespread by the end of the eighteenth century, while a few even had the advantage of defence counsel by the middle of the century; furthermore, these lawyers' trial role may not have been as restricted in reality as in legal theory. Rules forbidding them from addressing the court and jury on behalf of the prisoner may have been frequently ignored in practice (they were only finally fully abolished in 1836).

However, Flanders, a few years earlier, would certainly have been unrepresented, even though she was monied, unless a point of law arose. As there were only 338 barristers practising in all of the central courts (King's Bench, Common Pleas etc) as well as at *nisi prius* (civil jurisdiction) at Assizes it would, in any event, have been difficult for most criminal trial defendants in the early eighteenth century to be represented.[59] To some considerable extent this was compensated for by the very active role, by modern standards, that was taken in judicial proceedings by eighteenth century Judges, who usually do appear to have

---

58. See Shapiro, A., "Political Theory and the Growth of Defensive Safeguards in Criminal Procedure: The Origins of the Treason Trials Act of 1696". *Law and History Review*, vol.11, no.2 (1993), at p.215. This Act placed on a statutory footing something that had sometimes been allowed beforehand. In 1684, at the Old Bailey, a Mr Ralphon was told that he could have had counsel as "it was not denied in cases of treason" (OBSP, January 17-18).

59. Lemmings, D., *Gentlemen and Barristers* (1990), p.123.

been careful to ensure that most defendants received some semblance of "due process".[60] This attempt at fairness is reflected in the fact that between the sixteenth and eighteenth century the acquittal rate in such trials was between a quarter and half of those indicted.[61] This is on a par with modern levels and significantly higher than acquittal rates for the Victorian period. Thus conviction was certainly not an inevitability. Henry Fielding, in 1754, genuinely, and probably with some accuracy, felt that the worst "villain upon earth is tried in the same manner as a man of the best character who is accused of the same crime".

The trial of the Jacobite conspirator, Christopher Layer, who had been involved in Atterbury's plot, and which dominated the newspapers for part of 1722 (when *Moll Flanders* was first published), throws an interesting light on the potential effect on criminal procedure when competent counsel were present, a very different matter from Flanders' trial. Layer had been arrested for conspiring, in Leytonstone in Essex, to raise "an armed force and troops of soldiers" to advance the Jacobite cause. He was consequently accused of high treason, for which he was entitled to have the assistance of counsel at his trial at the court of King's Bench in Westminster that year, as provided for by the Act of 1696. The *London Journal* of the same year produced a "large and impartial abstract of the tryal" in a weekly supplement. The influence of counsel at his trial can possibly be seen in the care that was taken to exclude written statements of Layer's preliminary interrogation "these minutes of the examination were not offered to be read as evidence, it not having been either read to Mr Layer at the time he was examined, nor signed by him; but the witnesses gave an account of his confession viva voce, look'd to their notes to refresh their memories".[62] This was an early manifestation of an evidential rule that was to become well established in the English law (until the advent of the audio taping of interviews in the 1990s made it

60. Hay, D., "The Criminal Prosecution in England", *Modern Law Review*, vol.47 (1984), p.5.
61. Baker. J.H, *Crime in England*, ibid.,p.23 and Lemmings, D., *Gentlemen and Barristers* (1990), p.123.
62. *The London Journal*, February 9, 1723.

redundant).

That advocates zealously defended their clients even in a sensitive case can be seen in the words of the Lord Chief Justice who presided over Layer's trial, and who was to note "these counsel have been permitted to say whatever they thought proper for your service,and I heartily wish that I could say ... that they had not taken a greater liberty than they ought to have done". Judges in such political cases did tend, of course, to be quite heavily "establishment" orientated.

In James II's reign the position of Judges had been precarious but lucrative. If they did not follow the government approved line they could quickly find themselves out of office; those that were "reliable" could expect advancement. This, along with a naturally bloodthirsty disposition, probably explains some of the enthusiasm of Jeffreys at the Western ("Bloody") Assizes of 1685, having thus made a good impression he was swiftly promoted to Lord Chancellor by the King.[63] Those Judges who kept their offices could also make thousands of pounds a year (in 1691 an ordinary Judge of the court of King's Bench made over £2,000). Their position (and the penalty for independence) became a little less precarious after 1688, but few Judges would wish to risk political disfavour, at least until the Act of Settlement of 1700 had provided that Judges should be made *quamdiu se bene gesserint* and that their salaries should be established, removing fears of dismissal or a salary cut if they lost Royal approval. Even in Layer's case, the presiding Judge's summing up of the case to the jury, though biased, was certainly not outrageously so, as he firmly directed them that they should "discharge the part of honest men, consider and weigh well the evidence ... if you are not satisfied these things are true, then you'll acquit him".

Judges in the eighteenth century were normally very reluctant to accept guilty pleas in capital cases, not least because a trial (never very long in any event) might provide them with mitigating features that would justify a recommendation of reprieve. Thus they would often actively attempt

---

63.　Although famous for a cavalier disregard for the niceties of criminal procedure, Jeffreys had an excellent reputation as a Judge in civil matters.

to dissuade the defendant from such a course, and the records frequently refer to the courts trying to discourage such pleas. In February 1687, when a French woman, Mary Hoby, accused of the murder of her husband, pleaded guilty on her arraignment at the Old Bailey "... the Court with all possible tenderness, let her know the danger and the consequence of her confession and offer'd her yet the liberty to depart from her plea, and take her tryal if she thought fit".[64] Earlier, in 1680, when Thomas Nevil was accused of burglary from a shop and horse theft he "voluntarily pleaded guilty", and, the account notes that "nor could he be persuaded to do otherwise", his reason being, apparently, an awareness of the overwhelming nature of the evidence against him, leading him to have "no hopes on life".[65] As a consequence of this judicial reluctance, very few defendants pleaded guilty even where the case against them appeared very strong (probably fewer than one per cent), the opposite to the present day situation (in which inducements in the form of more lenient sentences are offered to defendants if they admit their guilt).

However, in many cases, in lieu of a guilty plea, there appear, from the Sessions' Papers, to have been frequent instances in which the defendant only nominally defended the charge, sometimes not making any reply at all to the allegations made in court. Thus, in 1694, when John Riggs was accused of burglary and came to give his account of events it was noted that "the prisoner had very little to say on his own behalf"; while at the same Sessions, Henry Hawkins from Holborn "gave but a very slender account of his life and conversation" to the court when he stood trial for stealing a saddle from a stable. Not surprisingly, both men were convicted.[66]

By pleading "not guilty" there was also the possibility of putting pressure on prosecution witnesses to tailor their evidence to suit the defendant. Sometimes this could be the result of intimidation, as Fielding was to note in 1751. However, often it was also the result of a successful

---

64.   *A Hellish Murder Committed by a French Midwife on the Body of her Husband.* Published by Randall Taylor (1688).
65.   OBSP, April 26 to April 28, 1680, p.3.
66.   OBSP, February 21-23, 1694, p.4.

appeal to the compassion of the prosecution witness, which allowed him not to forfeit his recognizance (because he had in fact attended to give evidence) while not suffering the guilty conscience of being responsible for a hanging over a small theft.[67] In a considerable number of cases, of course, the prosecution witnesses failed to appear, whether through accident or conscience, despite risking the loss of their recognizances. This might only be known at the last minute (as is often still the case today) also encouraging not guilty pleas. Mary Knight and Hannah Jones, who were indicted for the burglary of one Peter Combely's house (they were accused of stealing a great coat and other unspecified goods) were not unique in finding that "... no evidence appearing against them, they were acquitted".[68] This may have been the situation with Flanders and explain her "not guilty" plea, despite the apparently strong evidence against her.

Deliberately refusing to plead at all (standing "mute of malice") would have had horrific consequences as it would have led to the imposition of the *peine forte et dure*. This meant that the defendant would be taken back to prison and tied down while a flat board, placed on his (or her) chest was progressively loaded with iron weights, until they expired (or begged to be allowed to make a plea). This happened in the case of Edward White, who, strangely, given that he already stood convicted of other serious burglaries, when accused of another burglary in Shadwell in 1681, "obstinately refusing to plead, was ordered to the press".[69] The sight alone of the press could induce a change of mind. In January 1723, when the footpads William Spiggot and Thomas Phillips (previously operating on Finchley Common) were returned to Newgate after refusing to plead, Philips had a change of heart as soon as he saw the weights, though Spiggots held out till he was bearing 200lb, before begging to be allowed to make a plea. At times in the eighteenth century "muteness" may have been mitigated by jailers initially applying lesser penalties to see if they

---

67. Green, A.G., *Verdict According to Conscience* (1985), p.362.
68. OBSP, December 11-14, 1689, p.4.
69. OBSP, December 7-8, 1681, p.3.

could induce a change of decision, by, for example, the tight binding of the thumbs with whipcord. The torture was finally abolished in 1772, and deliberate "muteness" in court deemed (for the next 50 years) to be the equivalent of a guilty plea. Nevertheless, before this date, a few brave individuals occasionally had recourse to refusal to plead, perhaps as a result of a wish to spare their families the shame of a conviction, or a fear that the Crown would forfeit their property (as a convicted felon) if they were convicted (though in this period this was normally a theoretical rather than a practical risk, as juries usually returned verdicts stating that the convicted had "no goods" for this purpose).

Some prisoners may not, in any event, have been in a totally fit state to make a defence. Drink was present even in the court. According to John Hall, unless they could afford to pay half a crown to go into the more comfortable "Bail-Dock", "where criminals are secured" the Newgate inmates, "rcscmbl[ing] so many sheep", when waiting in the densely crowded "hold" of the Old Bailey, before their trials, would usually "claim 12 pence apiece of the youngest for hold-money" with which thcy "make shift to get drunk before they go up to the Bar to be arraigned or try'd".[70]

Then as now, when proper and coherent defences were advanced by the accused they were of a varied nature. The most successful, if the prisoner had not been arrested at the scene of the crime, was alibi, ideally supported by perjured (or truthful) witnesses. Others would include an allegation of mistake by the prosecutor, sometimes backed up by a suggestion of drunkenness on his or her part, or even malicious fabrication; when Daniel Ashford was accused of rape in 1689, although there was apparently a degree of corroboration it was observed that "in the whole course of the Evidence there was abundance of malice appeared, which weighed so heavily with the jury, that they acquitted the prisoner".[71]

In a surprising number of cases, where the victim had handed money over to the defendant, and both were males, the defence was an allegation that the money had been given voluntarily by the victim to buy the silence

---

70.   *Memoirs ...* (1708), *ibid.*, p.32.
71.   OBSP, December 11-14, 1689, p.3.

193

of the accused, the latter person having witnessed him in "the Act of Sodomy" (potentially a capital offence). This was the case with one Thomas Elves who was accused of robbery from William Helliwell in 1720. Unfortunately, when asked by the court whether he had anyone to speak for his character (crucial to establish the plausibility of such a suggestion), he was forced to reply "no, I have no soul to speak for me", and was swiftly convicted. The account makes clear it was "not the only instance" reported where a "villain" had tried to escape justice by accusing his prosecutor of "this detestable crime".[72] As this case indicates, a crucial component in a successful defence was often the ability to call character witnesses, especially men of some standing, who would give evidence in court on behalf of the accused. Reputation was a vital commodity for a defendant, if only to decide whether his or her version of events was potentially plausible. Where present it could be very effective in deciding an ambiguous situation in the prisoner's favour. Thus, when Jane Walker was accused of stealing five shillings from Elizabeth Earle in Fleet Street, in 1689, "the prisoner having credible persons to clear her reputation [she] was discharged".[73] Similarly, when in 1694, Thomas Achust of Ludgate was accused of "clipping the current coyn of this kingdom" he called several men to speak to his character. His defence was that the special shears found in an old coat in his closet had been left two years earlier by a previous occupant of the room, not, on the face of it, perhaps the strongest of cases. However, "he called several witnesses to justify his honesty", and was found not guilty.[74]

Many techniques used for assessing witness or defendant reliability were the same as those employed by jurors today. Did the accused or witness appear nervous or "shifty"? When John Barret from Whitechapel was allegedly found in a house (not his own), that had been previously locked, and was subsequently charged with burglary, although "the prisoner denied it" he "faulter'd in his allegations ... so he was found

---

72. *Select Trials at the Sessions House in the Old-Bailey*, vol.1, 1720-1723. Printed by John Applebee (M.DCC.XCII), p.11.
73. OBSP, December 11-14, 1689, p.3.
74. OBSP, February 21-23, 1694, p.3.

guilty".[75] Juries generally appear to have been careful to give the benefit of any ambiguity in the evidence to the accused. Any real doubt about the provenance of stolen goods, the identity of the felon, or the possibility of honest mistake was usually given to the defendant. At the same Sessions that saw Barret convicted, Susan Stanley of Stepney was accused of stealing a silver seal, a key and 17s. in money from one John Metcalfe. However when the woman was searched for possessions, "the prosecutor could swear but to one half crown, that the woman had, which he might easily mistake, so she was acquitted". Ten years earlier, in 1681, when Thomas Squires was accused of stealing a gun from a gun-smith's in St Pauls, Covent Garden, although the case was "proved upon him by many shrewd circumstances" he was still acquitted because the prosecutor was not "able positively to fix it home".[76] Similarly, when in 1694 Richard Harding was accused of picking the pocket of one Jonathan Miller of his gold and silver coins he was also acquitted because "the prosecutor could not swear he was the person that pick'd his pocket, the money being found on the ground between the prisoner's legs, he was acquitted".[77] Cases based on purely circumstantial evidence were also usually treated with caution. In 1697 when Jane Watson, a housemaid, was accused of concealing the birth of her bastard child and then feloniously strangling it, soon after delivery (sadly a not infrequent occurrence amongst domestic servants afraid of losing their positions), which baby was later found hidden in a box in her room by her master who had been alerted by blood stains, her defence that the child was still born was accepted, there being "no marks of violence".[78]

An examination of such contemporary records as are available, such as those of the Old Bailey proceedings, reveal, for the most part, a reasonable (and rational) attempt at determining the truth of a case, and, usually the possession of an open mind by both Judges and jurors. Indeed, later in the century the very conservative jurist William Paley in his

---

75.   OBSP, December 10-11, 1691, p.3.
76.   OBSP, December 7-8, 1681, p.3.
77.   OBSP, February 21-23, 1694, p.1.
78.   OBSP, December 8-11, 1697, p.1.

Principles of Moral and Political Philosophy (1785) was to assert that juries were too quick to acquit, being too willing to give the defendant the benefit of any doubt; "I apprehend much harm to have been done to the community, by the over-strained scrupulousness, or weak timidity of juries, which demands often such proof of a prisoner's guilt as the nature and secrecy of his crime scarce possibly admit of".

This "open mind" can be clearly seen at work in numerous contemporary hearings, especially those where the instinctive sympathies of the jurors may not have been with the defendant. For an example can be cited the case of an Italian, Joseph Baretti who was accused of the murder of a man (apparently Welsh) in a London street in October 1769, allegedly stabbing him with a knife that he was carrying. He (Baretti) had apparently been accosted in a particularly lewd manner by a prostitute whom he struck. The woman raised a commotion and he was pursued, having been identified as a "Frenchman" by a group of men, one of whom he struck three times (and killed) with his pocket knife, when cornered by the group. There was a clear dispute as to the evidence. Barretti was able to call a number of character witnesses to vouch for him, including Dr Johnson and the actor David Garrick. Even so, it was a case where considerable violence had been used against a Briton, apparently acting purely out of a (possibly misguided) sense of chivalry and national pride. Thus, at first sight it was not not a case that would pre-dispose the defendant to the jurors' favour. Even so, the jury at the Old Bailey on October 20, 1769 acquitted him not only of murder but also of manslaughter, finding him to have been acting purely in self-defence.[79] Perhaps even more significantly, when, in 1694, a real Frenchman, John Carath of the parish of St Annes stabbed an Englishman to death with a sword, the latter having apparently attacked him with a cane, the jury swiftly returned a verdict of manslaughter only.[80] The injustices in the system (of which there were many) appear normally to have been due to structural causes in the process (for example, the speed and lack of depth

---

79.   Heppenstall, R. *Reflections on the Newgate Calendar* (1975), p.118.
80.   OBSP, February 21-23, 1694, p.1.

in hearings) rather than caused by an inherent personal lack of fairness on the part of the Judge and jurors.

The Verdict

The two serving maids were called to testify and presented a bleak picture of Flanders' involvement in the crime "... for though the thing was truth in the main, yet they aggravated it to the utmost extremity". At this time, the courtroom confrontation between accuser and defendant was relatively unmediated (by lawyers), and thus often quite dramatic. Defoe does not, however, record the precise nature of the questions asked by Flanders of the prosecution witnesses. However, she pretended in her speech (unsworn as it had to be at this time), that she intended to buy the goods she was accused of attempting to steal when she went into the building. This was to the great amusement of the court, and also rather implausible given that it was a domestic residence and "... no shop for the selling of anything". Judges in seventeenth and eighteenth century trials appear to have shown little reservation during the proceedings in revealing their points of view on the evidence to the jury.[81] Then as now, humour, despite the gravity of the proceedings, was not unknown in court. A burglar who was facing a hopeless case, in 1676, apparently even made a "joke" during his trial, at which "there was a great hoot in the court, but silence was straight commended".[82]

Despite the overt judicial scepticism, Flanders was convicted by the jury only of one felony (stealing the goods), not of the burglary (breaking in), which was of "small comfort" to her as the first would bring her a sentence of death in any event. On the facts of the case the jury's verdict was clearly a correct and sensible one. Burglary at this time appears to have required forcible entry to premises (rather than merely trespass) unless committed at night, although by the seventeenth century the term

---

81.   Green, T.A., *ibid.*, p.271.
82.   *A Perfect Narrative ...*, *ibid.*, printed for E. Olivier (1677), p.5.

was often colloquially applied to all housebreaking. That burglary, without forceful entry, had to be carried out at night appears to have been a fifteenth century innovation. In any event, whether her terminology was correct or not, housebreaking by day followed by the theft of more than 5s. had, quite early on, been made a felony without benefit of clergy.[83]

Whether all jury verdicts at this time were always so reliable given the circumstances in which the trials occurred is debatable. There must have been numerous cases of honest mistakes being made by that body, though if a trial Judge had doubts about a jury verdict he had the power (sometimes exercised) to recommend a Royal pardon.

Early Eighteenth Century Juries

There were firm limitations on who could serve on a jury. Jurors originally had to have a freehold of £20 a year, though this was broadened in 1692 to include men with £10 a year in freehold or copyhold land, in tenements, or in rents. The financial requirement so ensured that the trial jurors came largely from the middle groups of society.

The jurors were, thus, often the defendants' peers in only a strictly legal sense (ie, commoners rather than members of the nobility); frequently they were farmers in the country, tradesmen, merchants and successful craftsmen in the town. Generally, such people would probably be expected to have had a fairly conservative attitude to property rights, though, significantly, in two important types of cases juries were denied jurisdiction; these being namely game cases and excise prosecutions. The former is certainly not surprising as the game laws were the clearest illustration of "class legislation" in the eighteenth century; overtly in favour of the upper orders of society, and denying many people the right to kill game (designated birds and wild animals including pheasants and hares) on their own land. It is thus not surprising that this was entrusted to JPs (in rural areas always from the upper orders of society) rather than the "middling orders" who constituted the jury.

Although London was a huge city, the recurrence of some jurors'

---

83.   Sharpe, J.A., *Crime in Seventeenth Century England, ibid.*, p.107.

names on an annual basis mean that it can be said that jurors were drawn
from what was a tiny proportion of the population. As a result they
probably developed considerable familiarity with both substantive and
procedural criminal law as well as the Old Bailey Judges themselves.

At the end of the seventeenth and the beginning of the eighteenth
centuries prisoners would be tried in batches by the selected jurors, the
batches being anything from one to a dozen; six was quite a normal figure.
There would be hardly a pause between the trials, and the verdicts would
be given together, at the end of the group of trials. Jurors were said to be
taking notes at the Old Bailey in the 1730s, something that was probably
necessary if they were to correctly remember their verdicts in the different
cases, especially as only rarely did Judges find it necessary to sum up to
the jury.[84] Jury trial at this point was something of a mixed blessing,
though there were some potential advantages. In theory, a defendant could
challenge up to 36 potential jurors without reason (and more with cause)
using his peremptory challenge (finally only abolished in England after
being progressively reduced to three, by statute, in 1988, it survives in
America), though this was very little used by ordinary defendants accused
of felony.

The "new" system of reaching a verdict at the conclusion of each
individual case was only adopted at the Old Bailey in 1738, though it had
been in practice in other courts somewhat earlier. As a result, verdicts in
trials would often be quick, sometimes without even a retirement from
court. For example, the Middlesex jury that heard 21 cases over two days
in December 1679, deliberated just three times on verdicts on all the
defendants, returning an average of seven trial verdicts at a time.

It was customary in the early eighteenth century for the Old Bailey
Sessions to see two juries empanelled; appropriately, for a court with a
joint jurisdiction, one was drawn from the County of Middlesex, and the
other from the City of London, these normally hearing cases from their

---

84.   Beattie, *ibid.*, p.395.

own areas.[85]

As numerous offences had been removed from benefit of clergy, by Act of Parliament, during the seventeenth and eighteenth centuries, hundreds of people faced potential death sentences if convicted of many types of felony. Discretion, as a consequence, became all important. Jury mitigation, often referred to as "pious perjury", was very significant in effecting this. Juries did not think that all capital offences deserved the death penalty, and, for example, in larcenies removed from clergy, could find the defendant guilty of non-capital theft of less than 40 shillings from a house, or five shillings from a shop, or one shilling from the person, a "partial verdict", even when it was clear that the goods were valued at far more. Since *Bushel's* case in 1670 a Judge had been obliged to accept a jury verdict, whatever its basis, even when it went against his own legal direction, and was not able to take action against the jurors even when he disagreed with them.

He could, of course, use considerable moral pressure on them. In the American colonies, at any rate, there were well documented instances of this. In the trial for witchcraft arising out of the events at Salem in New England in 1692 the jury determining the fate of one alleged witch initially returned (unusually for that series of trials) a verdict of "not guilty", at which the Judge sent them back to reconsider their verdict (they changed their minds). Such things may have also gone on occasionally in England. However, in far more cases it appears likely that Judges actively connived with the jury in the commission of such "pious perjury", something that explains the almost routine returning of such verdicts in certain specific situations (such as the thefts by prostitutes from drunken "punters" discussed above, which regularly resulted in goods being valued at 10d. whatever their real worth). Some cases of this were extreme. For example, in one case, a theft of 23 guineas and goods from a house, which were later valued at £100 in the indictment, were declared by the jury to

---

85.　On the Old Bailey Sessions Papers (OBSP) generally see Langbein, J.H., "The Criminal Trial Before the Lawyers", p.274. *The University of Chicago Law Review*, vol.25, no.2 (1978).

be worth 39 shillings.[86]

So common was this down valuing that amongst some commentators there was a considerable degree of concern over the exercise of "pious perjury" during the eighteenth century; this was especially so amongst some legal writers, who felt that it was likely to damage the whole criminal justice system and encourage jurors to "forget their oath". Important amongst these critics were Henry Fielding in the 1750s and Martin Madan in the 1780s.[87] Research by J.A. Sharpe has suggested that at times, in seventeenth century Essex, perhaps as much as 20 per cent of Grand Larceny cases were deliberately undervalued by juries. Sometimes, of course, even the complainant in a criminal trial would commit "pious perjury" in advance, and deliberately undervalue his stolen goods to avoid the possibility of having an execution on his conscience. However, the significance of this form of mitigation can be exaggerated, especially in the London area. As most jurors in the City of London, repeatedly served on jury trials, giving them a probable familiarity with the law and courtroom conventions, and intimacy with the Judges their independence in practice from judicial directions was probably limited, especially in "run of the mill" felony cases. Most evidence suggests that nearly always the Judges and juries worked together in close harmony. The situations where they undervalued goods were, for the most part, probably conventionalized ones, approved by the judiciary; significantly, "pious perjury" only rarely led to outright acquittals. Indeed, some other, more "popular" commentators, felt that relations between trial Judges and jurors were often too close to be healthy. Sir John Hawles, a lawyer and author of *The Englishman's Right: A Dialogue Between a Barrister at Law and a Juryman* (1680) even felt (perhaps rather harshly if taken as a general proposition), that some jurors manifested a "slavish fear" of the Judges instructions, which encouraged them to "echoe back, what the bench would have done"; others were so keen for the status provided by the office of juryman that they would "not give a disobliging verdict, lest

---

86.   Beattie, *ibid.*, p.424.
87.   Green, T.A., *ibid.*, p.307.

they should be discharged, and serve no more".[88]

However the situation, in Flander's case, "pious perjury" on the part of the jury does not appear to have availed her, perhaps because her goods were worth so much more than the 40s. limit (being valued at £46 in total). She was swiftly convicted of a death penalty count, albeit acquitted of another serious charge (the burglary).

Flanders' Sentence

The next day, having been convicted, she was carried down to receive the death sentence. When prompted to speak in her own mitigation to the Judges "... for that they could represent things favourably for me" (ie, they could recommend a pardon from the death penalty), she pointed out that nobody had lost anything by her crime, and that it was her first offence (to conviction at least!), and that the potential loser (he had not actually lost any goods), the master of the house, "desired mercy might be shown" to her, which indeed he "very honestly did" (probably like many people, not wanting blood on his hands). The Judges however "... sat grave and mute", and then proceeded to pronounce the sentence of death. This was inevitable given the nature of the conviction; however, her mitigation was not a wasted or pointless effort, as the Judges also had the power to subsequently recommend a reprieve and transportation. Twelve days after receiving the sentence with other prisoners, the death warrant, the order for execution, was delivered, and Flanders' name was on it.

However, in this traumatic moment, her new Minister of religion, from outside the prison, arranged to give her spiritual advice and comfort and turned out to be a devout man who "broke into [her] very soul", unlike the prison Ordinary. He was so impressed with her apparent repentance and religious demeanour in the prison that he sought to intervene with the

---

88. See on this Linebough, P., "(Marxist) Social History and (Conservative) Legal History: A Reply to Professor Langbein", *The New York University Law Review*, vol. ix, no.2 (May 1985), p.233.

Recorder who had presided over Flanders' trial, to gain a reprieve. This was not uncommon, and was something which it was well in the Recorder's power to recommend.

Religious Conversions

A perhaps surprising number of condemned men and women at Tyburn made deeply contrite and penitent speeches at the gallows, though some showed defiance of the authorities to the end, some men openly blasphemed when advised by the Ordinary at the scaffold, as well as ignoring the preferred religious comfort and advice. Thus, in 1690, four of the eight felons due to be executed on one day "were very obstinate", refusing to give an account of their earlier "evil courses", and, despite having "good advice given them every day, yet they were not convinced of their trifling with the offers of grace and salvation, as if they believed not a future judgment, nor the eternal existence of their souls".[89] However, these men do not appear to have been typical amongst the condemned. The expressions of penitence from the scaffold were often quite formalized, usually emphasized how the committing of small sins had led the condemned man inexorably to the commission of larger ones and had a strong religious content.

Flanders was not unique in experiencing a religious conversion while in prison. In Newgate some people were obviously readily open to spiritual redemption, if only as a defence to the terror awaiting them. Some "converts" were very likely dissembling, in the hope that this would secure a reprieve as Charles Wesley, a great prison preacher later in the century was to freely admit "so often have I known [conversions and repentance] vanish away as soon as ever the expectation of death was removed". Some, however, do appear to have made sincere and deep religious conversions, such as that of the robber Mathew Lee, who on the eve of his execution in 1752 told his Minister that "... Jesus Christ hath

---

89. *A True Account of the Behaviour, Confession, and Last Dying Speeches of the Eight Criminals that were Executed at Tyburn on Monday, January 26, 1690.* Printed for Langley Curtis (1690), p.1.

washed away my sins in his own blood";[90] or John Lancaster, whose procession to Tyburn in 1748 was like a revival meeting if Wesley is to be believed.[91] Cynicism can thus be taken too far, it was still very much an age of faith, if to a markedly smaller degree than the century that had gone before. Christianity still provided the most important intellectual reference point for most people. That Flanders did not totally lapse afterwards, even if somewhat moderating her enthusiasm, would suggest that she at least was amongst the sincere ones. Defoe certainly wished the novel, as well as providing entertainment, to be seen as a portrait of spiritual redemption.

Shortly after her religious conversion Flanders learnt of her reprieve from the Minister "who had obtained a favourable report from the Recorder" in her case. While it was for the Monarch to authorize a reprieve, and some, like the future George III often assiduously attended to reprieves in person, they usually followed the advice of the trial Judge (such as Flanders' Recorder).[92] Though these men could be greatly variable in their personal willingness to make such a recommendation, a first offence was usually a reason for reprieve, if the offence was not so serious as to prevent this.[93] Because of this process, Flanders was spared her life, unlike some of her "worst comrades" in crime who went "out of the world by the steps and the string".

Intercession on the part of the condemned was widespread and was done by many levels of society (though obviously the higher the social status of the intervener the more effective it was likely to be). This can clearly be seen in the case of the fraudulent clergyman Dr Dodd, later in the century. Dr Samuel Johnson, who felt that this cleric had been treated harshly, even organized a campaign on his behalf which included writing letters to Lord Mansfield, the then Lord Chancellor, and a 20,000 signature petition being presented to Lord Percy. Despite this, these

---

90.   Quoted, V.A.C. Gatrell, *The Hanging Tree, ibid.,* p.379.
91.   Linebaugh, P., *The Tyburn Riot Against the Surgeons, Albion's Fatal Tree, ibid.,* p.87.
92.   Shaw, A.G.L., *Convicts and the Colonies* (1966), p.29.
93.   Shaw, A.G.L., *ibid.,* p.30.

representations were unsuccessful, partly because the unfairness of hanging other more commonplace men for the same offence and reprieving Dodd was well apparent to the authorities (again, perhaps, being indicative of a desire to at least appear even-handed in the administration of justice). However, in many cases such intercession was successful, the system apparently accepting that it was evidence that someone was a sufficiently useful member of society to be deserving of clemency despite having had the misfortune to be convicted of felony. Thus, when in 1754 Mary Squires was convicted of robbery in a case that many thought was misconceived, the *Newgate Calendar* could note that "some gentlemen who had heard the trial, being dissatisfied with the evidence which had been produced, made such application, that a free pardon was granted to Squires".

Function of Pardons and Reprieves in the System

Even before 1700, in the late seventeenth century, reprieves had already become a fundamental element in the administration of criminal law, Judges recommending certain people for pardon in a circuit letter at the conclusion of their Assize or Old Bailey sessions.[94] It was subsequently open to the King to approve this recommendation, and to issue the pardon via the Chancery. These recommendations were also often used by Judges where they felt that a jury which had convicted had been too harsh, or where there was a doubt about the legal basis of the conviction. So, for example, where a man in Kent in 1729 was, despite the guidance of the trial Judge, convicted of murdering his son, by beating and whipping him when he had a fever (the Judge thought the violence had not been excessive or the implement used for the beating improper), the Judge simply stayed the execution of the convicted man (as it was within his normal power to do) and applied to the King for a pardon.[95]

Pardons and reprieves were an especially common feature of the eighteenth century justice system, their importance advancing with the

---

94.   Beattie, J.M., *ibid.*, p.431.
95.   Beattie, J.M., *ibid.*, p.96.

development of the "bloody code", that was creating new capital offences and abolishing clergy for others. About half those sentenced to death in the century were reprieved and transported to the colonies or imprisoned instead.[96] Indeed, in the period 1701 to 1725, 67 per cent of Old Bailey capital convictions appear to have resulted in a reprieve (though this fell considerably for a period thereafter); by the start of the following century the figure was even higher. As the reformer Sir Samuel Romilly was to note of the "bloody code" in 1810 "these sanguinary statutes however, are not carried into execution".[97] He further observed "that for some time past the sentence of death has not been executed on more than a sixth" of all condemned men and women.

It has been asserted, with some truth, that the general "rule of thumb" discernible in the way in which the bloody code worked was that Judges passed and upheld the death penalty on pre-1688 capital offences and usually transportation on post-1688 capital offences (especially after the 1718 Transportation Act). This was particularly marked in the post-1750 period but also clearly manifest before.[98] There were some exceptions to this general tendency, especially with regard to capital crimes that had become much more prevalent in the eighteenth century due to changing economic conditions, such as various types of fraud.

However, for much of the eighteenth century after 1725 London was at variance with the rest of the country in having a relatively low rate of reprieves, the rate of executions compared to the number of death sentences passed tending to be much higher in the Metropolis for most of the 1700s than in the provinces. For example, of 527 people sentenced to death in London in the period 1749 to 1758 some two-thirds were actually executed, compared to about a quarter on the Norfolk circuit.[99] The reasons for this are not totally clear, though no doubt London's apparently more pressing criminal problems contributed to it as well as a belief in the possibly greater exemplary effect of a London execution

96. Hay, D., in *Albion's Fatal Tree, ibid.*, at p.43.
97. *Observations on the Criminal Law of England*, p.3.
98. McLynn, F., *Crime and Punishment in Eighteenth Century England* (1991), xii.
99. McLynn, *ibid.*, p.258.

at Tyburn. Also probably significant was the fact that it was harder in a large and mobile city like London to establish previous "character" by producing reputable witnesses to vouch for it, something that was always an important factor in determining pardons, than may have been the case in more static rural societies.

After 1660 the most common policy was to grant a reprieve, accompanied with the substitution of another punishment, such as transportation (especially after the 1718 Act came into force). This, in turn, giving the Judges enormous scope to decide who would go to America for seven to 14 years, and who would be hanged.

From the statistics women appear to have fared better at trial with regard to pardons than did men.[100] Children, as well, despite well publicized and notorious exceptions, were often granted clemency in this manner, after being convicted of felonies. This was especially significant in the case of very small children, who even if legally guilty of very serious matters were also frequently reprieved. For an example of this can be cited the case of the 10-year-old, William York, who, while living as a pauper in the poorhouse of Eye in Suffolk murdered a five-year-old girl because, according to the *Newgate Calendar,* "the child fouled the bed in which they lay together, that she was sulky and that he did not like her". He selected a knife and carefully "cut her wrist all round to the bone" an operation he repeated at her "other wrist, her elbows and left thigh". He then washed the body himself and buried it in a dunghill to avoid discovery. When he was examined by a magistrate "he showed very little concern and appeared easy and cheerful". Although sentenced to death he was reprieved several times on account of his age and eventually pardoned. This greater leniency towards women and children may have helped Flanders.

Later in the century Blackstone was to attempt to justify the discretionary element involved in the process, fearing that "the exclusion of pardons must necessarily introduce a very dangerous power in the Judge or jury, that of construing the criminal by the spirit instead of the

---

100.   Beattie, *ibid.*, p.438.

letter".[101] He was, however, well aware of Cesare Beccaria's then recent criticisms of the exercise of such discretion, noting that "pardons (according to some theorists) should be excluded in a perfect legislation where the punishments are mild but certain."[102] This was a view that was to triumph in early to mid-nineteenth century penology. Even before Beccaria, however, Henry Fielding had voiced concern at the effect of pardons in his *Inquiry*. He felt that "from the hopes of a pardon, at least with the condition of transportation" felons could receive encouragement when facing the risks inherent in their activities.

Nevertheless, late in the eighteenth century, the discretionary system was still receiving substantial intellectual support. It was expressly identified and approved of by William Paley in his famous *Principles*, first published in 1785, who said that the law "sweeps into the net every crime, which under any possible circumstances may merit the punishment of death: but ... a small proportion of each class are singled out, the general character, or the peculiar aggravations of whose crimes, render them fit examples of public justice". In some respects this neatly summarizes a widespread eighteenth century view of the operation of the justice system.

The Fate of Flanders' Colleagues

Although Flanders had escaped the noose, six of her fellow convicted felons were to be executed "... some for one crime, some for another and two for murder". In their distress, they made a "dismal groaning" from the condemned hole, where they were kept. The Ordinary "...was busy with them, disposing them to submit to their sentence". Even knowing of her own narrow escape from joining them, Flanders did not have the courage or composure to watch them being put into the customary carts, to be taken to Tyburn for execution. She cried for two hours, after their departure, unlike a few of the other inmates who, with true gallows

---

101.   Blackstone, W., *ibid.*, vol.iv, p.390.
102.   Blackstone, *ibid.*, vol.iv, p.390.

humour "... brutishly huzzaed and wished them a good journey".

Tyburn

Tyburn was the principal, though not the only, place of execution in London (pirates like Captain Kidd in 1701, for example, were normally hanged at Execution Dock by the Thames, near Wapping, and there were regular executions at Kennington Common and Smithfield).[103] Additionally, sometimes, any street could become the location for an *ad hoc* hanging, using a portable or specially erected gallows, to specially denounce a particular crime that had been committed in or near it. Tyburn was situated near to present day Marble Arch, to the West of London. It remained London's premier hanging spot till 1783 when its location was moved to Newgate itself.

The procession to Tyburn, from Newgate prison, was a public occasion. Prisoners were allowed to dress as they pleased, most choosing their best clothes, a few shrouds in preparation for their approaching deaths, and some wearing white cockades to proclaim their innocence of the crimes for which they were about to be executed. The widespread desire to appear smart (if at all possible) at execution, even prompted the legendary highwayman Dick Turpin to purchase a "new fustian frock and a pair of pumps" to be hanged in. As John Hall observed in 1708, for a man to go to his death in a dirty shirt if he could possibly avoid it, "... were enough to save the hangman a labour, and make a man die with grief and shame of being in that deplorable state". This was also probably popular with the executioners themselves, as, in theory the hangman had property in the dead felons' clothes, though the crowd sometimes prevented them exercising this right. In any event, it appears that the normal custom was for the relatives of the executed man to make a "bargain" with the executioner for the clothes, "which they purchase at a market price", so that they were not removed from the bodies of their loved ones.

---

103. By an old custom pirates' bodies would be hung in chains by the Thames so that they were washed by the water of three tides.

The condemned would usually be transported in open carts, though a few men of "quality", such as Lord Ferrers who was hanged in 1760 for murdering his valet, or the Reverend Dr Dodd who was hanged in 1777 for forgery, were allowed to drive to their deaths in private carriages. Ferrers' coach was even drawn by six black plumed horses. Those women to be burnt or men to be hung drawn and quartered (usually for coining), would customarily be drawn to Tyburn by a sledge. On the way, prisoners would be permitted to stop at public houses for refreshment or to speak to their relatives in the crowd, making the journey a long drawn out affair, usually lasting at least two hours. By ancient tradition, the procession often stopped at the Crown Inn near St Giles Pound, where the prisoners were allowed a drink, a custom that went back to the time when the historic Lazar house, that had been there previously, had given a bowl of ale to the condemned. Jack Sheppard, on the way to his own death, stopped at the City of Oxford tavern where he drank a pint of mulled sack, a procedure in which he was joined by the appropriate officials in attendance (the City Marshal, Under Sheriff, etc.). At Tyburn itself they would be ministered to by the Ordinary and usually allowed (and sometimes encouraged) to make a final speech before execution, though this was occasionally drowned out by the noise of the crowd.

Execution in the Eighteenth Century

That Flanders should be terrified by her possible impending fate, and horrified by that of her unreprieved colleagues, is quite understandable. The execution scene was to be depicted, graphically, later in the century, by William Hogarth in the print of "Thomas" the "Idle Prentice" at Tyburn (etched in 1747). He is carrying his own coffin in readiness, in his cart, with the Ordinary travelling in front by carriage, while pick-pockets, totally unabashed, "work" the crowd. It was an awful and terrifying death. Those to be executed were pushed off the back of the cart and strangled, taking usually at least five minutes to die, and occasionally as much as 15 or 20 (in the 1600s, Samuel Pepys had unsuccessfully advocated the introduction of silk ropes that were "soft and sleek" to ensure a closer fit, and thus a swifter death, than that provided by the normal hemp ropes used). Jack Sheppard, for example, was recorded as having died "with difficulty and was much pitied by the surrounding multitude", this was especially so as this popular criminal hero, whatever his earlier irreverence, had "behaved with great decency at the place of execution".[104] Normally, according to Hall, before they were pushed "their caps are pull'd over their eyes". Between 1571 and 1759 felons were hanged from "Tyburn's triple tree", a triangular three limbed construction, each crossbeam of which could take up to eight men.[105] It was not till the 1880s that fully effective "drops", inducing a swift death (by breaking the neck, rather than strangulation) were introduced, though the drop itself was old at this point (it was first used, singularly ineptly, to execute Lord Ferrers in 1760).[106] Sometimes concerned relatives or the executioner would pull on the hanging man's legs to expedite the process. There were even a few cases where a "hanged" man was revived afterwards, such as the famous "half hanged Smith" (one John Smith, a habitual burglar who was later transported to Virginia), who was reprieved 15 minutes into his execution in 1705. This felon was later able to give a graphic account of the early stages of such a death; after coming to in a local tavern he stated that "... he, for some time was sensible of very great pain, occasioned by the weight of his body, and felt his spirits in a strange commotion, violently pressing upwards; that having forced their way to his head, he, as it were, saw a great blaze, or glaring light which seemed to go out at his eyes with a flash, and then he lost all sense of pain". On his revival he suffered an acute case of pins and needles, unlike some, he was later reprieved rather than having to go through the process again.

Those to be executed for treason, if men, experienced an aggravated form of death (the use of which was uncommon in England compared to the situation in much of the rest of Europe). This can be summed up in

---

104. Earlier, Sheppard, although he had regularly attended prayers in the chapel and "behaved with decency there" in private "affected mirth" before going, and subsequently, "... endeavoured to prevent any degree of seriousness among the other prisoners on their return".
105. Laurence, J., *ibid.*, p.43.
106. Gatrell, VAC, The Hanging Tree (1994), p.54.

the sentence handed down to the Jacobite plotter Christopher Layer in 1722 after his conviction for the offence of high treason: "you, Christopher Layer, be led to the place from whence you came, and from thence you are to be drawn to the place of execution, and there you are to be hanged by the neck, but not till you are dead, but you are to be cut down alive, and your bowels to be taken out, and burnt before your face; your head is to be sever'd from your body, and your body to be divided into four quarters; and that your head and quarters be disposed of where His Majesty shall think fit".[107] The sentence continued even after death as, with regard to Layer's remains, "his quarters were delivered to his friends, who put them into a hearse and sent them to Mr Purdy's an undertaker ... and his head was the next morning fixed on a pole at Temple Bar". This was a common place for traitors' heads to be mounted. For example the Cromwellian Major General Harrison's head was mounted there after his own execution in this manner in 1666 (it stayed there for many years), an event at which, if Samuel Pepys is to be believed, he showed considerable fortitude "looking as cheerful as a man could in that situation". These cases, like the burning of women, were comparatively rare, being confined to treason (including coining), and sometimes mitigated by the executioners to some degree. As William Blackstone was to note, in 1769, there were very few cases in the eighteenth century of people being burnt or disembowelled without first being strangled "... and those accidental or by negligence". He also observed that contemporary English practice on punishment and execution, though apparently "disgusting" was relatively lenient compared to the "... shocking apparatus of death and torment, to be met with in the criminal codes of almost every other nation in Europe".[108]

Execution day would be well signalled to the Newgate inmates as, in accordance with a bequest made in 1605, the big bell of St Sepulchre's Church was rung on the night preceding every execution of convicts confined at Newgate, as well as on the morning of the execution itself.[109]

---

107.   *The London Journal*, March 4, 1723.
108.   Blackstone, W., *Commentaries* (1769), Book iv, p.371.
109.   Radzinowicz, L., *ibid.*, vol.1, p.173.

That is why, on the execution day that she escaped through her reprieve, Flanders was saluted "... with the tolling of the great bell of St Sepulchre's". Eight times a year (following the Bailey Sessions), between two and a dozen people would be hanged and the bell rung.[110] Additionally, the Beadle to St Sepulchre's was paid from an endowment to read an exhortation to the condemned the evening before their executions, in which he beseeched them all to: "... keep this night in waking and hearty prayer to God for the salvation of your own souls".[111]

In the early eighteenth century London executions were becoming progressively more rowdy. This was probably a result of a combination of population growth, transport improvement, increased alcohol consumption and improved advance publicity for executions (via the growing press), which in turn allowed large crowds, often numbered in their thousands, to assemble in readiness at Tyburn. These were not just the "vulgar" citizens or mob, all classes would attend. Later in the century James Boswell was to visit the scene because, as he freely admitted, "in my younger years I had read in the *Lives of the Convicts* so much about Tyburn that I had a sort of horrid eagerness to be there". Having got there, though, the awful spectacle depressed him and induced a profound attack of melancholy for several weeks: "I was most terribly shocked".[112] Stands were sometimes erected at Tyburn, to provide for paying spectators, with an unimpeded view of the proceedings, and were known as "Mrs Proctor's Pews" (on one famous occasion a dozen people were killed when one of them collapsed). These stands can also be clearly seen in Hogarth's later portrayal of the execution scene. By 1725 many of the earlier vestiges of solemnity at an execution were disappearing, with some executions taking on a grotesque, almost carnival like, atmosphere. In that year a mob, drunk on gin and other spirits, that was lining the procession route to Tyburn, even fought with the military guards to reach the prisoners.[113] So many

---

110.   Gatrell, V.A.C., *The Hanging Tree* (1994), p.30.
111.   Besant, W., *London in the Eighteenth Century* (1908), p.547.
112.   Boswell, J., *London Diary*, May 4, 1763, Heinemann edn (1950), p.252.
113.   Cockburn, J.S., "Punishment and Brutalization", *Law and History Review*, vol.12, no.1 (1994), p.166.

people lined the route for the execution of a celebrated felon that Sheppard had hoped to make a final escape, and thus cheat death, by cutting himself free with a concealed knife (discovered just before the procession left Newgate) and throwing himself into a dense group of sympathetic onlookers by the roadside. Had he managed this, the escorting troop of soldiers and band of constables may well have been unable to recover him before he was spirited away by elements in the crowd.

As with pilloried prisoners the reaction to the condemned by the crowd would depend greatly on the nature of the crime for which they were to be executed. Some would be cheered; some, like the widely hated Jonathan Wild, were abused and pelted at the gallows (so much so that his executioner had to speed up his hanging; his knowledge that this was likely may explain his unsuccessful attempt at committing suicide in Newgate the previous night with an overdose of laudanum). Those guilty of sexual crimes, or crimes against children would also receive considerable abuse. A brave end was usually well appreciated by the spectators. An anonymous contemporary account showed that some of them, at least, disliked a man to "... snivel to the Ordinary, and die a dunghill [coward] at last". As John Hall observed in 1708, "there is a great deal of glory in dying like a heroe, and making a decent figure in the cart". The considerable display of aplomb by Lord Ferrers, may also explain the respectful treatment that this aristocrat received from the crowd at the gallows in 1760. Indeed, the London crowd of the early eighteenth century appear to have increasingly appreciated a display of public bravura rather than penitence, perhaps indicative of some decline in religion or a change in social attitudes. One observer from the period, Bernard De Mandeville in 1725, even felt that some condemned prisoners were increasingly going to their deaths not only "drinking madly" but also "jeering others that are less impenitent". De Mandeville also noted that some sections of the crowd did not seem to be greatly moved or edified by the terrible spectacle, nonchalantly saying that "there is nothing in being hang'd, but a wry neck, and a wet pair of breeches". Sometimes the "mob" would attempt to secure the bodies of popular felons which were being removed to the Surgeon's Hall for public dissection, or to be covered in pitch prior to being hung in chains on a gibbet as a warning to other criminals; they were often successful in this despite the guards.[114]

The fatalistic attitude of many is caught by the final verse of Jack Sheppard's *Last Epistle,* published in *The Daily Journal* in 1724.[115]

"Oh! then to the tree I must go;
The Judge he has ordered that sentence.
And then comes a gownsman you know,
And tells a dull tale of repentance.
By the gullet we're ty'd very tight;
We beg all spectators, pray for us.
Our peepers are hid from the light,
The tumbril shoves off, and we morrice [dance]."

Because of these apparent changes, by the start of the 1750s many writers, such as Henry Fielding, felt that the scene at Tyburn was rapidly becoming counter-productive, providing moral support from the unruly crowds to many convicted felons rather than a complete severance of social solidarity. He lamented that because of this the "thief's procession to Tyburn, and his last moments there are all triumphant" rather than shameful.[116] This feeling that the ceremony itself might be becoming damaging, was fairly widespread. In 1784 the radical John Wilkes expressed the view that the Englishman's famous bravery and disdain for death was nurtured by such gruesome public spectacles. This, along with the pressing policing considerations in supervising the unruly crowds at Tyburn and along the route of the two hour procession led, towards the end of the century, to a move in venue from Tyburn to outside Newgate Prison itself. However, even then, as James Boswell was to record in his *The Life of Johnson,* this was not universally supported. Dr Johnson

---

114. Something that was allowed in restricted cases since Elizabethan times, and expanded after the 1752 Murder Act. Surgeons Hall was, appropriately, located till 1809 in the Old Bailey. The new method of "hands on" training for surgeons made their appetite for corpses considerable.
115. November 16, 1724, it took up half the front page.
116. Fielding, H., *Inquiry, ibid.,* p.122.

(admittedly by then in a minority) felt that there was little to say for it, arguing that "... it is not an improvement; ... the old method was most satisfactory to all parties; the publick was gratified by a procession; the criminal was supported by it".

The hangmen of the era were traditionally known as "Jack Ketch" after the real name of a famous executioner of the 1660s, a man whose name was to become the synonym for English hangmen for the next two centuries. The original Ketch, perhaps revealingly, was noted for his professional incompetence and even felt it necessary to publish an article defending himself against criticism for his mishandling of the execution of Lord Russell in 1683. In this he attributed the blame for the bungled decapitation to Lord Russell's failure to position his neck appropriately! However, he also bungled the execution (again, as appropriate in a treason case involving an aristocrat, by beheading) of the Duke of Monmouth two years later, taking at least five strokes to remove his head.[117]

Executioners were paid a small stipend as a retainer, as well as on a piece-work basis for each execution they actually carried out (they were also often paid, between executions, to carry out the whippings of vagrants, supervision of the pillories etc.). They were further able to supplement their incomes (sometimes very significantly) by selling off pieces of the hemp rope that had been used in the execution of notorious criminals (though the one used for Lord Ferrers' had been, allegedly, made of silk). These pieces of rope were often much sought after as souvenirs by the public. Many of the men who carried out this office were themselves little different to those they executed, indeed several, such as Pascha Rose, who was hanged at Tyburn in 1686, or John Price, who was executed at Bunhill Fields in 1718, met an identical fate to that of their professional clients.[118]

Those to be executed, especially if for a notable crime, would often be expected to make a final speech at the scaffold. These were usually

---

117. Robin, Gerald D., *The Executioner: His Place in English Society* (1953), p.242. The last nobleman to be beheaded for treason appears to have been Lord Lovat in 1747.

118. Laurence, J., *ibid.*, p.99.

quite stylised and conventional in content, in part no doubt the result of assiduous promptings and suggestions by attending chaplains. So common was this for major felons that the Jacobite Christopher Layer even felt it was necessary to publicly justify a lack of a final speech at his place of execution and as a result: "at the fatal tree he delivered a paper to Mr Walter Price, the under-sheriff, importing, `that as he had resolved to employ all the time allowed him at the place of execution in devotion, instead of a speech to the spectators he had committed his thoughts of all worldly affairs to writing'".

The circumstances attendant on executions were well known to Londoners, and regularly featured, or were referred to, in their popular entertainments. Thus "Polly", in Gay's *The Beggars' Opera,* when envisaging the highwayman MacHeath's imminent execution was painting a well known scene when she observed, "methinks I see him already in the cart, sweeter and more lovely than the nosegay in his hand! ... I hear the crowd extolling his resolution and intrepidity! ... What vollies of sighs are sent from the windows of Holborn, that so comcly a youth should be brought to disgrace! ... I see him at the tree! The whole circle are in tears! ... even butchers weep! ... Jack Ketch himself hesitates to perform his duty, and would be glad to lose his fee, by a reprieve".

Transportation

Flanders' reprieve was on condition of transportation to the American colonies. She was subsequently put on board a ship in the Thames with 13 hardened criminals from Newgate, having spent a further 15 weeks, after her sentence was commuted, in prison.

The proportion of transports coming, like Flanders, from London or its environs, was particularly high. One estimate places those from the Metropolis and the South-Eastern counties at half of an estimated total figure from England of 36,000, in the period from the 1718 Act to the Revolution of 1776 (which brought a temporary end to the practice, until it was redirected to Australia), though this number may well be on the low side.[119] Indeed, though impossible to estimate precisely how many were transported to America in total, from the 1650s onwards, some estimates place it as high as between 50,000 and 100,000 people, with 2,000 a year making the voyage in the early 1770s.[120] Others place it significantly lower, at least 30,000 people and possibly 50,000, though this figure does not include the significant numbers of Irish transports.[121]

Unlike Flanders, most transports were male (about 80 per cent) and in their late teens or twenties (about 75 per cent). Despite this, several were, like Flanders, in their 50s and 60s. On the ships *Gilbert* and *Jonathan*, which left London for Maryland in 1721 and 1724 respectively, of the total of 153 convicts embarked, seven were over 50, and one over 60.[122] As well as reflecting the disproportionate amount of males compared to females involved in crime, it has been argued that the relatively small proportion of women amongst the transports also reflects a disposition on the part of the courts to treat women more leniently, in this respect, than men. According to this school of thought the courts were more reluctant to order females to be transported, and as a general rule, according to this interpretation, Judges and juries favoured banishment across the seas only for those women (perhaps like Flanders) who were perceived as constituting a serious threat to society (and thus, in turn, suggesting that female transports were normally involved in more serious crimes than many of their male counterparts).[123] Generally, the transports who were sent across the Atlantic, other than some of the small number of Scottish ones later in the century, were guilty of neither major felonies

---

119. Along with 13,000 from Ireland and only 700 from Scotland. See on this Ekirch, A.R., *Bound for America: The Transportation of British Convicts to the Colonies, 1718-1775*.
120. Barnes, H.E., *The Story of Punishment* (1972), p.71.
121. See Radzinowicz, L., *ibid.*, vol.5, p.468.
122. "Bound for America: A Profile of British Convicts Transported to the Colonies 1718-1775", reproduced in *Crime and Justice in American History* (1991), Monkonen, E. (ed), vol.1, p.99.
123. "Bound for America: A Profile of British Convicts Transported to the Colonies 1718-1775", reproduced in *Crime and Justice in American History* (1991) Monkonen, E. (ed), vol.1, p.98.

(for which they would have been executed), nor, apart it appears from significant numbers of those sent from Ireland, were they merely vagrants, beggars or petty thieves. Many, if not most, of those transported were guilty of clergyable "grand larceny".[124] Most transports after 1718 had committed non-capital felonies for which they could claim benefit of clergy to avoid the death penalty, the Transportation Act of that year empowering the courts to banish such clergied offenders for seven years.

The earlier practice of reprieving prisoners from execution on condition that they agreed to transport themselves to the colonies first became common after the Restoration in 1660.[125] It had, however, an ancestry going back to 1597, when courts of Quarter Sessions were empowered to "banish" beyond the seas vagabonds and sturdy beggars "who will not be reformed of their roguish kind of life". This law appears to have been very little used (if at all). In 1617, however, greater provision was made for its employment by an Order of the Privy Council which stated that subjects of the King who had committed offences which "though heynous in themselves, yet [are] not of the highest nature" might be reprieved from execution if they were also people "who for strength of bodye or other abilityes shall be thought fitt to be imployed in forreine discoveryes or services beyond the seas". Provided, that they were not guilty of murder, rape, witchcraft or burglary. In the 1660s transportation was made an available punishment, in lieu of death, for a restricted selection of offences, in particular theft from military stores, convicted "Moss-troopers" from the border country in the north of England who were guilty of pillaging and those convicted of fire raising.

In the period 1655 to 1699 it would appear that about 4,500 convicts were sent to the Americas.[126] Other than those sent under the few minor statutes permitting transportation as a legal sentence (such as the Act of 1666 dealing with the border Moss Troopers), nearly all transports to

---

124.   "Bound for America: A Profile of British Convicts Transported to the Colonies 1718-1775", reproduced in *Crime and Justice in American History* (1991) Monkonen, E. (ed), vol.1, p.104.
125.   Shaw, A.G.L., *Convicts and the Colonies* (1977), p.28.
126.   Sharpe, J.A., *Crime in Seventeenth Century England* (1987), p.147.

America in the seventeenth century went as a condition of a Royal Pardon; exile, as Blackstone later noted, being a punishment that was "unknown to the common law". The normal procedural way of effecting this was first established under the Republic, in 1655, and continued after the Restoration; it was to be the normal way of providing for transportation until 1718. Thus, chronologically, according to the novel, it was almost certainly the manner by which Flanders would have gone to America. In 1655 prisoners who had been convicted of minor felonies at the Surrey Assizes were first given conditional pardons, with the condition being that "... every of them shall be ... transported beyond the seas to some English Plantacon with all convenient speed and if they or any of them shall refuse to bee transported being thereunto required or make any escape or retourne to England within tenn years after theire said transportation without lawful licence first had then this present pardon to them ... to be null and voyd".[127] Thus, premature return would, of course, automatically mean their execution.

Subsequently, transportation was used for some offenders who had pleaded benefit of clergy, and for others reprieved through the Royal prerogative of mercy as death was considered too harsh in their particular cases. They would normally have sued for a conditional pardon under the Great Seal (conditional on transportation). Flanders' Lancashire husband was transported under such circumstances having made (under pressure, and very unusually it appears) an "offer of a voluntary transportation" in exchange for not being prosecuted to trial.

Thus, strictly speaking, as a matter of pure law in the 1600s, transportation was not usually a sentence in its own right (except where statute specifically so provided) but a condition precedent to receiving a pardon; those who accepted it between 1655 and 1718 avoiding their death sentences (though this seems to have been overlooked with regard to the 800 captured prisoners who were transported to the West Indies after Lord Chief Justice Jeffreys' "Bloody Assizes", trials that were notorious for their disregard of normal legal procedures, following the

---

127.   Smith, A.E., "The Transportation of Convicts to the American Colonies in the Seventeenth Century", *American Historical Review*, vol.39 (1934), p.232.

battle of Sedgemoor in 1685).[128]

The Transportation Act (passed in 1717) which came into force in 1718, greatly increased the extent of use of this punishment, placing it on a sound statutory basis. After 1718 it was very unusual for a prisoner to be left to make his own arrangements to transport himself, though a few men of higher social position were still allowed to transport themselves after that date, most were carried by specifically appointed men, such as the individual merchant who had the contract for Newgate and the Home Circuit.[129]. The usual period was for seven years, though in some serious cases 14 could be ordered. Part of the motivation behind the growth of this punishment was set out quite explicitly in the Preamble to the Transportation Act of 1718, saying that such a law, as well as deterring criminals would provide labour since "... in many of His Majesty's Plantations in America there is a great want of servants". The explanation for the introduction of the new power contained in the Act was also attributed by contemporaries to a variety of other factors. One journal felt that it was because "the Kingdom being all on a sudden almost over-run with thieves and their abettors, and great numbers of persons, to whom Royal pardon had been extended upon condition of transporting themselves to the West Indies, neglecting to perform the said condition and returning to their former wickedness ... the Transportation Act passed, for clearing the nation of these vermin".[130]

However, the new provision's main penal function was to provide a viable secondary punishment to the death penalty (imprisonment being comparatively little used, until the 1760s, as a main punishment in its own right, except for beggars and vagrants sent to the Bridewell and other houses of correction).[131] It was aimed primarily at "any person convicted for an offence for which he is liable to be whipt or burnt in the hand" (ie,

---

128.   Defoe always felt that this and the hundreds of attendant executions should be contrasted with the comparative "leniency" of the Hanoverian regime towards the Jacobites.
129.   Beattie, J.M., *ibid.*, p.509.
130.   *The Original Half-Penny London Journal*, Tuesday April 1, 1725.
131.   See below, p.238.

clergyable first offenders).

The apparently large number of executions at the time did engender alternative suggestions that were even more drastic than transportation, including that some convicts should be made into complete slaves instead of temporarily indentured servants "every one must allow that it is the part of good policy to reap public benefits from private evils".[132] Nevertheless, the impact of transportation on English penal practice was immense. This can be seen very readily in the balance of disposals after a normal Old Bailey Sessions. A typical division from the 1670s (that of the Sessions that took place from April 30 to May 2 in 1679) resulted in 14 people sentenced to be executed (nine men and three women), 19 to be "burned in the hand" (ie, clergied) and released and only "two received the Mercy of the Court for Transportation". In contrast, the Sessions that finished at the start of May 1724 produced only three death sentences, with three men to be burnt in the hand and also to receive alternative punishments (such as whipping), three simply to be whipped and 24 to be transported (though this was probably a slightly extreme case, most Sessions producing more death sentences).[133]

The prisoner's voyage to America took from eight to 12 weeks. Most prisoners were held in leg irons, between decks, in conditions of considerable unpleasantness. Between 1725 and 1736 one in five died during the sailings. The dangers of the voyage out can be seen in the case of William Parsons, who was transported in 1749 for counterfeiting. Of the 170 convicts embarked with him on board one Captain Dobbins' ship in the Thames, 50 died on the voyage. On reaching Maryland Parsons swiftly absconded, turned highwayman and with the money he made returned to England where he continued his criminal activities, though he was ultimately executed for returning prematurely from transportation (a capital offence in its own right).[134]

---

132. Proposals to the Legislature for Preventing the Frequent Executions of Convicts. In a letter to the Right Honourable Henry Pelham, p.26 "by a student of Politics", 1754.
133. *Daily Journal*, May 4, 1724.
134. *The Newgate Calendar, ibid.*, p.262.

Women fared, if anything, better than men on the voyage across the Atlantic. Figures from the landing dockets for a sample of 19 voyages from 1719 to 1736 suggest a mortality rate of 15.6 per cent for men and 13.7 per cent for the women. In part it may have been slightly lower amongst females because of a reduced level of alcohol consumption amongst them. As the eighteenth century progressed, however, it would appear that the voyages became safer, certainly the mortality rates on the much longer voyage to Australia, which replaced America in the 1790s (after the Revolution of 1776) were relatively modest.

Under the 1718 Act the court had the power to make over offenders "to any such person as shall contract for the performance of such transportation ... and they shall have property and interest in the service of such person for such term of years". The indentured convicts were usually sold in America to planters or other colonists by the contracting merchants who had carried them across the Atlantic. However, after the voyage a wealthy convict could buy his or her own freedom, though of course not allowed to return to England for seven years. Despite this, since even healthy unskilled convicts could sell for £10, as indentured labourers, this was likely to be very expensive and beyond the means of most transports.[135]

Fortunately, Flanders was rich and well able to afford the cost of her freedom. However, in this she was certainly not unique; in 1754 an alleged perjurer, Elizabeth Canning bought her freedom with popularly subscribed money after she was transported. Although widely believed to be innocent, as *The Newgate Calendar* was to note "she was transported to New England on July 31, 1754, having first received some hundreds of pounds collected by the bounty of her friends and partizans. She was afterwards reputably married in America".

If the money was available, not only could freedom be purchased at the end of the journey, but the voyage itself made much more comfortable. Indeed, Flanders was able to allay her husband's fears over transportation by pointing out that "if he had money ... he might not only avoid the

---

135.   Shaw, A.G.L., *ibid.*, p.35.

servitude, suppos'd to be the consequence of transportation but also any unpleasantness of life in America and on the way to it". This was also well evidenced by contemporary cases. *The Gentleman's Magazine* for July 1736, reported that a group of five lawyers, sentenced for stealing books from the library of Trinity College Cambridge, went to the port by hackney carriage and were accommodated "with the captains cabin, which they stored with plenty of provisions etc.for their voyage and travels".[136]

Flanders' Voyage

Thus, Moll Flanders was following a common practice for rich transportees in paying for luxuries. Her special treatment cost her £20 and some tobacco for the ship's captain; this was certainly a reasonable price to pay to escape the ship's hold. This was especially so as the captain took her and her sea-sick husband on shore with him when they harboured in Ireland, en route for America, "... in kindness to [her] husband, who bore the sea very ill".

Earlier in her life (the first time Flanders voluntarily went to America as an "honest" woman) her mother in Virginia had told her daughter (as it was to transpire), that she was herself a transported felon, remarking as well to her that "some of the best men in the country were burnt in the hand, there's Major Banks says she, he was an eminent pick pocket. Justice R. Blank was a shoplifter. Both of them were burnt in the hand", the sign of a previous offence that had attracted benefit of clergy. She had then shown her daughter a "very fine white arm" and hand which were branded on the palm, as was the practice in such cases. Some transports genuinely did do well, though Defoe, worldly man though he was, appears to have had a rather optimistic view, and tended to ignore the many unfortunate ones amongst them; some were cruelly whipped and ill-treated

---

136.   Quoted A.G.L. Shaw, *Convicts and the Colonies* (1966), p.36.

by their new masters.[137] Indeed it was only in 1705 that a law made it necessary to get a JP's order before it was permitted to flog a European servant naked, failure to do so still only bringing a penalty of 40s. (sadly this law does not appear to have extended to the native Indians or negro slaves). Perhaps not surprisingly, many of these indentured servants appear to have fled from their masters to the sanctuary of the nearby forests and mountains of that vast country.[138] The harshness of life for some of them can be seen in a letter by a near contemporary transport of Flanders, one Richard Frethome, who wrote that since he had landed he had eaten nothing but pease pottage, had no shirt to wear, no shoes to put on, and had to work from dawn to dusk. So demoralizing was this that he "... thought no head had been able to hold so much water as hath and doth daly flow from my eyes". He died a few months after writing. Adversity was especially likely if the individual lacked clerical skills or basic literacy that might allow them a better employment. Later in the century, Oliver Goldsmith was to record the experiences of another English transport in this respect "when we came ashore, we were sold to the planters. I was bound for seven years and as I was no scholar, for I had forgotten my letters, I was obliged to work among the negroes".[139] Thus Flanders' mother was certainly exaggerating when she told her daughter that "many a Newgate bird becomes a great man" in America, though there were a few recorded cases of this happening.

However, in fairness it must be noted that Defoe's optimistic appraisal was also a widely held contemporary view, one writer on Virginia even remarking that "... few of them ever lived so well and so easily before [they were sent to America]".[140] Fifty years later William Eden, the future Lord Auckland, and himself a strong opponent of the excessive use of capital punishment, said, in his *Principles of Penal Law* (1771) that criminals transported to the Americas "merely transferred to a new country ... as fertile, as happy, as civilized, and in general as healthy as

---

137.   A.G.L. Shaw, *ibid.*, p.32.
138.   Barnes, H.E., *The Story of Punishment*, 2nd edn (1972), p.72.
139.   *The City of the World* (1762) Everyman edn (1934), p.222.
140.   Barnes, H.E., *ibid.*, p.72.

that which he hath offended" and feared that the punishment might even operate as a "temptation to the offence". However, even allowing for exaggeration, it is still the case that those who had good masters were certainly much better off than they had been in Newgate.

For many "respectable" inhabitants of the American colonies, the convicts sent over from England and Ireland were not at all welcome, and were often perceived as a social menace who needed to be subjected to severe discipline if they were to be effectively controlled.[141] They appear, at times in the 1700s, to have virtually been social "pariahs". In 1767, for example, Benjamin Franklin (then in England) noted in his articles and public letters that the Americans remembered the Act authorizing transportation to the colonies (that of 1718) as the "most cruel insult that perhaps was ever offered by one people to another, that of emptying our gaols into their settlements". He felt that it was an insult that had been further aggravated by the "barbarous ill-placed sarcasm" shown in a report from the Board of Trade, when one of the colonies complained of the Act. The report, in ignoring the objection, bluntly stated "it is necessary that it should be continued for the better peopling of your Majesty's colonies". This was a theme he was to return to in 1770, giving an "American" point of view, with particular reference to occasional English criticisms of the apparently harsh treatment sometimes meted out to the transported prisoners. He observed that "honest hired servants" were treated as mildly in America as in England. But the "villains" transported to the Americas necessarily had to "be ruled with a rod of iron". He also observed that when the colonies had introduced laws of their own banning the importation and sale of transports these had been over-ruled from London, and asked Englishmen why "if mild laws could govern such people, why don't you keep and govern them by your own mild laws at home?" In reality, however, transports do not seem to have committed a particularly high proportion of crimes in colonial America.

Most of them went to Virginia (as did Flanders initially) or Maryland,

---

141.   See Letter from Benjamin Franklin to the Printer of the *London Chronicle*, May 9, 1759.

where agriculture was more labour intensive than further North and greater numbers of workers needed (in 1700, England's American colonies still only had a combined population of perhaps a little over 260,000 people), although many other American colonies also took some. Flanders was also very fortunate (and unusual) in that her Lancashire husband was able to accompany her, having escaped conviction on an evidential technicality (poor identification), on the proviso that he too agreed to be transported to America.[142]

Flanders in the New World

Flanders' money, and contacts, ensured them a good future in the New World. She later moved to Maryland and bought a plantation there, which, with the advice of a helpful Quaker, they planted with tobacco. They were assisted in this having themselves "bought us two servants, (viz) an English woman-servant just come on shore from a ship of Liverpool, and a negro man-servant". Her husband was speedily both busy and content with his new lot, enjoying, in particular, the abundant hunting available in the area. As a result, the pair of them were able to reflect how much better their lives were "not than Newgate only, but than the most prosperous of our circumstances in the wicked trade that we had been both carrying on".

Flanders subsequently found, to her delight, that she had also inherited another plantation from her mother that had been given to her (Flanders') American son to hold on her behalf as a trustee. She was thus a rich woman. Overjoyed by this she made her son a present of a gold watch that she had brought over from England, though she did not "... tell him that [she] stole it from a gentlewoman's side, at a meeting-house in London"!

---

142.   This may be a legal flaw in Defoe's work; the circumstances in which such "deals" were struck (if at all), and their legality, are little documented.

Flanders Reform and the Remainder of her Life

The limit of Flanders' transportation (in her case the normal seven years, though in some serious cases it could be 14) having passed by a year, she returned home to England on a visit, when nearly 70 years of age. This was comparatively rare for transports, most of whom were well settled in the Americas after their periods were expired. She decided to stay in the "mother" country, and was later joined by her husband (whose transportation time was also over). She spent the remainder of her life, comfortably settled, and in "sincere penitence" for her earlier sins; though, as Defoe ambiguously noted in his preface to the novel, not always "... so extraordinarily penitent as she was at first".

Chapter 6

Historical Analysis of Aspects of Moll Flanders' Criminal Career

"Immorality is without doubt the present reigning distemper of the Nation." Daniel Defoe, The Poor Man's Plea (1698).
"Law is a bottomless pit."
Dr Arbuthnot, "The History of John Bull" (1712).

Flanders was not a "typical" criminal if such a thing existed in the late seventeenth and early eighteenth century; no one who first embarked on a criminal career at the age of 48 could be. Again, it should be stressed that at this time most criminals, even adults, were probably casual opportunists, rather than hardened and skilful professionals like Flanders (who managed to make many hundreds of pounds over a 12-year long career). Few contemporary criminals had her intelligence or social graces (she was clearly a precursor of the type of professional pickpocket able to infiltrate middle and upper class environments, who in the next century would be referred to as a member of the "swell mob").[1] However, her experiences of crime and the penal process in London are illustrative of a policing and criminal justice system that was already under severe structural stress and which was not fully able to cope with the rapid changes under way in the wider society. In this,

---

1.   Chesney, K., *Victorian Underworld* (1970), p.150.

there may be a few parallels with the present, albeit very different, age, with its overcrowded prisons and, until recently, seemingly inexorable rises in the apparent rate of crime, and with a wide range of proposed "solutions" to the problem being simultaneously advanced from many different quarters (as was the case in 1722).[2] In particular, Flanders' criminal career raises a number of important historical and, from the criminological perspective, theoretical, issues, and also illustrates many key features of underworld life in late seventeenth and early eighteenth century London which are worthy of more detailed further consideration.

Function of the Individual in the Criminal Justice System

Flanders' experiences vividly illustrate the crucial importance of the individual at this time to the operation of the criminal justice process. As well as the central importance of the prosecutor, there was that of informers, accomplices giving evidence and the rewards given to many individuals to ensure that the system worked effectively. The inability on the part of the state to mobilize a powerful institutional response to crime meant that alternative strategies to combat it were necessarily encouraged. Because the formal policing provisions were so weak, whether in the form of the constables, watchmen or the policing abilities of the regular army (which in those days itself presented enormous problems to the civilian population generally when mobilized to deal with order, as is evidenced by the regular petitions for their removal once they had been billeted on civilians), there was no alternative. Throughout the seventeenth and eighteenth centuries the state depended on the individual citizen (often acting in his own self-interest), to be policemen of their society (though not quite in the manner of the modern notion of "community policing"). The population, was, as appropriate, bribed, exhorted, rewarded, threatened or coerced into filling the many gaps left by the formal agents

---

2.   *Cf.* Judge Eric Stockdale and Silvia Casale, *Criminal Justice Under Stress* (1992), p.3.

of policing.[3] This, of course, resulted in the devolution of responsibility onto ordinary people. Popular altruism played a relatively small part in this process. The system was heavily reliant on making it in people's personal interest to enforce the law, either by providing cash incentives to informers and thief takers, by relieving those who had arrested and prosecuted felons from onerous parish duties in recompense, or by allowing those same felons to save their own skins at the expense of their erstwhile comrades by giving information and accomplice evidence. In addition, the system was normally dependent on ordinary people, at the scene of the crime, taking the burden of pursuing, arresting and prosecuting criminals.

Even the formal policing agents, responsible for supervising the inception of the process, were still amateur people (both constables and JPs). Other "amateurs" were responsible for indicting and convicting felons, as members of the Grand and Petty Juries. The use of private initiatives and incentives was even extended, in an extreme form, to pirates or buccaneers who, operating as "privateers" under letters of "marque", were often effectively given a legal status (provided they were selective in their targets), during the long years of war from 1689 until the peace of Utrecht in 1713. Peace often made this no longer readily feasible, and many of them then necessarily returned to indiscriminate piracy. Even after 1713, however, a proclamation offering free pardons to all who surrendered before September 1718 and a reward of £100 for every pirate ship taken can be seen to have reinforced the private role.

This emphasis on amateurs and private citizens inevitably resulted in a considerable degree of arbitrariness in the criminal justice system. Firstly, there was the question of detection (as today) then apprehension, both often contingent on the support of local people via a capture as a result of the "hue and cry" and assistance with detection. Although in theory the "hue and cry" needed a constable to raise it, the term was also used, informally, to refer to any popular pursuit of a fleeing felon. In its

---

3.   Rock, P., *Law Order and Power in Late Seventeenth and Early Eighteenth Century England*, p.242.

formal sense, by the eighteenth century it posed serious problems, contingent as it was on the pursued individual(s) being unable to travel with any speed to a refuge that would confer anonymity. In any sense of the word, this was something that did not apply to London, being traditionally most effective against strangers in rural areas. Its raising was little regulated, being dependent on local officials.[4] A popular local man in an unseemly neighbourhood would consequently be very difficult to detain. A stranger in a "good" neighbourhood, especially if not very sturdy, much easier. There had next to be the willingness, on the part of the victim, to make a decision to prosecute and incur the inconvenience and expense of finding a constable and magistrate, paying the fees and recognizances, attending court, etc., (many cases were probably given up at this point and dealt with informally). Even if matters were taken to court there had to be a successful prosecution in front of a jury (never a foregone conclusion). The process did not stop with a guilty verdict, punishment itself was variable; on occasion exemplary, but frequently commuted.

Nevertheless, the apparent amateurism of the system did have some strengths, for all its inefficiency. Indeed, recent years have seen a re-emergence of a belief in the need to get ordinary people involved in law enforcement through mechanisms such as local watch schemes, serving as special constables, impact statements in court, etc., rather than leaving it solely to the specialists and professionals (ie, the police and lawyers), and suggesting that to some limited extent the policing wheel has turned "full circle". Others have called on individuals to regain control of the prosecution process, a control that was lost in the nineteenth century.[5]

Whatever the merits, or lack of them, of the early eighteenth century system, the unpredictable nature of criminal justice in Flanders' lifetime, so different in many ways from the situation a 150 years later, is particularly well portrayed in Flanders' case. By a "whisker", she escaped

---

4.   Rock, P., *Law Order and Power in Late Seventeenth and Early Eighteenth Century England*, p.242.

5.   See for example Nils Christie, "Conflicts as Property", *British Journal of Criminology*, vol.17, no.1 (1977), p.1.

hanging and ended up going to a life of prosperity in America.

An Era of Change in Criminal Justice

The portrayal of Flanders' career is thus particularly valuable as a counterpoint to the penal changes that were already under way and due to develop much further in the hundred or so years after Defoe was writing. However, it should be noted that even in the early 1700s the penal process was already significantly less arbitrary than the situation a hundred and fifty years before (the mid-sixteenth century), when branding and release and the death penalty were the main available choices of punishment. By the end of the eighteenth century, with the modern police force still several decades away, law enforcement and criminal justice had been further transformed, to a marked extent, from the system that Defoe portrayed. By the end of the 1830s it was totally altered, with a police force willing, at least in serious cases, to take the decision to prosecute out of the hands of the individual, while at summary trials (increasingly important by then in the extent of their jurisdiction) cases were often presided over by professional stipendiary magistrates in the big cities, especially in London. With regard to trial on indictment, the jury trial had effectively almost reached its modern form and was a very different institution to that which Defoe knew, with single trial considered verdicts delivered on their own rather than in batches, legal representation in serious cases and a less assertive judiciary, etc. Significant reform in the substantive criminal law had also occurred. The "Bloody Code" had collapsed after the mid-1820s, as the work towards criminal law reform began to bear fruit. Sometimes these changes are seen as being the result of the inspiration provided by Sir Samuel Romilly (1757-1818) and the utilitarian philosophers, foremost amongst them Jeremy Bentham, these men in turn resulting in a vitally influential Parliamentary Committee of Inquiry under the chairmanship of Sir James Macintosh (1765-1832) strongly supported, as it was, by Sir Robert Peel. However, to an extent, these writers and politicians appear to have caught the more widespread "spirit of the age" in pressing for reform. The report of the Macintosh

Inquiry became the basis for a series of Acts passed in the period from 1820 to 1830, abolishing capital punishment for most of the nearly 200 offences that it was theoretically available for. In 1820 the law making theft of 5s. worth of goods from a shop a capital offence was repealed. In 1822 it was abolished for a hundred assorted offences, and in 1832 for stealing horses and sheep. After 1838 no one was executed other than for murder, attempted murder, treason, arson or piracy with violence (after 1860 no one other than for murder or, very occasionally, attempted murder). The report also produced legislation that greatly rationalized the remainder of the criminal law, for example replacing dozens of the laws dealing with different types of theft with a single consolidating Act.

A vivid illustration of the transformation in criminal policy and procedure can be seen by comparing the differences between the method of arrest, trial and the potential sentences for pick-pockets of high value goods, such as watches, in the 1720s and those in the mid-Victorian period. In the former case the accused had usually been detained by a crowd (normally including the loser), had received trial on indictment at the Old Bailey, and, if convicted, usually faced death or transportation. As an illustration of the latter situation can be taken the experiences of two male pickpockets that were taken into custody by a detective after they attempted to steal a watch from a gentleman near the Thames, in 1862. Not only were these two men arrested by an undercover policeman but Henry Mayhew could quote a police officer as saying that they were "brought before Westminster Police Court", ie, were tried summarily, by a professional salaried stipendiary magistrate, and were "sentenced each to three months' imprisonment".[6]

It is, however, also important to appreciate that the appearance of random arbitrariness in the early eighteenth century can be exaggerated. Flanders' was not a typical case. Initially, in the years before and immediately after the Second World War, the difference between the theoretical and the actual application of the criminal law at this time was viewed by legal historians as illustrative of the inefficiency of the

---

6.   Mayhew, H., *London Labour and the London Poor*, vol.4 (1862), p.192.

seventeenth and eighteenth century criminal justice system. This can be considered to be the "traditional" view in legal history. In the past twenty years this has been strongly, and very plausibly, challenged by academics who see, from a wide variety of perspectives, "method in the madness".

An important start in this process was made by Douglas Hay in 1977 who saw the selective enforcement of the law as a valuable tool of class power.[7] However, it is not necessary to accept Hay's radical thesis without failing to appreciate that there were other processes at work than pure "capriciousness". Arguably, there was a real attempt by the courts to distinguish between felons who warranted clemency by reprieve or being allowed benefit of clergy and those who did not. Perhaps, in this, the law implicitly recognized that being on the wrong side of the law was a realistic possibility for many poorer people, and sought to distinguish amongst them between the "deserving" and "undeserving". This can be particularly seen in an analysis of the types of crime that regularly attracted clemency and those that did not. Because horse theft was usually calculating, committed for financial advancement alone, and often showing demonstrating professional sophistication it was rarely reprieved. Felons who took jewels and goods from houses for resale were also usually executed. However, those who were convicted of burgling houses to steal food were normally spared. In East Sussex, for example, in the late seventeenth century, 70 per cent of the latter were reprieved while 60 per cent of the former were executed. Designated and punished "criminals" can thus be said to have been the products of a combination of their own conduct, past and present, and the decisions of those who observed, accused, examined, indicted, tried and sentenced them.[8]

Of course some of the subtleties of this system of discretion were probably lost in the huge anonymity of London, where "reputation" was a less easy commodity to establish. This may explain why reprieves were less common there (for much of the 1700s) than in the provinces. There

---

7.   See *Albion's Fatal Tree, ibid.* On the "radical" perspective generally see below, p.259.

8.   Cynthia Herrup, *Law and Morality in England, Past and Present*, no.106 (1985), p.123.

were also, inevitably, the unlucky, those morally deserving of reprieves who did not get them, and the fortunate, who received them when they did not deserve to do so (perhaps like Flanders).

Punishment

Flanders' exposure to the punishments of the period is also highly illustrative of a system that was already changing, and about to undergo a further even more rapid transition. With the introduction of transportation, widespread from 1718, the death penalty, although increasing in theoretical availability under the "Bloody Code" could in practice be mitigated by sending convicts to America.[9] As a result many executions were commuted to this punishment, for many of the "new" capital offences this being almost routine, and the great bulk of executions being for the same offences that had attracted death prior to 1688. The large number of capital offences should not obscure this important fact; additionally, many of the new offences were the result of a lack of consolidating Acts (such as the separate Acts allowing death for damaging each of the different London bridges), passed in a random and haphazard manner, and sometimes included statutes that were virtually never applied (such as an obscure Act of 1716 that made it a capital offence to mutilate trees which ornamented gentlemen's gardens).[10]

Already some of the popular views as to its efficacy that were to bedevil transportation till its near abolition in Australia, in the 1840s, had emerged, namely that it was not a "real" punishment. At this point these were certainly without foundation, though perhaps not so much in the 1840s, when some of the distinctions between normal emigrants and convicts in conditions of life became attenuated.

However, many of the ancient and archaic aspects of punishment still

---

9.   In fact, the several hundred new capital offences in the eighteenth century were responsible for less than a third of all executions in the period. Douglas Hay, *Albion's Fatal Tree, ibid.*, p.50.
10.   See Hostettler, J., *The Politics of Punishment* (1995), p.95.

survived in the 1720s; for example, burning for female coiners, disembowelling and quartering for male ones, the stocks, pillory and branding. It should, nevertheless, be remembered that there was some ground swell of opinion against these survivals long before the formal inception of reform at the end of the eighteenth, and in the early nineteenth centuries, and a widespread feeling that the law on punishment would benefit from rationalization. There was already a considerable historic ancestry for such a view in 1722. For example, during the Commonwealth there had been the establishment of Sir Mathew Hale's Law Commission of 1652. One of its members, William Sheppard (d.1675) had produced an agenda (little of it appears to have been totally original to himself) that included appeal courts, trial without jury for small civil actions and, from a penal aspect, abolition of imprisonment for debt, reform of the prisons themselves, restrictions on the use of the death penalty, abolition of benefit of clergy, amongst other suggestions, though this produced few tangible results, especially after the Commission became sidetracked into other issues. Thus, to some extent, the later reformers were merely crystallizing ideas that were already in much wider general circulation. Decades before them, Dr Johnson had noted that draconian punishments did not seem to deter crime, believing (possibly mistakenly) that "rapine and vice are hourly increasing" and that the lack of differentiation in punishment might actually encourage property offenders to commit murder to avoid capture, on the basis that the penalty could be no worse: "a thief seldom passes much of his time in recollection or anticipation, ... nor, when the grave closes upon his companion, has any other care than to find another".[11] He felt that the answer was to introduce a "scheme of invigorating the laws by relaxation, and extirpating wickedness by lenity", even citing the works of Thomas More in support. Dr Johnson, like Henry Fielding, was also well aware that the disproportionate penalties for relatively small property crimes weighed heavily on the minds of potential witnesses and prosecutors, while

---

11.   Still an ongoing debate in criminal justice, as Lord Chief Justice Taylor's criticism
        in 1996 of the Home Secretary's proposals for mandatory life sentences for repeat
        offenders such as rapists demonstrates.

additionally observing that "from this conviction of the inequality of the punishment to the offence proceeds the frequent solicitation of pardons". This also led him to believe in the pressing need for increased leniency, believing (correctly) as he did that laws against "wickedness" are ineffectual, "unless some will inform, and some will prosecute; but till we mitigate the penalties for mere violations of property, some will always be hated, and prosecution dreaded ... what is punished with severity contrary to our ideas of adequate retribution, will be seldom discovered".[12] Like many others, he also felt, on ethical grounds alone, that the penalty was often quite disproportionate to the crime "who can congratulate himself upon a life passed without some act more mischievous to the peace or prosperity of others, than the theft of a piece of money". Certainly, the neighbouring legal jurisdiction of Scotland appears to have been more selective in its infliction of the death penalty (and also transportation, only a total of about 700 Scotsmen going to the Americas this way in the 1700s) without great difficulties arising, though, of course, it had no equivalent of London's crime problems to police.

Within little more than a hundred years of Defoe's writing the penal system had been radically transformed, with the death penalty greatly limited, and the unruly public display of a Tyburn execution long moved to Newgate (from 1868 it was even carried out, as Fielding had advocated over a century earlier, in private). By the mid-nineteenth century the pillory (ended in 1837, two years before most American States banned it), branding and whipping in public had also been abolished, having largely fallen into desuetude long before.

Prison as a punishment in its own right had also become of central importance to the system, though this had come quite late in the eighteenth century. Even in 1776, it would appear, from John Howard's survey that well under 20 per cent of the prison population were undergoing sentences as a punishment, as opposed to being debtors (often in special and different debtors' prisons) or prisoners awaiting trial, transportation or execution. However, by the 1840s, prisons had, to a considerable extent,

---

12.   *Rambler* 114, April 20, 1751.

been transformed to regulated and disciplined environments based on cells and a tightly scheduled day, run closely by the turnkeys, rather than the loosely controlled, corrupt and often squalid institutions of Flanders' day with their large amount of prisoner self-regulation. In some ways this was a massive improvement, the prisoners lived in infinitely more hygienic conditions and were usually better fed, if they were poor, than had previously been the case. However, the isolation of the prisoners in the new regimes of the classic "penitentiaries" (less common than might be imagined, local jails were often much slower to change) may have contributed to an increase in mental illness amongst the inmates. This appears particularly to have been the case in the United States where such experiments in "new" prison regimes were taken further than in England, especially in Pennsylvania.

Illustrative of the changed attitude towards the purpose of imprisonment and punishment are some of the theoretical proposals towards the end of the eighteenth century from men such as Jeremy Bentham (they were rarely fully implemented). Bentham proposed a "Panopticon or The Inspection House" in a paper of 1787, in which the prisoners were "secluded from all communication with each other" in their own small cells. At all times they would be under the permanent observation of an inspector with an "apparent omnipresence" but who himself could not be seen. Rigid segregation meant that there would be no opportunity for "quarrelings, nor confederatings, nor plottings to escape; nor yet any whips or fetters to prevent it".[13] A more different vision of the nature and purpose of a prison to that of Flanders' Newgate would be hard to imagine, though whether it would be superior might be debatable. By the end of the eighteenth century there were already some tangible changes in English penal establishments themselves. For example, amongst the new English county prisons, that at Wymondham in Norfolk, built in 1784 by Sir Thomas Beevor, under the inspiration of John Howard's writings, provided for the segregation of petty and first offenders from hardened criminals, separate cells for night time,

---

13.   Bentham, J., in the *Works of Jeremy Bentham*, London (1791).

separation of incorrigible prisoners from the remainder, and the existence of a well equipped prison workshop to employ the able-bodied inmates.

The explanations for this change have varied from the influence of Methodism and the "Quaker conscience" of reformers (such as John Howard), to the requirements of a newly dominant bourgeois to organize society on sound commercial lines, to separate the "dangerous" classes from the "normal" working class and to regulate the former in large numbers. Probably neither is totally satisfactory.[14] The first ignores the structural changes in the nature of English society, while the latter is rather contrived and views the belief systems of the English middle and upper classes in an excessively monolithic fashion. It also suggests a more complete change than may, in reality, have been the case. Additionally, Michel Foucault, a strong exponent of the latter view, ignores the important regulating function, centuries earlier in England at least, of the Houses of Correction (in the early 1600s essentially a combination of prison, hospital and workhouse with a strong reformatory ethos) and overlooks the relatively slow changes in some local jails up to the mid-nineteenth century.[15]

However, both schools of thought can find some empirical support. By the 1770s there was clearly in existence a group of scientifically minded individuals who were, to an extent, transforming the practice of institutional hygiene, whether in prisons, troopships, hospitals or insane asylums (such as the doctor, William Smith, who wrote a denunciation of the conditions in London jails in 1776). These men, often physicians like the Quaker John Fothergill (who was also a friend of Howard's) saw hygiene as intimately linked to the improvement of the poor, along with visibility (by the opening up of the city's criminal classes to inspection). Additionally, there had been the emergence of a new philosophical basis for the reform of penal institutions. From the 1770s English materialism, drawing inspiration from the earlier work of John Locke and other

---

14.　For a review of this see Michael Ignatieff (1981) "State, Civil Society and Total Institutions: A Critique of Recent Social Histories of Punishment", in Tonry, M., *et al.* (eds) *Crime and Justice, An Annual Review of Research*, pp.153-192.

15.　*Discipline and Punish* (1977).

philosophers who rejected the existence of "innate ideas" provided an apparently rational rebuttal for the concept of original sin and innately "incorrigible" criminals. This in turn then stressed the importance of environment in character formation and thus provided a cogent intellectual underpinning for changing the latter's (ie, criminals') socialization, through, for example, the mechanism of reformed prisons, rather than seeing felons purely as the result of an inevitably innate propensity to crime.

This group of reformers were to be backed from the latter part of the eighteenth century by the reviving political radicals to be found on the more unorthodox wing of the Whig party. These radicals were frequently merchants and tradesmen, often from an urban environment and Nonconformist (especially Quaker or Unitarian) in religion. They saw reform as an effective way of dealing with the problems of the poor. It was felt that a more hygienic, disciplined atmosphere could combat this apparent poor socialization of the "lower orders"; as John Mason Good, the physician of Cold Bath Fields prison was to put it in 1795, "the poor ... feel not from want of education, the same happy exertion of delicacy, honour and moral sentiment which everywhere else is to be met with".[16]

Not all of the themes behind early eighteenth century penology have been irreversibly confined to penal history, occasionally resurfacing as they do, in modern debates. According to Graeme Newman, Professor of Criminal Justice at the University of Albany, it is important to bring back a concept of shame in punishment that has been lost in the rather clinical modern types of penalty, and that it may even be that this "will certainly mean revisiting and perhaps updating penalties once discarded as barbaric".[17] Additionally, at a time of fairly limited privatization in the English penal system, the City of Fullerton, in California, has gone a step further and also re-introduced "superior accommodation" cells, rented out at $100 a night to convicts who wish to "avoid spending time in the county jail". Inmates under this regime will either have their own cells

---

16.   Ignatieff, M., *A Just Measure of Pain* (1978), p.59.
17.   *This Will Hurt: The restoration of Virtue and Civic Order* (Digby Anderson ed) Social Affairs Unit (1995).

or be housed with other "fee payers", something that would have been well understood by Defoe's contemporaries in Newgate.

Influence on America

The English criminal justice system of the seventeenth and early eighteenth centuries is, of course, also historically very important as the one that was largely inherited by the American colonies, and thus, after 1776, the United States of America. Flanders would have found the courts of Virginia and Maryland readily comprehensible in English terms.

The colonial systems inherited lay justices (usually appointed by the governor of each colony), responsible for trying minor cases individually (and so approximating to English petty sessions), or more serious ones in panels, with juries, twice or four times a year (like the English Quarter Sessions). Punishments included the same emphasis on corporal penalties (such as whipping and branding) and a similar slow move towards greater use of imprisonment towards the end of the eighteenth century. The colonies even had their own equivalent of transportation, namely "banishment" from the individual colony. The policing agencies included, as in England, nightwatchmen and part-time constables. Interestingly, the latter also manifested the same problems of recruitment as in the "mother" country, so that, for example, in 1712 the colonial assembly in Philadelphia passed a law providing for a penalty of 10 pounds for anyone refusing to serve in the office (a fairly close figure to the London one of the time).[18] This continuity is not surprising; the colonies had sought to apply the common law from their beginnings, the Charter of Virginia of 1609 even expressly stating that their system of law was to be "... as near as conveniently may be ... agreeable to the laws, statutes, government, and policy of our realm of this England". The English common law was usually dominant, unless there was some specific exception, based on a

---

18.   Walker, S., *Popular Justice: A History of American Criminal Justice* (1980), p.20.

local custom or law.

As a result, they inevitably faced many of the same penal problems and had recourse to the same solutions. This even manifested itself, in some of the colonies, to the extent of regularly applying the anomalous doctrine of "benefit of clergy", which was only abolished in America in the 1780s. Even then, abolition was not, it appears, because it was necessarily felt to be archaic, but because changes in penal practice, such as the growth of the prison, meant that it was no longer needed. It seems to have fulfilled much the same purpose as in England in mitigating the harshness of the common law.[19] The colonial courts in Maryland and Virginia appear to have particularly regularly applied benefit of clergy, in much the same circumstances as the "mother country".

In other ways, however, the American colonies also early showed their individuality. The Americas do not appear to have participated in the explosion of capital offences that characterized the England of the "Bloody Code", most colonies having only a dozen or so offences which theoretically carried death (though these offences would also encompass the overwhelming majority of the English cases in which a death sentence was actually administered).[20] In the Quaker Pennsylvania, the death penalty was even abolished in the late seventeenth century for most crimes, though forcibly restored by the British Government in 1718. Because of the early creation of the office of District Attorney (also sometimes called the County Attorney) the colonies appear to have been faster than England in reducing the role of the private prosecutor in initiating criminal legal action (though the latter was still very important). Lawyers were also given greater theoretical powers at an earlier date in the criminal trial process than in England (though these were probably comparatively rarely exercised in practice).

Inevitably, attempts to *precisely* imitate the English courts in the differing circumstances of a vast and thinly populated land like America

---

19.   Sawyer, K.J., "Benefit of Clergy" in Maryland and Virginia, p.49, *American Journal of Legal History*, vol.xxxiv, No.1 (1990).
20.   Walker, S., *Popular Justice: A History of American Criminal Justice* (1980), p.12.

were doomed to being rather unsuccessful. Such attempts were also not helped in the late seventeenth and early eighteenth centuries by a judiciary that was often poor in quality, and sometimes very corrupt (though it should be observed that the standard of Judges in 1680s England was also often not very high). As a contemporary pamphlet noted these American Judges, being ignorant of the law themselves (they were often merchants and planters by training, and lacking a legal background or training unlike English Judges), were unable to avoid the snares of "clerks and other such small dealers in the law" who had come out from England, and who though "ignorant of the law" had "... so much knowledge of the forms, as to be able to perplex, delay and confound all the business of the courts there".[21] Additionally, the smaller scale of towns and populations meant that some efforts to duplicate the English system were often fairly cosmetic. Thus, the same Judge and court might sit to hear differing types of case under a confusing variety of titles taken from the Westminster courts, such as that of Chancery or Common Pleas.[22]

Each colony was unique in its system to some extent. Maryland, in 1700, was divided into eleven counties in each one of which there was a "county court" complete with "several justices", the use of petty juries and "several attorneys or pleaders at Bar". These courts, approximating to English Quarter Sessions, sat six times a year but only to deal with misdemeanours and minor felonies "... the punishment whereof doe not extend to life or member". More serious cases were always remitted to the "provincial court" (roughly approximating to English Assizes or the Old Bailey). A broadly similar system prevailed in Virginia, where serious criminal cases were heard at a "general court" in front of a jury consisting of six men from the county where the crime had been committed, the: "... rest of the jury to be made up of standers". This court, which had the governor and his council members as Judges, conducted its proceedings: "... according (or as near) to ye com[m]on & statute laws of England as

---

21. *The Present State of Justice in the American Plantations* (1704), Anon. Possibly by Thomas Hodges.
22. Surrency, E.C., "The Courts in the American Colonies", *Amer. J. Leg. Hist.* (1967), vol.11, p.256.

ye circumstances of the country will admit".[23]

Professional Crime in London in the Period

Flanders is a manifestation of the existence of sophisticated professional crime in London, something that was to reach its apogee in Jonathan Wild at the time Defoe was writing the novel. Jonathan Wild allegedly divided the Metropolis up into districts and parcelled it out amongst different gangs. At his trial in 1725 he was accused on his indictment of being a "confederate with great numbers of highwaymen, pickpockets, housebreakers, shoplifters and other thieves" and with having "formed a kind of corporation of thieves". Some of these allegations were clearly exaggerated, indeed it has been suggested that there were probably not more than 10 large gangs, containing a total of 150 members at the time.[24] Wild even dressed as befitted his position as a prosperous man of consequence: "he dressed in lace clothes and wore a sword" and also, as Defoe noted in his history of the criminal "openly kept his counting-house or office, like a man of business, and had his books to enter everything in with the utmost exactness and regularity". Indeed Wild, according to Defoe in his *Account* "acquired a strange, and indeed unusual reputation for a mighty honest man". Wild *was*, in fact, running a business. Losers of stolen property visiting his office near the Old Bailey (he later also opened a second one) had to "first deposit a crown; this was his retaining fee". Defoe himself, having had a silver-topped sword stolen "had occasion, ... to wait upon Mr Jonathan with a crown in [his] hand". Perhaps because the value of the stolen item was small he did not gain much of Wild's attention and the business proved abortive, though another person, a woman who had had a gold and jewelled watch stolen in a more "material affair was treated with respect by Mr Wild, and a pot of tea

---

23. Report on Court Procedures in the Colonies (1700), from the reports of six colonies as a result of a request from the Lord Justices and Privy Council in England. Reproduced in *American Journal of Legal History,* vol.9 (1965).
24. Speck, W.A., *Stability and Strife, England 1714-1760* (1977), p.60.

brought out in form". His "business" ultimately even extended to running a large sloop to transport high value stolen goods which it would have been hard to sell in England, to Holland (and, on the return journey, to bring back contraband brandy). As a result, it has been suggested, very plausibly, that by the 1720s professional crime had become a major problem in London; as the contemporary Henry Zuch said, robbery "... in the Metropolis ... is become a science". However, although in early Georgian London the professional criminals were undoubtedly a significant part of the criminal scene, the bulk of criminals were still non-professional "for every Wild or Sheppard there may have been a thousand opportunistic pickpockets or shoplifters, concerned with immediate survival".[25]

Role of Women in London Crime

Flanders, of course, is the central character in the novel, and that a woman should be portrayed as succeeding for so long in such a hazardous career is worth consideration. With her governess and teacher Flanders constituted an all female operation. Women appear to have been particularly involved in receiving stolen goods, and it is thus appropriate that the governess is another female. The highwayman, Jack Sheppard, in his early days of crime (stealing from his employers' houses) at the start of the 1720s, had been heavily dependent on female fences, such as "Edgeworth Bess" and another woman, who went by the rather unprepossessing name of "Maggot". At a more mundane level, Elizabeth James and her daughter were typical of the breed, being a widow and spinster living together in Holborn in 1684; following the robbery of a poulterer, in which amongst other things, turkeys, capons and chickens were taken, their premises were found to be full of poultry and they were indicted for "receiving those goods, and harbouring the said robbers"[26]

---

25.   Sharpe, J.A., *ibid.*, p. 117.
26.   OBSP, January 17-18, 1684, p.2.

However, female involvement in crime was certainly not limited to this speciality.

When considering gender and crime there are two key issues that confront criminologists: the extent to which women are involved in crime, and the degree to which they are recipients of differential treatment in the criminal justice system. Flanders' sex, appropriately for the period, signifies the relatively full role (by modern standards) that women played in London crime of the period (significantly she compares herself to Moll Cutpurse, the notorious seventeenth century female receiver and organizer of London crime). Admittedly, Defoe had a rather "modern" attitude to women, manifest for example in his proposals for a woman's "Academy" in an *Essay on Projects* (1697). However, the evidence very strongly supports the notion of a greater female involvement in crime than at present. If anything, the role of women in criminal activity appears to have greatly declined as time has progressed from this period, this being especially marked in the later nineteenth and early twentieth centuries; by 1847 they formed 27 per cent of defendants on indictment, by the 1890s only 19 per cent, a figure that was to continue to fall in the twentieth century. Even today, at the end of the twentieth century, female criminals do not appear to have developed quite the role or influence that their unliberated London sisters had in Flanders' period. Much academic work in recent years suggests that in the late twentieth century not only is women's share of recorded crime low (though slowly increasing) but that this can also be substantiated by self-report studies and other non-official measures as being representative of their contribution to "real" levels of crime as well. The current figure of less than 2,000 women in a prison population for England and Wales of over 50,000 was not remotely the case in Flanders' period. Even in John Howard's time, significantly later in the eighteenth century, women made up almost a quarter of Newgate's criminal inmates. This trend has been found to have been particularly manifest in the London area. A detailed study of the gender of defendants tried at the Old Bailey, between the 1680s and 1912 (effectively the point of demise of the Old Bailey Sessions Papers) indicates that women constituted over a third of the caseload at the Old Bailey in the late seventeenth and early eighteenth century, after which period they declined steadily; additionally, much (though not all) of the reduction appears to reflect a "real" change in involvement, rather than a differential in methods of disposal. It suggests that women were once "heavily involved in the criminal process" in a way that is no longer the case.[27]

This phenomenon invites explanation, though this is not easy to establish, and is something which has been attempted by much recent academic work in the area.[28] Defoe was writing in an era when the "theoretically" secondary position of women was almost unquestioned. That being the case why were females, proportionately to males, so much more likely to have recourse to crime than at the present?

A possible reason might be that in the unusual environment of a huge city like London (unusual when compared to a rural area) the normal social and cultural checks and controls that limited country women from embarking on crime were not present to anything like the same degree. According to this explanation the attenuation of "traditional" social controls attendant on moving to the urban environment, and which produced a greater degree of crime in both sexes worked, proportionately, to an even greater extent in women than men. According to this paradigm, rural life was particularly restrictive for females; girls and young women were surrounded by powerful social constraints that did not exist to anything like the same degree in the city and its urbanized environs, explaining not only higher crime rates generally but also a significantly greater proportion of female participation in crime.[29] There is also the possibility that informal social control mechanisms that were particularly employed in rural areas, against women, such as the "chariavari", the

---

27. See on this Feeley, M. and Little, D., "The Vanishing Female: The Decline of Women in the Criminal Process, 1687-1912", *Law and Society Review* 25 (1991), p.719; and Feeley, M., "The Decline of Women in the Criminal Process: A Comparative History", *Criminal Justice History*, vol.15 (1994), p.235.
28. See Zedner, L., "Women, Crime, and Penal Responses: A Historical Account". At p.247 in Michael Tonry (ed), *Crime and Justice; A Review of Research* (1991).
29. Beattie, J.M., *The Criminality of Women in Eighteenth Century England, ibid.*, p.96.

playing of raucous music outside the offender's residence, were especially weakened in an urban environment.

Much research does suggest that in the eighteenth century, city women were much more heavily involved in crime than those in other, more rural parts of England, and also committed much more serious types of property offence as well.[30] Urban women were, it appears, engaged in roughly the same range of crimes as men and in the same patterns of offending, though to a slightly lesser degree. Not only is the apparently heavier involvement of women in crime in the seventeenth and eighteenth centuries compared to the following periods a European-wide phenomenon (rather than a purely English one), but also the heavy weighting in favour of urban women compared to rural females for the commission of such offences applies to other cities in Europe (rather than simply London). In some countries it was sometimes even more notable than in England. In the Dutch cities of the period, about 20 per cent of those prosecuted were women; though occasionally, in Ghent and Amsterdam, it even approached half (perhaps in part, in the latter case, because many men from the city were at sea for long periods). In the town of Leiden women constituted between 41 per cent and 44 per cent of those prosecuted between 1678 and 1794. Although much less involved in violence, they heavily outweighed the men in the "craft" crimes of receiving and fencing stolen goods (65 cases compared to 39) and were only marginally behind them for conventional theft.[31] Significantly, this pattern of greater urban female involvement in theft appears to be borne out by crime statistics from the more rural American colonies as much as the English countryside. In colonial Massachusetts, of the 224 serious cases of felony with which women were charged between 1673 and 1774, two-thirds

---

30. Zedner, L., *ibid.*, p.316. Additionally, at the end of the eighteenth century some work suggests that women made up only 12 per cent of accused in the home counties, suggesting again the unusual nature of London crime, see Frances Heidensohn, "Gender and Crime", *Oxford Handbook of Criminology* (1994), p.1004.
31. Kloek, E., "Criminality and Gender in Leiden's Confessieboken 1678-1794", *Criminal Justice History*, vol.11 (1990), p.8.

appear to have been charged with murder and manslaughter (especially infanticide and the killing of family members), sexual offences and, in the early (pre-Salem) period, witchcraft, rather than "instrumental crime" (although most other forms of crime were represented to some degree).[32]

Other studies have linked the possible decline in female crime participation to a reduction in women's status generally, in the early 1800s, this being linked to the erosion of the traditional small scale "family economy" in the nineteenth century in the face of industrialization. It has been suggested that because their financial contributions to the family economy suffered a reduction attendant on this process, this in turn produced a loss of status perhaps encouraging them also to take a more secondary role in criminal enterprises as well as legitimate ones.

At a less sophisticated level of analysis, there may have been a practical explanation for high female involvement in eighteenth century crime. Women in the period were heavily associated with a number of employments, such as running pawn and "dolly" shops or as household servants, that provided the easy opportunity for certain types of criminal activity, such as receiving and disposing of stolen goods and of domestic theft. Indeed, much modern research has suggested that the limited entry into crime of women in modern times is simply a consequence of reduced practical opportunities (compared to men) for them to do so, "organized crime isn't an equal opportunity employer"; Flanders does have an entrée to such a life (through her acquaintance with the governess) and thus an opportunity to participate. John Beattie has also suggested that rural women would be confined to a more limited range of employments than their city counterparts, where there was a greater range of opportunities, though many of these city employments were occupations which by their nature could be precarious or seasonal, domestic service, shop work, textile working and market gardening. It was more common for women in London to be alone, working, in contact with the wider world and more

---

32.   Data from Hull, N., *Female Felons: Women and Serious Crime in Colonial Massachusetts* (1987).

vulnerable to economic fluctuations.[33] Many women over the age of 60 were still dependent on their own efforts to support themselves, in part because of their longer life expectancy; this might include crime or dealing in illicit goods. This probably applied to a particularly high proportion of poorer London women, and was especially so when increased military recruitment took away hundreds of men to the army and navy. To this extent Flanders' governess was typical.

Women were also more likely than men to have direct responsibilities for families and children, putting them under special pressure to "provide" when times were harsh. It does also appear that in this era women's theft were characterized by a greater willingness to take very practical items, especially things like clothes, things that men might ignore. A classic illustration might be the case in 1739 in which Elizabeth Reynolds and a friend, Martha London, were accused of robbing one Ann Hornby of her stays, apron, gown and cloak. The defendants had offered the victim accommodation for the night but first told her that she must take off all her clothes in the street so that they could be examined to "see if they were clean"! When the victim refused they struck her and took them anyway. The victim went off "crying and roaring" but (in part because Reynolds had a cast in her eyes and a scar on her face) was able to circulate an accurate description leading to their arrest by the victim with a constable, in an alley near Bishopsgate. Although on the way to the watch house they tried to threaten her to say to the Judge that "I was very much in liquor, and pulled off my cloaths, and gave em away myself", the victim refused, and the two were subsequently convicted and sentenced to death, though, interestingly, the jury explicitly "recommended them to the mercy of his majesty".[34]

Flanders' sex also raises the vexed question that still troubles modern criminology as to the extent to which women being "processed" in the criminal justice system were, and are, treated differently to men. This can either be better, as members, albeit fallen, of the "fair" sex (sometimes

---

33.   Beattie, J.M., *ibid.*, p.243.
34.   OBSP, January 17-20, 1739.

termed the "chivalrous" approach), or worse because of their especially degraded status in being females who would resort to crime. Certainly many of the statistics at the turn of the seventeenth century seem to better support the existence of a degree of "judicial chivalry", with a greater willingness to commute death penalties and the attendant lower percentage of executions of women at Tyburn. To this extent, Flanders (and her mother), being transported rather than hanged are representative of what appears to have been a general trend of the era. Of course, the ability to "plead one's belly", gave them an apparently widely used avenue of defence not open to men; as the condemned John Hall wryly observed in 1708 "upon this point the women have a great advantage over the men". The benefit of the doubt appears to have normally been given to the woman in this situation, and once commuted (actually in theory "postponed") such sentences rarely appear to have been carried out in practice, especially if they were truly pregnant.

A reluctance to execute women in the early eighteenth century was also present in other European countries. An analysis of the prosecutions in the town of Leiden in Holland produces this as the main instance of differential sentencing, or penal "double standards". Until about 1750 female burglars were usually sentenced to life imprisonment or banishment, while males ones were normally sentenced to death.[35] Similarly, in Frankfurt am Main, in Germany, the city council regularly sought the expertise of women to establish or confirm pregnancies in female suspects (though there, after about 1650, they seem to have been replaced by male doctors), and as in England pregnancy had a moderating effect on capital punishment; out of fourteen cases between 1573 and 1662 suspended for pregnancy only two were executed after giving birth.[36]

---

35. Kloek, E., "Criminality and Gender in Leiden's Confessieboken 1678-1794", *Criminal Justice History*, vol.11 (1990), p.21.

36. Boes, M.A., "Women and the Penal System in Frankfurt am Main 1562-1696", *Criminal Justice History*, vol.13 (1992), p.63.

Versatility of Criminal Careers

Flanders' career also illustrates the versatile nature of crime in this period, with an attendant lack of "career" specialization. This is also entirely consistent with modern studies of twentieth century thieves; "hard core" criminals tend to be willing to try a number of different ventures as the opportunities present themselves. Then, as now, only a few concentrated solely on one form of activity. Although Flanders put her main efforts into stealing gold watches from well-to-do women, she was prepared to turn her hand to almost any other criminal opportunity that came along, and even, initially, to return to a "normal" and lawful life. Her criminal career is thus largely an unstructured one. Despite some contemporary portrayals of rigid segregation between criminal types other authentic seventeenth and eighteenth century life histories of criminals suggest versatility was more common than speciality. Moll Cutpurse was a pickpocket turned fence; the highwayman, Mulled Sack, had started his criminal career as a highway robber before becoming a pickpocket (a downwards if less risky step).[37] This downward move was not at all unusual. Captain Richard Dudley also went from being a highwayman to a burglar after his gang was destroyed. Despite having formerly been gallant enough to escort a wounded man whom he had shot to a nearby village, so that he could secure medical assistance, as the *Newgate Calendar* was to note, when "deprived of the chief of his own forces, he entered the house of an old woman in Spitalfields, gagged her, bound her to a chair, and rifled the house of a considerable sum of money, which the good woman had been long in scraping together". This woman subsequently smothered to death when she fell over in her tightly bound condition. Jack Sheppard had been a burglar and highwayman (in this latter occupation his career appears to have lasted only a few weeks and netted about two guineas in loot). An even more marked illustration of the unstructured nature of crime at this time, with an attendant low level of sophisticated organization, can be

---

37.   McMullan, J.L., *The Canting Crew, ibid.*, p.108.

seen in the career of the notorious highwayman Dick Turpin.[38] Despite being seen as the apotheosis of organized crime at the time, his career included being a sheep and cattle thief, a deer poacher, a smuggler in Canvey Island in Essex, a horse thief, a burglar and, of course, a highwayman. Perhaps significantly he was executed for horse theft not for robbery. His famous joining up with another celebrated highwayman, Mathew King, was the result of the chance meeting when he attempted to rob King on the road, King asking "what dog eat dog"? ie, it was totally *ad hoc* in its arrangement. Interestingly, Flanders' long criminal career also suggests that Defoe felt that early eighteenth century society may have been vulnerable to a thief who was willing to take pains and to approach her work with a degree of skill and care.

---

38.   Sharpe, J.A., *Crime in Early Modern England 1550-1750*, p.107.

Chapter 7

Theoretical Criminal Analysis of Flanders' Career

"Wherefore, till the nobility, gentry, Justices of the Peace, and clergy will be pleased either to reform their own manners, and suppress their own manners, and suppress their own immoralities, or find out some method and power impartially to punish themselves when guilty, we humbly crave leave to object against setting any poor man in the stocks, and sending them for the house of correction for immoralities, as the most unequal and unjust way of proceeding in the world."
Defoe, "The Poor Man's Plea" (1698).

Modern Criminological Paradigms Illustrated by Flanders' Career

Much of the *modus operandi* of the street criminals of Flanders' time, including her own stratagems, has altered little in almost 300 years, providing a modern urban reader with a strange sense of familiarity. For example, a London Underground publication from 1995, *Travelling Safely by Tube,* advises passengers to "beware if you are suddenly jostled or if there is a sudden argument or commotion. Incidents can be staged to distract you while a pickpocket steals from you", something with which Flanders and her "teacher" would have readily concurred!

This being the case, it is also interesting (and sometimes amusing) to examine her career to see if it would support any of the wide variety of modern theoretical paradigms that have been developed in the twentieth century to explain crime. Most theoretical interest in crime and analysis of the justice system in the early 1700s has focused on two important topics: the potential existence of an extensive criminal "subculture"; and the class and social structures underlying the existing justice and penal system of the time. These two areas can both find some illuminating episodes in Defoe's novel.

Subcultural Explanations for Crime in the Era

Arguably, one the most important themes that has been considered in analysing crime in London in this era, is the existence (or lack of it) of an extensive criminal subculture in the Metropolis; that is a large group of people with values that were separate from, and contradictory to, those of the wider "respectable" society, this group often being popularly portrayed as the criminal "underworld". From this perspective, Flanders' socializing with her governess, a highwayman, the teacher and her other accomplices in the early stages of her career, and her willingness to reside at points in one of the London "sanctuaries", such as the Mint, could support such an explanation for her later activities; she mixes heavily with a group of Londoners who certainly do not have "positive definitions" towards law abiding conduct. Can a large and identifiable "criminal underworld" with its own culture be identified? On this issue the evidence is contradictory. At one point such a notion had strong support from several social historians; however, this has waned in recent years, as the emphasis has increasingly been on the apparent "normality", lack of differentiation (from the wider society), and mundaneness of most London criminals, including those who were executed. The notion of significant amounts of crime in London being the work of a socially distinct underworld is one that in the last twenty years has found relatively little favour amongst academics, the only recent exception (to even a limited extent), being John McMullan's *The Canting Crew* (1984).

At first sight the evidence for such a group of individuals, Defoe's "nimming clan" or, as Flanders calls them, the "fraternity" does appear quite convincing, as much of it is drawn from contemporary literary accounts that focused on the linguistic and geographical peculiarities of some groups of criminals. That there were social groups in the city and its suburbs at this time that held values that were markedly different, and at variance, to those of the mainstream society is certainly true. The important question is their extent, were they localized pockets or a homogeneous group? The sixteenth century had seen an apparent reduction in the previous importance of the family as the basic "criminal unit" (which it seems to have been in the medieval period) and the emergence of new forms of underworld association. These groups were localized to the extent that they were often concentrated in the criminal "sanctuaries" but they could also be found, to some extent, in most areas. The lack of clear social stratification in London at this time (compared, for example, to the period from the 1840s onwards) meant that these areas were also, usually, geographically, close to areas providing potentially rich targets. From many accounts it appears they had also evolved their own argot, or thieves "cant", with "files" busy "drawing" from "cullies" with the assistance of their accomplices and then dividing up their "snappings".[1] Thomas Dekker had produced a book, *Lantern and Candlelight*, on the jargon of London thieves as early as 1608. This was something that Defoe was also keenly concerned with. Thus, the reformed criminal narrator in his *Street Robberies Consider'd* (1728) had composed a Short Canting Dictionary so that "whenever any person hears such a language, speech or cant; or what you please to call it, let them take care of the speaker; for they may depend on't they are certainly of the nimming clan, and therefore to be avoided".[2] To an extent this work appears to be a derivative of earlier cant dictionaries, for which there had been a near mania in the early 1700s; according to these dictionaries there were numerous special "underworld" words and phrases, enough to amount almost to a separate language; thus, a "jet" was a lawyer, a "betty" a picklock, "popps" were pistols, "nimming" was stealing, "snafflers" were

1.   McMullan, J.L., *ibid.*, p.163.
2.   *Ibid.*, p.29.

highwaymen, "harmenbeck" a constable, a "snip" was a cheat while "trine" were gallows (or Tyburn in particular). John Hall also drew up a short account of such language, in his *Memoirs* of 1708; many of his definitions do concur with Defoe's 20 years later; these also included numerous words to describe in detail the differing types of "theft from the person" and their perpetrators, including such specialities as "tail-drawers", men who "take the gentlemen's swords from their sides, at the turning of a corner or in a crowd".

According to Hall there was also a degree of solidarity and hierarchy amongst the town's criminals. Thus he felt that "a pickpocket is no more a companion for a reputable house breaker, than an informer is for a Justice of Peace". While, when in difficulties, he felt that "friendship is a virtue oftener found among thieves than other people; for when their companions are in danger, they venture hardest to relieve them". This last point certainly might apply to Flanders' governess. With regard to the most "hard core" gang members, Hall felt that there were also definite "rites of passage", a new man "is never thought worthy of being incorporated into a gang, till he has done some responsible piece of villainy to deserve it". Earlier, Mathew Hale had been of the opinion that the poor families "which daily multiply in the Kingdom" passed on a different cultural tradition to their offspring as they often brought up their children to a life of "begging or stealing, or such other idle course, which again they propagate to their children, and so there is a successive multiplication of hurtful or at least unprofitable people".[3]

However, it must be remembered that since the sixteenth century the notion of a cohesive criminal underworld had made "good copy" for writers and popular theatrical drama for playwrights, and thus was almost certainly greatly exaggerated. Many "cant" words appear, on examination, to have been colloquialisms that were in widespread use amongst the poorer elements of London society. The supposed degree of criminal

---

3.   From the Preface to *A Discourse Touching Provision for the Poor*. Written by
      Sir Mathew Hale, late Lord Chief Justice of the Kings Bench, Printed for William
      Shrowsberry (1683).

specialization also appears to be totally unsupported by the lives of most famous criminals of the time, many of them changing their lines of criminal activity on a regular basis, as opportunity presented itself.[4] The speed with which they would often impeach each other when detained also needs to be considered in assessing the degree of social cohesion present amongst them. There undoubtedly were thorough going criminal subcultures in the Metropolis in 1700, but they were probably, for the most part, very small and localized in extent, and not a large scale "alternative" society to the mainstream one.

Radical Interpretations of Crime and the Penal Process in 1700

A criminologist, or historian of crime, with a more radical perspective might focus on the social control mechanisms to which Flanders was exposed during her criminal career. This has been a well worked theme since the mid-1970s. According to Douglas Hay the large degree of discretion facilitated the use of the law and courts "as a selective instrument of class justice" at a time when other social control mechanisms, such as religion, were declining. In some areas, this thesis asserts, eighteenth century criminal procedure amounted virtually to a "ruling class conspiracy" against the lower social groups, though it was not a formal conspiracy but one based on the "common assumptions" of the conspirators. Hay would thus probably find the discretion inherent in the prosecution and pardon process that brought Flanders to trial, convicted, condemned and then saved her, highly indicative of the system; its apparent arbitrariness being possibly illustrative of the suggestion that such discretion was a potentially crucial tool in the preservation of power by the "political nation", being vital to the "legitimization of force".[5]

The delighted reaction of the crowd to the detention of the mercer

---

4. On the versatility of criminal careers, see above, p.252.
5. See Hay, D., "Property, Authority and the Criminal Law", in *Albion's Fatal Tree* (1977), p.62. This collection of essays was highly influential in influencing the debate.

might also be suggestive of an early manifestation of proletarian class consciousness, as sometimes portrayed, amongst others, by Peter Linebaugh; though some radical criminologists might be disconcerted at the apparent evidence of popular antipathy towards the mistakenly taken young man (suspected of pickpocketing), the continuing reality, in any form, of the "hue and cry", or the determination of the maids (much greater than their master's) to give evidence against Flanders.

Thus it can be argued that this evidence in the novel of popular participation in the policing process reinforces the view that the law was not simply a tool of political repression, substantial parts of it must have had considerable legitimacy in the eyes of ordinary people of the time. Policing London, with its huge size, labyrinthine design and lack of a regular police force, would have been impossible without this legitimacy. Far more than today the "public" were a crucial facet of the criminal justice process, and the system could not have functioned at all without some acceptance of its value. While some elements of Hay's analysis may be correct it also produces a schematic interpretation that does not fit easily with the somewhat haphazard nature in which many aspects of policing were carried out at the time. Additionally, many criminals, although poor, were not destitute, they appear often to have been people, such as servants, who were in regular employment and who were suddenly confronted by temptation. It has been remarked, with some truth, if perhaps a little robustly, that to turn most of these "little crooks" into class warriors requires "rose coloured glasses of the deepest hue".[6] At the lowest level quite humble men were crucial, in an official capacity, to the administration of justice, whether as constables, watchmen, witnesses, prosecutors and members of the "hue and cry". There were comparatively few gentry amongst prosecutors, and many quite ordinary people. Inevitably in such a socially mixed city, administration of the justice system required the authorities to steer a delicate path between firmness and leniency (with public order being a prime factor in determining the balance). The likely popular reaction to judicial activity was clearly a

---

6.   Langbein, J., "Albion's Fatal Flaws", *Past and Present*, vol.98 (1983), p.101.

factor in the formation of those decisions, sometimes moderating them. However, to say as Linebaugh does that in the 1700s "London proletarians, excluded from the hegemony, held the law in contempt" flies in the face of much contrary evidence.

The degree of ordinary awareness, and apparent acceptance of, the law can also be seen in aspects of popular culture; for example, a late seventeenth century ballad titled, the *"Bricklayers Lamentation from Newgate"*. In this account (possibly apocryphal) one Dick Lambert who was one of a team of brickmakers stole his fellow's bread and cheese, which resulted in the other members of the team holding a detailed and accurate mock trial:

> "A Judge, and a jury, and a clerk did appear, a sheriff, and also
> a hangman was there. The Judge being sat and the prisoner
> brought forth, the plaintiff he there on a brickbat took oath."

It resulted in a conviction and a "branding" of Lambert as a clergied offender as well as (incongruously) a mock hanging (he was quickly cut down). The disrespect to the "official" system shown by the "Judge" and "hangman" resulted in their being carried off to Newgate![7]

This does not mean that the criminal justice system as applied was accepted in its entirety (or, by some sections of the community probably at all), very clearly it was not. However, it is, perhaps, a mistake to view the gentry's obsession with pheasants and hares, as exemplified in the notorious Game Laws of the period (first introduced in 1671), which meant that to hunt "game" (as opposed to "vermin" like rabbits) required an estate of £100 a year (even on a would be hunter's own land), as typical of the whole of the criminal justice system of the period. It is also easy to be excessively attracted to modern notions of the non-coercive aspects of class rule, supposedly transmitted through the agencies of socialization (such as Gramsci's concept of "hegemony"), when considering what was

---

7.   Sharpe, J.A., in "Popular Culture in Seventeenth Century England" (1988) ed,
      Reay B., at p.261.

still a very much less sophisticated society than that of today.

Nevertheless, Defoe himself was well aware of a class bias in law enforcement, most notably examined in the *Poor Man's Plea* in the *Shortest Way with Dissenters* (published in 1703).[8] He freely asserted in this work that the laws of the realm were become "Cobweb Laws, in which the small Flies are catch'd, and great ones break through". The differential application of these laws meant that the provisions against drunkenness and lewdness were never invoked against the gentry and rich merchants, while gentlemen were also "... allow'd the full career of [their] corrupt appetites, without the restraint of laws". In the early years of the eighteenth century the comparison between the criminal underworld and that of high office and politics was a popular source for literary satire. In the year following the publication of *Moll Flanders*, John Gay sent a private letter observing (several years before he further explored the theme in *The Beggars Opera*), "I cannot wonder that the talents requisite for a great statesman are so scarce in the world since so many of those who possess them are every month cut off in the prime of their age at the Old-Baily".[9] As the beggar remarks at the end of *The Beggar's Opera* (1727) "through the whole piece you may observe such a similitude of manners in high and low life, that it is difficult to determine whether (in the fashionable vices) the fine gentlemen imitate the gentlemen of the road, or the gentlemen of the road the fine gentlemen ... the lower sort of people have their vices in a degree as well as the rich and they are punished for them". This evidently touched a chord with many Londoners, the play had an unprecedented opening run of 62 nights in 1728. Even the young Henry Fielding, in his playwright phase (before censorship encouraged him to enter the magistracy), was to touch on this aspect of differential justice. In *Rape upon Rape* Justice Squeezum announces, in similar vein to Defoe, that "the laws are Turnpikes, only made to stop people who walk on foot, and not to interrupt those who drive through them in their coaches".[10]

---

8.   Oxford (1927), pp.1-20.
9.   Quoted by Thompson, E.P., in *Social History Journal*, "Eighteenth Century English Society", vol.3, No.2, at p.142.
10.   At Act II, scene ii.

At the time that Defoe was writing the novel, the "political nation" was at one of its most corrupt stages ever, often venal to a degree that would seem astonishing even a hundred years later. Outright political bribery was common at the very highest level, including the Royal court. Huge sums of money were made by Whig parliamentarians out of their offices (also explaining the amounts they were willing to pay to secure election, and the hostility of the minor Tory gentry who were excluded from the process). Men like Walpole, Newcastle and Chandos overtly dealt in offices, crown lands and government perquisites, freely using their influence and patronage to advance themselves and their allies. Robert Walpole openly thought that there was "nothing more reasonable and just" than using his office to help his friends. The "Bubble" year was perhaps indicative of a society that had become excessively acquisitive and unregulated at its higher levels; the almost hysterical greed for South Sea shares resulting in frenzied trading in Garraway's Coffee House in the City's financial area, right up to the "crash" itself in August of that year.

Thus, although radical interpretations of the operation of the justice process are often unfair and possibly even "fundamentally mistaken", sometimes involving what Professor Langbein has referred to as "ugly" allegations of class bias, something that is often unsubstantiated by the records available, and also occasionally attributing such bias where it clearly did not exist, they do perhaps provide a useful corrective to an excessively adulatory view of the system.[11]

---

11.   There is a useful dialogue between "conservative" and "radical" views in John
        Langbein's "Albion's Fatal Flaws", *Past and Present*, vol.98 (1983), and Peter
        Linebaugh's "A Reply to Professor Langbein", *New York University Law Review*,
        vol.ix, No.2 (1985).

Chapter 8

Early Eighteenth Century Explanations of Crime

"George Wych, convicted of robbing on the highway, was near 18 years old of a good family, brought up at Westminster School, which leaving, he join'd himself with whores, thieves, and such like other abandon'd wretches, gaming away his money and sometimes his cloaths: at last he ran away from his mother, his father being beyond sea; and never appeared again till taken up for two robberies. He seemed to have but little contrition but what proceeded from the near approach of death."
With him was his accomplice, 30 year old William Williams who: "said his business was to travel the country as a chapman, that the course of his misfortune was poverty which he was reduc'd to by his wife's sickness."
"The Monthly Intelligencer", March, 1731 at p.126.
"An Account of the Malefactors executed at Tyburn".

Although much of Defoe's writing suggests an instinctive anticipation of some twentieth century criminological paradigms, his era had no significant theoretical basis to fully explore deviancy. That being the case, there was a tendency to fall back on a number of stock explanations for crime. In the late seventeenth and early eighteenth centuries the causes of crime often appeared to be fairly obscure, sometimes even inexplicable, to many thoughtful people.[1] Neither economic necessity or mental disturbance were felt to be very satisfactory, though both were occasionally hinted at. Some connexion between indigence and crime, however, was appreciated by many seventeenth and eighteenth century commentators. Many of the writers and lawyers of the period addressed their minds to the likelihood of such a relationship when considering the need for the provision of poor relief, and some even wrote in detail specifically on the issue. This was true, for example, of Defoe, Fielding and Colquhoun. Ever since the newly mobile society of late and post medieval England had emerged, it had become increasingly apparent (at least from Tudor times onwards), that simply whipping the large numbers of vagrants on the roads and streets was not putting an end to the problem. The great common lawyer Mathew Hale, in the 1600s, when considering this topic had been firmly of the opinion that not only was it morally right to help the poor, but that it was also an "Act of Great Civil Prudence and Political Wisdom". This was because "where there are many very poor, the rich cannot long or safely continue such", not least because necessity made men of "fiery or active institutions rapacious and desperate". He also felt that although England had severe laws against theft "possibly more severe than other nations" yet "the jayls are never the emptier".[2]

Equally, however, indiscriminate alms giving was also widely felt not to be helping the situation. Defoe, though well aware of the plight of the poor, certainly did not believe in such unselective charity; in *Giving Alms No Charity* (1704), he expressly asserted that "people have such a notion in England of being pitiful and charitable, that they encourage Vagrants, and by a mistaken zeal do more harm then good". He felt that charity should be given not to beggars, but to poor families with many children that had lost their breadwinner. The difficulties in providing poor relief were apparent to the legislature as well. There were numerous statutes from early on in the eighteenth century regulating or amending such relief

1.   See on this Lincoln B. Faller, "In the absence of adequate causes: efforts at an etiology of crime", p.55.
2.   From the Preface to "A Discourse touching Provision for the Poor" (1683).

and the manner in which it was to be provided, though their success was often very limited.

However, as Henry Fielding was to point out (though himself a strong believer in effectual provision for the poor), not all poor men stole. Similarly, the popular criminal accounts of the period often concentrated on men and women of good family who had "gone to the bad". These were men such as Christopher Slaughterford, who was hanged at Guildford in 1709 for murdering a woman, despite having been born to "very honest and respectable parents" and having been carefully brought up within the "precepts of the Church of England".[3] That many of the worst felons came from the most respectable backgrounds was a particularly recurrent theme of popular literature. Typically, John Hutchins, a solicitor (in that period admittedly a sometimes dubious profession compared to that of attorney), who was executed "on a Gibbet erected in Fleet Street" in 1684 for the murder nearby of a waterman, was apparently "descended of honest and industrious parents".[4]

Thus poverty, in itself, was not viewed as an adequate explanation for crime. Other possible causes were also considered. Sometimes heredity could be identified as a possible factor in explaining an individual's deviance. This was noted, for example, of the highwayman William Barton, who was hanged in the same year that Defoe was writing his account of Flanders, and of whom it was said "that his father had been always of a restless temper and addicted to every species of wickedness" so that he "seemed to have inherited a sort of hereditary wildness and inconstancy".[5] Flanders' own mother as a prostitute and petty criminal, had given her a bad start to life from this aspect, something specifically alluded to by Defoe. A bad upbringing could also, in extreme cases, take the blame, an example being that of Captain John Stanley who in 1722 was executed for murdering his mistress with a sword. His own father, a soldier, had apparently encouraged him to such swordplay at the early

---

3.   Faller, L., *ibid.*, p.60.
4.   "A True Account of the Behaviour, Last Dying Words and Execution of John Hutchins, the Solicitor". Printed by E.R. for R. Turner (1684), p.2.
5.   Faller, L., *ibid.*, p.56.

age of five. The notorious Captain Richard Dudley had also shown early criminal tendencies when he stole 30s. from his sister at the tender age of eight. Despite this, many, like John Hall, in trying to identify a "character" for the "merry transitory life of a thief in general", were more struck by how indulgence on the part of "doating parents" rather than harsh treatment, appeared to encourage later deviance on the part of their children. Thieves, he felt, were "generally born of good and honest parents" who unfortunately humoured their children in their "stubbornness".[6]

Normally, however, contemporary writers did not see something special that distinguished the "felon" from others (unlike their late Victorian successors, such as Lombroso, busy searching for physical signs of "atavism"). As a result, they often fell back on innate human wickedness and depravity to explain the crime they saw around them. This was possible in an era which was still relatively religious, if less so than had been the case in the previous century. This can be seen clearly in the case of one John Benlofe, who was executed at Tyburn in 1690 for burglary and trying to murder his master, although that gentleman had apparently set "a good example before him". Despite this, Benlofe had mixed with "vain company ... relaxed the fear of God and omitted prayer". As a result he had not been able to "... strictly guard his heart from the breaking out of evil inclinations".[7]

Another very common theme of the era was the way in which minor sins had led their perpetrators inexorably on to major ones. Absence from church, drinking and swearing eventually and inevitably culminating, for example, in highway robbery or murder. As Hall observed of felons generally "he begins first with the little sins that Youth is capable of committing (which is lying and pilfering)". Hutchins, similarly, apparently spent his considerable inheritance by early "betaking himself to lewdness and debauchery". This was also a regular phenomenon of many "Last

---

6.   Hall, J. (1708), *ibid.*, p.2.
7.   "A True Account of the Behaviour, Confession, and Last Dying Speeches of the Eight Criminals that were Executed at Tyburn on Monday, January 26, 1690". Printed for Langley Curtis (1690), p.1.

Dying Speeches" at the scene of execution, which often explicitly supported such an explanation for later more serious crime, including that which had led to the condemned man's execution. Typical of these was that of the wife-killer, John Marketman, who told the assembled crowd that early in life he "had been very disobedient to his too indulgent parents, and that he had spent his youthful days in profanation of the sabbath and licentious evils of debaucheries".[8] Also significantly, William Hogarth's "idle prentice" was portrayed by him, (in 1747), at the start of a career that would ultimately lead to murder and execution, playing dice in a London churchyard during divine service.

Even men who proclaimed their innocence of the crimes for which they were condemned could sometimes see their sentences as the due reward of providence for earlier lives and bad conduct. When Thomas Cook, a prizefighter (the prejudice that this caused was apparently "a very unlucky thing for him"), was executed for the murder of John Cooper, a rather zealous constable, in a disturbance in Mayfair in 1702, he accepted this interpretation of his fate. The case against him was not strong; indeed, it was "amongst the number of those that are looked upon as hard cases", certainly "the greatest part of the evidence [against him] was founded in hearsay".[9] Cook steadfastly denied his guilt to the end, despite the efforts on the part of the Newgate Ordinary to make a clean breast of matters, "much endeavours were used to bring him to a confession, if he knew himself guilty". It appears that in part he was refused a reprieve and made an example of because he "had expressed himself in strong terms against reforming [ie, active] constables" (he was, however, given an initial reprieve on the way to Tyburn for the first time and subsequently taken back on a second occasion). Nevertheless, in his dying speech, at Tyburn, on August 11, 1703, he very gamely stated that since it was his "misfortune" to die such a shameful death he must "look upon it as an affliction from God Almighty". This resignation may have been linked

---

8.   Sharpe, J.A., "Last Dying Speeches": Religion, Ideology and Public Execution in Seventeenth Century England. *Past and Present*, vol.107 (1985), p.145.

9.   Although sometimes frowned on, and considered as of less weight, this was still usually admissible at the turn of the seventeenth century.

to his ready acceptance that in his early life, in Gloucestershire, he had stolen sheep and "done many ill things", while later, in London, as he also willingly acknowledged, he had been a "grievous sinner, a great swearer and drinker, an adulterer, a prophaner and lewd wretch". If this had not been enough to call down divine displeasure, he had even resisted attempts to "crack down" on vice, not only resisting a new (and perhaps rare) breed of more interventionist constable, but also being a "sworn enemy to those who were employed in the reformation of manners". He made a devout end, telling the Ordinary at the gallows that he had never felt so much joy in his life as he had "since his coming into the cart" that took him to Tyburn and his death. While he was in the middle of his final prayers "the cart drew away, and he was turned off".[10]

These dying speeches appear to have been "genuine" declarations, those to be executed having little reason to dissemble, although they were probably heavily prompted into using such a standardized form by the clergymen who attended the condemned at the gallows. Execution was an experience that not only "concentrated the mind" but needed to be prepared for. Indeed, it was the manner in which murderers had denied this chance to their victims that added such a horror to their crimes. Thus, when George Caswell, a "gentleman" came to confess to the Ordinary (Samuel Smith) before his execution in 1691, for the murder of Andrew Hickson, an acquaintance who was killed as a result of a drunken quarrel, the factor that "multiplyd his terror" and which was viewed as the "great aggravation of the crime" was that he had "thrust a man out of the world so unprepared for death".[11] Obviously, in such a psychological environment, the dire consequences of earlier irreligion by the condemned would be particularly stressed. The *Newgate Calendar*, for example, was to attribute Wild's fall to his having, when young, come across and read books that unfortunately contained the "abominable doctrines" of Deism

---

10.   *A Select and Impartial Account of the Lives and Dying-Words of the Most Remarkable Convicts from the Year 1700, down to the Present Time*". Printed by J. Applebee (1745), vol.1, (2nd edn), pp.39-45.

11.   "The Confession of George Caswell Gent. Executed at Tyburn on Monday, December 21, 1691 ..." Printed for Langley Curtis (1691).

and Atheism. These were especially prone to corrupt, as the atheist "having nothing after this world to hope or fear" was, as a consequence, careful only to secure himself from detection, this being the only social limitation on indulging his base urges. As this suggests, however, it seems from this that at the time it was readily accepted that nearly all people had to wrestle with such depraved, and potentially criminogenic, impulses (unlike the situation in the late nineteenth century).

A woman, or women, could also sometimes be blamed for leading a man astray; one prisoner at the Old Bailey, in 1677, after his conviction for burglary (of the Mace and two Privy Purses from the Lord Chancellor!) even "complained to himself of lewd and lascivious women, saying that they were the cause of his and many other mens vice". At which view the writer of the pamphlet narrating details of the trial heartily concurred concluding his account with the imprecation "from such vile women that brings many a man to sudden death good Lord deliver us all".[12]

Human wickedness, it was felt, could be especially powerful when joined to social pretentiousness, or some other folly. The thief, and former articled attorney, George Griffiths, who was executed for stealing from his master in 1700 "very justly attributed his misfortunes to the associating with persons who were his superiors in point of circumstances, and the making an appearance which he was unable to support". Similarly the traitor William Gregg (who worked for money not Jacobite ideology), and who was executed at Tyburn in 1708, noted at his execution that "the want of money to supply his extravagances had tempted him to commit the fatal crime which cost him his life".[13]

These explanations are, of course, generally inadequate to most modern thinkers, and to an extent were not even totally satisfactory by the mid-eighteenth century to men like the Fielding brothers (magistrates

---

12. "A Perfect Narrative of the Apprehension, Tryal and Confession of the Five Several Persons that were Confederates in Stealing the Mace and the Two Privy Purses from the Lord High Chancellor of England" (1677), printed for E. Olivier, p.5.
13. Wilkinson, G.T., *Newgate Calendar* (1816 edn).

in turn at Bow Street) writing from the 1740s onwards. Henry Fielding himself noted, in 1752, that "no disorders ever spring up without a cause". Even Fielding, however, still attributed the apparently growing level of crime to irreligion. In *Examples of the Interpretation of Providence in the Detection and Punishment of Murder* (1752), he stated that the main social problem of the era was the "general neglect (I wish I could not say contempt) of religion, which hath within these few years so lately overspread the whole nation". He also felt that particularly severe crimes, such as murder "would out", naturally, because "the divine providence hath been pleased to interpose in a more immediate manner in the detection of this crime than any other ... and the most unaccountable indeed miraculous means, by which the most secret and cunning murders have often been detected". This was closely repeating a view that had been advanced several decades earlier by Defoe himself, when writing *Moll Flanders*. Flanders was clearly of the view that the "necessity of nature" worked so strongly in this area that sometimes even "the minds of those who are guilty of any atrocious villany; such as secret murther in particular, ... have been oblig'd to discover it".

However, with the limited theoretical explanations at their disposal, writers of the period, though able to hint at other possible factors, sometimes very obviously, for example, in works such as Bernard Mandeville's *Fable of the Bees* (1714),[14] and also in some of Defoe's own writing, had few ready alternative theoretical paradigms to apply to the explanation of crime. Those early writings which did hint at attempts to form a more scientific explanation, even when they anticipated later theoretical approaches to deviance (which they often did), subsequently tended to be "childless", petering out and being repeated anew (but not advanced) by other, later, writers. They have as a consequence been termed "shadow criminology", lacking in a theoretical structure and

---

14.   Like his contemporary Defoe, Mandeville was a Londoner, though by adoption, having been born in Holland. Although roundly condemned at the time from many quarters his most famous work shows an incisive if cynical analysis of society.

disciples to further explore, develop and transmit them.[15] They were usually the work of people such as lawyers, magistrates, prison chaplains and interested writers like Defoe (though few of the others were as well equipped as he was), amongst several other professions which contained people who had special reasons for having an interest in the subject.

It was only in the latter half of the eighteenth century that the first signs of a recognizably "scientific" (and thus modern) criminology can be seen, much of it in what became known as the "classical" tradition; for example, the works of Beccaria and Bentham. Indeed Beccaria's *Dei Delitti e Pene* (of 1764) has been termed the first naturalistic explanation of crime, one that did not base itself largely on concepts of sin and demonology.[16] In part this appears to have been linked to a growing dissatisfaction with religious dogma and supernatural interpretations of the world.

Prior to about 1740 there had been a belief, if waning, in the guiding hand of providence and a belief in God that had provided a rational basis for good conduct. This had been weakened significantly by changing intellectual attitudes. Such diverse factors as the European wars of the 1750s and the great Lisbon earthquake of 1755 also contributed to the erosion of faith and an attendant reliance on supernatural interpretations of society, and encouraged, in turn, a search for alternative explanations for human deviance and a new basis for morality. To this extent, Defoe, essentially a puritan, can be seen as being a late exponent of a tradition of criminal interpretation that had been dominant for hundreds of years, but which was about to lose much of its intellectual foundation. In part this tradition viewed society as an "organic" entity in which crime like all forms of human wickedness (particularly murder) might inevitably expect its due rewards, often in this world, and certainly in the next. At the start of the eighteenth century nearly all sides in the debate as to the severity and extent of punishment, whether those who supported a harsh imposition of the death penalty on a regular basis (including, to an extent,

---

15.   See on this, "Introduction" by Paul Rock to *History of Criminology*, Dartmouth (1994), p.xiii.

16.   Jenkins, P., "Varieties of Enlightenment Criminology", *Brit. J. Criminol.*, vol.24, No.2, April 1984, p.112.

Defoe) and those (often Dissenters) who felt that the existing use of the gallows was too vindictive and a waste of human life, couched their arguments in theocentric terms. They appealed to a particular image of God's justice to justify the degree of temporal punishment. Judges and authors thought of justice in terms of a divine model in which human justice was located within a hierarchy in which God was firmly at the apex. As John Waugh was to expressly warn in 1717 "vengeance belongs unto God as the Supreme Lord and Judge of the world; and unto magistrates, as commissioned by Him for the execution of it".[17] The law itself and its administration was full of religious or quasi-religious solemnities; for example, Judges' duties were often expressly described as being "solemn" and "sacred". This can again be seen to be present in numerous executions of the period. By way of illustration, can be considered the case of John Marketman, who had murdered his wife while drunk in 1680, and executed, at his own request, in the Essex parish of West Ham to the east of London rather than in the county Assize town of Chelmsford. He was led to the scaffold by his mother where the preacher, fulfilling the same role as the Newgate Ordinary in such situations, urged him to take comfort from the fact that he was a "monument to divine justice; and that in and thorow you, God sheweth the consequences of a sinful and wicked life".[18] It should, perhaps, also be borne in mind that the last trial for witchcraft in England only occurred in 1712 (though it was very rare after 1660).[19]

Even in the early 1700s, Defoe himself had produced an amalgam of many "practical" measures to deal with crime along with his moralistic analysis. This sometimes bordered on the fatuous as can clearly be seen in his treatise *A Warning to House-Keepers* (1728). Having noted that "the

---

17. McGowen, R., "The Changing Face of God's Justice: The Debates over Divine and Human Punishment in Eighteenth Century England". *Criminal Justice History*, vol.ix (1988).

18. Sharpe, J.A., "• Last Dying Speeches': Religion, Ideology and Public Execution in Seventeenth Century England". *Past and Present*, vol.107 (1985), p.144.

19. Technically, witchcraft was not a crime; people were convicted of keeping familiars and cursing others pursuant to being witches.

season chiefly for breaking into houses is during the winter, and long nights" the narrator's suggestions: "I would advise every housekeeper to have a dog" are almost banal! There was, however, already a significant difference in tone over some matters between Henry Fielding writing in the early 1750s, and Defoe, less than thirty years earlier. God, Fielding felt (although he fully accepted the role of providence), might need some practical assistance in discovering criminals in this world, and there were, he also observed, possibly structural explanations for crime (as well as solutions) other than pure human wickedness.

However, compared to the relatively small distinction between Fielding and Defoe, the difference between Defoe's work and Jeremy Bentham's detailed analysis of criminal motivation in his *Introduction to the Principles of Morals and Legislation* of 1789 is enormous; the sea change of the Enlightenment had separated the two. Illustrative of this change of approach can be seen to be Bentham's highly technical discussion of a robber's motivation; he observed that the sight of successful robberies worked on potential felons by "weakening the tutelary motives which tend to restrain him from such an action, and thereby adding to the strength of the temptation".[20] He was already a huge distance from Defoe, although writing only 60 years later.

Despite the apparent simplicity of much of their analysis, perhaps care should be taken about being "condescending" towards the earlier writers on crime. No doubt a commentator of Defoe's era would marvel at the intelligent men and women who have made profitable academic careers out of explaining this phenomenon (crime) and yet are still no more able to produce conclusive arguments or effective "cures" than their early eighteenth century ancestors.

Certainly, Flanders, in the early 1700s (or, in theory, the early 1680s), sees the explanation of her deep involvement in crime in a fairly straightforward way, namely as a manifestation of her own wickedness (albeit with some seriously mitigating circumstances, at least at the start of her career). Like Edmund Kirk in 1684, when explaining how she came

---

20.   Bentham, J., *Introduction to the Principles of Morals and Legislation* (1789), ch.xii.

to commit her crimes, she might dismiss the "slender inducements I had thereunto" and confess that it was caused by her "own vile and corrupted heart".[21] As a deeply religious man, one who in 1726 had written *The Political History of the Devil,* and who felt that it was unlikely "that there is or has been one council of state in the world ... where the devil ... has not sat as a member" this is an attitude that Defoe would personally have strongly supported.

21.   "Dying Advice" (1684), quoted Faller, *ibid.*, p.52.

Conclusion

Defoe brings to his story of Flanders' criminal life a balanced account, exposing the horrors and brutalities of the justice system of his time while also being very aware of the highly destructive, and socially corrosive, reality of professional crime in this era. Flanders' conduct in the novel, stealing from children and from desperate people while their house burnt down, getting servants into difficulties with their masters, contemplating murder, etc., could only contribute to a damaging of the sense of community and trust in the City of London and its environs. It was all the more reprehensible as she persisted in it long after she was, herself, financially secure.

Defoe saw her life as a warning (as well as entertainment). Indeed, in his preface to the work he himself, appropriately for a man with such a practical turn of mind, suggests that the criminal incidents contained in it "give us excellent warning in such cases". This was a theme that Defoe was generally very mindful of (in part, of course, he had to advance it as a justification for publishing such a salacious work), and even expressed directly via the characters in the novel, so that the governess tells Flanders that a thief is a "... creature that watches the advantages of other people's mistakes". Flanders herself also observed that her narrative "if duly considered, may be useful to honest people, and afford a due caution". At some points Defoe's advice on practical crime prevention is consequently even quite explicit; for example, when Flanders having abortively attempted the theft of a gold watch from a woman notes that "the woman whose watch I had pull'd at was a fool" because "had she with a presence of mind needful on such an occasion, as soon as she felt the pull, not scream'd out as she did, but turn'd immediately round, and seiz'd the next body that was behind her, she had infallibly taken me. This is a direction not of the kindest sort to the fraternity"; but "tis certainly a key to the clue of a pick-pocket's motions, and whoever can follow it, will certainly catch the thief as he will be sure to miss if he does not".

This combination of perspectives, humane, realistic and extremely practical, allied with a realistic mixture of sensitivity without sentimentality is, perhaps, not totally surprising in an educated man who had been both a Newgate inmate and in the pillory, and yet who had also mixed with the highest ranks of society and who was subsequently, in 1728, able to write authoritatively on street robberies. It has, however, produced an invaluable criminal biography as a record of the times.

Select Bibliography

N.B. Many works consulted, especially contemporary sources, are cited only in the footnotes.

Bailey, S.H., and Gunn, M.J., *The Modern English Legal System*, 2nd edn (1990).

Bailey, V., ed, *Policing and Punishment in Nineteenth Century Britain* (1981).

Baker, J.H., *An Introduction to English Legal History*, 3rd edn (1990).

Barnes, H.E., *The Story of Punishment*, 2nd edn (1972).

Beattie, J.M., *Crime and the Courts in England 1660-1800* (1986).

Beier, A.L., *Masterless Men* (1985).

Bentham, J., *Introduction to the Principles of Morals and Legislation* (1789).

Beresford, M.W., "The Common Informer, The Penal Statutes and Economic Regulation", *Economic History Review*, vol.10 (1957).

Bessant, W., *London in the Eighteenth Century* (1908).

Birkenhead, Lord, *Famous Trials of History* (1926).

Birkenhead, Lord, *More Famous Trials* (1928).

Blackstone, W., *Commentaries on the Laws of England*, vols.iii and iv (1768).

Blewett, D., *Introduction to Moll Flanders*, Penguin edn (1989).

Boswell, J., *Boswell's London Diary 1763-4*, Heinemann (1950).

Browner, J.A., "Wrong Side of the River: London's Disreputable South Bank in the Sixteenth and Seventeenth Century." *Essays in History* (University of Virginia), vol.36 (1994), p.35.

Burke. P., *Popular Culture in Seventeenth Century London* (1976).

Chesney, K., *Victorian Underworld* (1970).

Clark, G.N., *The Later Stuarts 1660 -1714* (1956).

Cleary,T., Henry Fielding: *Political Writer* (1983).

Clerk, P., "Migration in England During the Late Seventeenth and Early Eighteenth Centuries", *Past and Present*, no.83, p.77.

Cockburn J.S. (ed), *Crime in England 1550-1800* (1977).

Cockburn, J.S., "Punishment and Brutalization in the English Enlightenment", *Law and History Review*, vol.12 (1994), no.1, p.155.

Colquhoun, P., *A Treatise on Indigence* (1806).

Cornish, W.R., *The Jury* (1968).

Cornish, W.R. and Clark, G.D., *Law and Society in England 1750-1950* (1989).

Crew, A., *The Old Bailey* (1933) .

Defoe, D., *The Letters of Daniel Defoe*, Healey, G.H. (ed) (1955).

Defoe, D., *Jonathan Wild* (1725).

Defoe, D. "The Poor Man's Plea", in *The Shortest Way with Dissenters* (1701).

Defoe, D., *A Tour Through Great Britain*, 2 vols. (1724-6).

Defoe, D., *Colonel Jack* (1722)

Defoe, D., *A Journal of the Plague Year* (1720).

Defoe, D., *The Complete English Tradesman* (1725).

Defoe, D., *Street Robberies Consider'd: The Reason of Their Being so Frequent* (1728).

Defoe, D., *A Warning for Travellers: with Rules to Know a Highwayman; and Instructions how to Behave Upon the Occasion* (1728).

Defoe, D., *A Warning to House-Keepers* (1728).

Defoe, D., *The Political History of the Devil* (1726).

Earle, P., *The Making of the English Middle Class, Business Society and Family Life in London 1660-1730* (1985).

Emsley, C., *Crime and Society in England 1750-1900* (1987).

Emsley, C., "The History of Crime and Crime Control Institutions c.1770-c.1945", p.149 in *Oxford Handbook of Criminology*, Reiner, R., *et al.* (eds) (1994).

Evans, R., *The Fabrication of Virtue, English Prison Architecture, 1750-1840* (1982).

Faller, L.B., "In the absence of adequate causes: efforts at an etiology of crime", in *Turned to Account: The Forms and Functions of Criminal Biography in Late Seventeenth and Early Eighteenth Century England* (1987), p.52.

Feeley, M., and Little, D., "The Vanishing Female: The Decline of Women in the Criminal Process, 1687-1912", *Law and Society Review* 25 (1991), p.719.

Feeley, M., "The Decline of Women in the Criminal Process: A Comparative History", *Criminal Justice History*, vol.15 (1994), p.235.

Fielding, H., *A Proposal for Making an Effectual Provision for the Poor* (1753).

Fielding, H., *An Inquiry into the Causes of the Late Increase of Robbers* (1751), Barnes and Noble edn (1967).

Fielding, H., *The Voyage to Lisbon* (1754), Everyman edn (1960).

Fielding, H., *Amelia* (1752).

Fielding, J., *A Plan for the Prevention of Robberies Within 20 Miles of London* (1755).

Gatrell, V.A.C., *et al.* (eds), *Crime and the Law, The Social History of Crime in Western Europe since 1500* (1980).

Gatrell, V.A.C., *The Hanging Tree* (1994).

Gay, J., *The Beggar's Opera* (1727).

George, G., *London Life in the Eighteenth Century*, 2nd ed (1930).

Gilmour, I., *Riot, Rising and Revolution. Governance and Violence in Eighteenth Century England*, p.356.

Green, A.G., *Verdict According to Conscience, Perspectives on the English Criminal Trial Jury 1200-1800* (1985).

Hay, D., *et al.*, *Albion's Fatal Tree* (1975).

Hay, D., "The Criminal Prosecution in England", *Modern Law Review*, vol.47 (1984), p.1.

Hay, D., *War Dearth and Theft in the Eighteenth Century: the Record of the English Courts, Past And Present*, no.95 (1983), p.117.

Hay, D., *Crime and Justice in Eighteenth and Nineteenth Century England* (1986).

Hepenstall, R., *Reflections on the Newgate Calendar* (1975).

Herrup, C., *Law and Morality in England, Past and Present*, no.106 (1985).

Herrup, C., *The Common Peace* (1987).

Hibbert, C., *The Road to Tyburn* (1957).

Hill, C., "Reformation to Industrial Revolution", *Penguin Economic History of Britain, vol.2, 1530-1780* (1992).

Holdsworth, Sir William, *A History of English Law*, vol.xii (1938).

Hostettler, J., *The Politics of Punishment* (1995).

Howson, G. "Who Was Moll Flanders?" *Times Literary Supplement* (January 18, 1968).

Howson, G., *Thieftaker General, The Rise and Fall of Jonathan Wild* (1970).

Howard, J., *The State of the Prisons*, 3rd edn (1784), Everyman edn (1929).

Ignatieff, M., "State, Civil Society, and Total Institutions: A Critique of Recent Social Histories of Punishment", in Tonry, M., *et al.* (eds) *Crime and Justice, An Annual Review of Research* (1981), pp.153-192.

Ignatieff, M., *A Just Measure of Pain* (1978).

Ingham, T., *The English Legal Process*, 5th edn (1994).

Innes J., and Styles J., "The Crime Wave: Recent Writing on Crime and Criminal Justice in Eighteenth Century England", *Journal of British Studies 25* (October 1986), p.380.

Jenkins, P., "Varieties of Enlightenment Criminology", *Brit. J. Criminol.*, vol.24, No.2, April (1984).

Johnson, C., (Defoe?), *Lives of the most Notorious Pirates* (1728).

Kayman, M.A., *From Bow Street to Baker Street* (1992).

Kermode, J., and Walker, G. (eds) Women, *Crime and the Courts in Early Modern England* (1995).

Kiralfy, A.K.R., *Potters Historical Introduction to English Law*, 4th edn (1958).

Landau, N., *The Justices of the Peace 1679-1760* (1984).

Langbein, J.H., "The Criminal Trial Before the Lawyers". *The University of Chicago Law Review*, vol.25, No.2 (1978), p.300.

Langbein, J.H., "Shaping the 18th Century Criminal Trial: a View from the Ryder Sources". *The University of Chicago Law Review*, vol.50, No.1 (1983), p.1.

Langbein, J.H., *Albion's Fatal Flaws, Past and Present*, no.98 (1983), p.96.

Laurence, A., *Women in England 1500-1760, A Social History* (1995).

Laurence, J., *A History of Capital Punishment* (1960 edn).

Lemmings, D., *Gentlemen and Barristers, The Inns of Court and the English Bar 1680-1730* (1990).

Linebaugh, P., *The London Hanged, Crime and Civil Society in the Eighteenth Century* (1991).

Linebough, P., "(Marxist) Social History and (Conservative) Legal History: A Reply to Professor Langbein", *The New York University Law Review,* vol.ix, no.2 (May 1985).

Mayhew, H., with Binney, J., *London Labour and the London Poor*, vol.4, "Those that Will not Work".

McGowen, R., "The Changing Face of God's Justice: The Debates over Divine and Human Punishment in Eighteenth Century England", *Criminal Justice History,* vol.ix (1988).

McMullan, J.L., *The Canting Crew, London's Criminal Underworld* (1984).

Page, L., *Justice of the Peace*, 2nd edn (1947).

Paley, W., *Principles of Moral and Political Philosophy* (1785).

Parker, G., *The Military Revolution* (1988).

Plumb, J.H., *England in the Eighteenth Century* (1950).

Priestley, P., *Victorian Prison Lives* (1985).

Radzinowicz, L., *A History of English Criminal Law*, vols.1, 2, 3, 4 and 5 (1948-1976).

Reiner, R. *et al.* (eds), *Oxford Handbook of Criminology* (1994).

Robb, G., *White Collar Crime in Modern England* (1992).

Rock, P., (ed), *History of Criminology*, Dartmouth (1994).

Rude, G., *Hanoverian London, 1714-1808* (1971).

Rude, G., *The Crowd in History* (Serif edn, 1995).

Sharpe J.A., *Crime in Early Modern England 1550-1750* (1984).

Sharpe, J.A., *Early Modern England, A Social History 1550-1760* (1987).

Sharpe, J.A., "Last Dying Speeches": Religion, Ideology and Public Execution in Seventeenth Century England. *Past and Present*, vol.107 (1985).

Shaw, A.G.L., *Convicts and the Colonies* (1966).

Shennan, J.H., *Liberty and Order in Early Modern Europe* (1986).

Shoemaker, R.B., *Prosecution and Punishment: Petty Crime and the Law in London and Rural Middlesex*, c.1660-1725 (1991).

Skyrme, T., *History of the Justices of the Peace* (1994).

Smith, A., *The History of the Lives of the Most Noted Highway-Men, Foot-pads, House-Breakers, Shoplifts, and Cheats of Both Sexes ... for Above 50 Years Last Past* (London 2nd edn, 1714).

Speck, W.A., *Stability and Strife, England 1714-1760* (1977).

Spierenburg, P., *The Prison Experience, Disciplinary Institutions and their Inmates in Early Modern Europe* (1991).

Stockdale, E., *et al.* (eds), *Criminal Justice Under Stress* (1992).

Stockdale, E., *A Study of Bedford Prison 1660-1877* (1977).

Stone, L., *The Family Sex and Marriage in England*, Harper Torchbooks edn (1979).

Stone, L., "Interpersonal Violence in English Society 1300-1980", *Past and Present* (1983), vol.100, p.22.

Summerson, J., *Georgian London* (1978).

Thompson, E.P., *Whigs and Hunters* (1975).

Tobias, J.J., *Crime and Industrial Society in the Nineteenth Century* (1967).

Walker, N., *Crime and Insanity in England*, vol.1 (1968).
Watts, M., *The Dissenters, from the Reformation to the French Revolution* (1978).
Wilkinson, G.T., *The Newgate Calendar (1816)*, Cardinal edn (1991).
Wilson, C., *England's Apprenticeship 1603-1763*, 2nd edn (1984).
Wrigley, E.A., "A Simple Model of London's Importance in Changing English Society and Economy 1650-1750", *Past and Present*, no.37, p.44 (1967).

Zedner, L., "Women, Crime, and Penal Responses: A Historical Account", p.247 in Michael Tonry (ed) *Crime and Justice; A Review of Research* (1991).

Contemporary Newspapers and Journals Cited

The Original Half-Penny London Journal
The Gentleman's Magazine
The London Journal
The Daily Courant
The Post-Man
The Monthly Intelligencer
The Spectator
The London Gazette

Contemporary pamphlets are cited in the footnotes, rather than the select bibliography; this being by title, date, publisher, and, if named, author (many are anonymous). I have followed Professor John Langbein in citing the series of pamphlets known as the Old Bailey Sessions Papers as "OBSP" followed by the date of the Sessions recorded. The normal introductory title to these papers varied with the decade, and publisher; a common one, from the early examples of the 1670s, beginning: "A True

Narrative of the Proceedings at the Sessions-House in the Old-Bayly ...". These papers are, as Langbein notes "probably the best accounts we shall ever have" of English criminal trial procedure between 1670 and 1730. Furthermore, his research has identified them as being accurate (if sometimes incomplete) accounts of the trials and defendants in the Old Bailey. I have therefore had extensive recourse to them in writing this book.

Index

(MF refers to Moll Flanders)